# GROUP TECHNIQUES

## How to Use Them More Purposefully

Robert K. Conyne
University of Cincinnati

Jeri L. Crowell
Wesleyan College

Mark D. Newmeyer
University of Cincinnati

Dr. Yuh-Jen Guo

PEARSON

Merrill
Prentice Hall

Upper Saddle River, New Jersey
Columbus, Ohio

**Library of Congress Cataloging-in-Publication Data**

Conyne, Robert K.
  Group techniques: how to use them more purposefully/Robert K. Conyne, Jeri L.
Crowell, Mark D. Newmeyer.
     p. cm.
  Includes index.
  ISBN 0-13-114988-1 (pbk.): 1. Group counseling. I. Crowell, Jeri L.
II. Newmeyer, Mark D. III. Title.

  BF637.C6C5718 2008
  158'.35–dc22                                                                    2007003829

**Vice President and Executive Publisher:** Jeffery W. Johnston
**Publisher:** Kevin M. Davis
**Editor:** Meredith D. Fossel
**Senior Editorial Assistant:** Kathleen S. Burk
**Production Editor:** Mary Harlan
**Production Coordination:** GGS Book Services
**Design Coordinator:** Diane C. Lorenzo
**Text Design and Illustrations:** GGS Book Services
**Cover Design:** Bryan Huber
**Cover Image:** Jupiter Images
**Production Manager:** Susan W. Hannahs
**Director of Marketing:** David Gesell
**Marketing Manager:** Autumn Purdy
**Marketing Coordinator:** Brian Mounts

This book was set in Century Light by GGS Book Services. It was printed and bound by R. R. Donnelley &
Sons Co. The cover was printed by R. R. Donnelley & Sons Co.

Pearson Education Ltd.
Pearson Education Singapore Pte. Ltd.
Pearson Education Canada, Ltd.
Pearson Education–Japan

Pearson Education Australia Pty. Limited
Pearson Education North Asia Ltd.
Pearson Educación de Mexico, S.A. de C.V.
Pearson Education Malaysia Pte. Ltd.

10 9 8 7 6 5 4 3 2 1
ISBN-13: 978-0-13-114988-5
ISBN-10:    0-13-114988-1

# Preface

We are delighted you are about to read this novel approach to understanding how to use group techniques! We hope it will make a positive difference in your group leadership skills.

Although several good books exist on the subject, our review suggested that there is a strong need for a textbook that clearly ties group techniques to a generic conceptual model that would be generalizable and adaptable across different contexts. In this book, we seriously consider the concept of the group leader as an "action scientist" and a "reflective practitioner," one who selects group techniques dependent on a working conceptual model that can be applied and evaluated. We show how group leaders can choose techniques purposefully, informed by the type of group at hand (we emphasize counseling and psychoeducation groups, but also present material related to task and psychotherapy groups in a separate chapter), a group's developmental stage, and applicable best practice guidelines. Moreover, we frame group techniques by their level of intervention (individual, interpersonal, group) and focus of intervention (cognitive, affective, behavioral, structural).

What results is a flexible, ecologically based model for selecting and applying group techniques—the purposeful group techniques model (PGTM). This model emerges from decades of study and experimentation and several years of trial-and-error testing in numerous training and educational situations.

The PGTM includes five steps:

1. **Identify** the group type (counseling, psychoeducation, task, psychotherapy), group developmental stage (beginning, middle, ending), and best practice area (planning, performing, processing) that is applicable.
2. **Analyze** the situation in terms of relevant ecological concepts of context, interconnection, social system maintenance, collaboration, sustainability, and meaning making.
3. **Review** possible group techniques considering focus (cognitive, affective, behavioral, structural) and level (individual, interpersonal, group).
4. **Select** a best-fit technique giving attention to evaluation criteria of adequacy, appropriateness, effectiveness, efficiency, and side effects.
5. **Implement** and **Evaluate,** allowing for continuation or changes in the future.

The PGTM builds from past contributions in group leadership training, including various critical incident models. A key approach, we think, to learning how to select and apply group techniques is to ground possible choices contextually. Therefore, the approach you will read about in this book is centered on presenting particular and specific critical incidents, which then are used to guide subsequent consideration.

In addition, we have collected and organized a vast array of group techniques that are available as a resource "toolbox" within the PGTM. These group techniques are contained in the appendix and are organized by best practice area (planning, performing, processing), group developmental stage (beginning, middle, ending), and by focus (cognitive, affective, behavioral, structural) and level (individual, interpersonal, group). Such a compendium of group techniques is a valuable resource to have at your disposal, but a caveat is in order. These techniques are not intended as stand-alone units but must always be considered within an overarching conceptual model, such as the PGTM.

This book can be read independently, as a stand-alone experience, of course. Yet, we think the best way to take advantage of its contents is to use it within some kind of educational or training experience. Reviewers suggested that starting with the last chapter (Chapter 11) might be valuable to some readers because that chapter provides a compact summary of key points covered in the text.

An important part of learning about using techniques is getting practice with actual group situations. We employ a critical incident format to simulate these situations. The critical incident format we incorporate is designed for experimentation, interaction, and group feedback. It is based on real-world group conditions, some of which (e.g., a critical incident involving a nurse) ask readers to expand their scope beyond typical counseling circumstances, to "think outside the box." We include such critical incidents because groups can be used in many settings, for many purposes, and with many populations, and we think it is important for group leaders to think in those terms.

Talking through and comparing choices of techniques, along with each person's rationale, will provide the richest of learning experiences. As one result, you will not only learn how to select and use group techniques but, more important, you will learn a lot about yourself as a person and as a group leader.

## Acknowledgments

We want to thank all those who have contributed to the development of this approach to selecting and using group techniques. The legions of students and workshop participants over the years, of course, are of primary importance. Our editors at Merrill/Prentice Hall—Kevin Davis, Meredith Fossel, and Mary Harlan—have been especially instructive and supportive, urging us to keep all the substance of this book and to communicate it as directly and clearly as possible. Kelly Keeler and Sharon O' Donnell handled project management and copyediting exquisitely. We especially want to thank the following reviewers who contributed to the strength of this final product: Fred Bemak, George Mason University; Breda Bova, University of New Mexico; Roberto Clemente, Roosevelt University, Chicago; Janice DeLucia-Waack, University of Buffalo, SUNY; Kevin A. Fall, Loyola University–New Orleans; Sally Hage, Teachers College, Columbia University; Jerry L. Johnson, Grand Valley State University; Chris McCarthy, University of Texas at Austin; William A. McDowell, Marshall University; Arthur R. Sanchez, California State University, Chico; and Conni Sharp, Pittsburgh State University.

This book is a product of a group effort, too, including a faculty member (Conyne) and two doctoral students specializing in group work. As any group we had our joys and our critical incidents along the way, the latter including dealing with a protracted illness, marriage and geographic relocation, an international child adoption, a university retirement, and finalizing of doctoral dissertations.

Finally, here's to good groups for you and our hope that this book will contribute to their effectiveness and to your enjoyment of them.

**Bob Conyne:** Special thanks to my deep and wide "group-work support network": students, graduates, workshop participants, colleagues, family, the Association for Specialists in Group Work (ASGW) and the Division of Group Psychotherapy and Group Psychology—indeed, the whole array of interconnected folks who have contributed so much in advancing group approaches to assist the health and well-being of people and settings. To my family group of Lynn Suzanne, and Zack who always instill hope and support. And to Rohs Coffee Shop, near UC, where we met many times while writing this book.

**Jeri Crowell:** Special thanks to Bob Conyne for inviting me to share in this book, for years of leading and coleading groups in classes, workshops, and programs about groups. Also, to Bob and his wife, Lynn Rapin, for connecting me with ASGW, and to all the wonderful group specialists who have mentored and supported me, including Bob Wilson, Mark Newmeyer, and Jim Trotzer. Above all, though, is my sincerest gratitude to my family for their support and love, especially my husband and best friend, Arthur Crowell.

**Mark Newmeyer:** Gratitude is extended to Bob Conyne for inviting me along on such a wonderful journey in writing this book. His friendship and mentorship are continual reminders of a key ingredient in group work—giving it away! Also, I must recognize all the members who have been a part of the various groups I have been privileged to lead over the years. Because of them I am keenly aware that I too have been given rich opportunities for personal growth that otherwise would have likely not occurred. I extend an appreciation to Rhoda Carnes for her feedback regarding the development of several critical incidents. Last, a profound thank you is extended to my wife, Amy, and daughter, Grace, for allowing me to frequently disappear to the computer.

# About the Authors

(L-R): Bob Conyne, Mark Newmeyer, Jeri Crowell

**Robert K. Conyne**, PhD, is professor emeritus and former director of the Counseling Program and of the Center for Ecological Counseling at the University of Cincinnati. He is a licensed psychologist and clinical counselor and a fellow in several divisions of the American Psychological Association, and in the Association for Specialists in Group Work (ASGW). Dr. Conyne has published 10 books, and over 200 scholarly journal articles and presentations in the areas of group work, prevention, and ecological counseling. He has received numerous awards, including the Eminent Career Award from the ASGW and the Lifetime Achievement Award from the Prevention Section of the American Psychological Association.

**Jeri L. Crowell**, EdD, is a professional counselor and currently the director of the Academic Center at Wesleyan College in Macon, Georgia. She counsels students with academic difficulties and works with students with disabilities, as well as with faculty. Dr. Crowell is a fellow with Preparing Future Faculty and is a nationally certified counselor with the National Board for Certified Counselors. She is active in professional organizations, including the ASGW, and Chi Sigma Iota, the international honor society for professional counselors, and the Center for Ecological Counseling. Dr. Crowell has received several awards for her academic performance at the University of Cincinnati, was recognized by the American Counseling Association as an emerging leader, and received the President's Award for Service to ASGW in 2005. She is published in the book *Critical Incidents in Group Counseling* (2004), and has contributed to multiple articles.

**Mark D. Newmeyer**, EdD, is an adjunct assistant professor of the Counseling Program and member of the Center for Ecological Counseling at the University of Cincinnati. He is a licensed counselor and a member of The American Psychological Association, the Association for Specialists in Group Work, Association for Counselor Education and Supervision, and Chi Sigma Iota, the international honor society for professional counselors. In 2004 the American Counseling Association recognized him as an emerging leader. Dr. Newmeyer has worked in a mental health private practice, a community agency, and a hospital psychiatry division.

# DISCOVER THE COMPANION WEB SITE ACCOMPANYING THIS BOOK

## THE PRENTICE HALL COMPANION WEB SITE: A VIRTUAL LEARNING ENVIRONMENT

Technology is a constantly growing and changing aspect of our field that is creating a need for content and resources. To address this emerging need, Prentice Hall has developed an online learning environment for students and professors alike—Companion Web sites—to support our textbooks.

In creating a Companion Web site, our goal is to build on and enhance what the textbook already offers. For this reason, the content for this user-friendly Web site is organized by topic and provides the professor and student with a variety of meaningful resources. Features of this Companion Web site include:

- **Counseling Topics**—17 core counseling topics represent the diversity and scope of today's counseling field
- **Annotated Bibliography**—includes seminal foundational works and key current works
- **Web Destinations**—lists significant and up-to-date practitioner and client sites
- **Professional Development**—provides helpful information regarding professional organizations and codes of ethics

To take advantage of these and other resources, please visit the Companion Web site for *Group Techniques: How to Use Them More Purposefully* at

**www.prenhall.com/conyne**

# Brief Contents

# Contents

## 6   Performance Techniques at the Middle Stage of Group Development: Connecting and Producing     96

## 7   Performance Techniques at the Ending Stage of Group Development: Consolidating and Forecasting     115

## Part IV: Techniques in Processing Counseling and Psychoeducation Groups     135

## 8   Processing Techniques to Use Within Group Sessions or Meetings     136

## 9  Processing Techniques to Use Between Group Sessions or Meetings  158

## Part V: Techniques for Additional Types of Groups  177

## 10  Group Techniques in Task and Psychotherapy Groups  179

## Part VI: Closure  205

## 11  Summarizing Group Techniques  206

*NOTE: Every effort has been made to provide accurate and current information in this book. However, the Internet and information posted on it are constantly changing, so it is inevitable that some of the Internet addresses listed in the textbook will change.*

# PART I

# Background for Considering and Using Group Techniques More Purposefully

The seminal social psychologist, Kurt Lewin, observed that "there is nothing so practical as a good theory" (Marrow, 1969). More astute words may never have been spoken as they apply to the choice and use of group techniques. As we will explain in Chapter 1, group leaders too often use group techniques in a kind of conceptual vacuum, where techniques are unexposed to and unguided by theory.

Of course, the proper use of group techniques is essential to group-work leadership. Group leaders must have at their disposal action steps they can take to propel a group forward and to address individual and interpersonal behaviors of members. But the choice and use of these techniques must be guided by a clear conceptual framework that gives rise to effective practice—that is, Lewin's "good theory."

In the first three chapters we describe what we think are good theory foundations upon which group techniques can be based and by which they can be guided. The result is a dynamic relationship between theory and practice. When put into practice, such a relationship can prevent an atheoretical, even a willy-nilly use of group techniques, akin to drawing blindfolded from a group techniques grab bag. Moreover, we strongly suggest that theory-guided practice in group leadership needs to be based on an ecological foundation (Bemak & Conyne, 2004; Conyne & Bemak, 2004; Conyne & Cook, 2004). An ecological foundation allows groups to be viewed as interdependent, dynamic entities that develop and exist within a larger context.

We suggest that the present dominant way of conceptualizing group work, which extrapolates substantially from Western theories of individually based personality development, largely misses the major salient properties and processes of groups that Kurt Lewin identified decades ago: interdependence, group dynamics, social climate, group development, experiential here-and-now processes, feedback, participant observation, and many others. In the intervening years, other substantial contributions have been added. For example, Lieberman, Yalom, & Miles (1973) introduced the importance of processing and meaning attribution, and the Best Practice Guidelines for Group Work (Association for Specialists in Group Work [ASGW], 1998) details guidelines for group leadership from planning through performing and processing. All of these resources, and others, we find as instrumental in their contribution to an evolving and appropriate good theory of group-work practice.

We built on the previously mentioned and other resources to create the model we present throughout this book to help guide the selection and use of group techniques. The Purposeful Group Techniques Model, which we abbreviate as PGTM, is the result. Chapters 1 and 2 introduce this model to support the proper selection and use of group techniques. Chapter 3 describes how to apply the PGTM in considering which technique to use for various situations.

So, the chapters in Part I provide a compatible intersection of conceptual and practical guidance to support a reasoned approach for group leaders when using group techniques. Subsequent parts will emphasize concrete opportunities for learning how to integrate the PGTM when leading counseling and psychoeducation groups, yet we also will address task and psychotherapy groups. But, first we focus on the foundation upon which the effective use of group techniques rests.

# Setting the Stage for Using Techniques in Counseling and Psychoeducation Groups

**ADVANCE ORGANIZER**

This chapter covers the following material:

**Ecology and Group Work**

**Metaphor of the Toolbox**

**What Are Group Techniques?**
*Specific or Broad in Scope*
*Ongoing Processes and Intentional Purposes*
*Planned or Unplanned*

**In Sum**

Group leadership is a very important function for counselors and other helpers, particularly because group counseling is being used more and more in schools and mental health agencies. Group counseling and other forms of group work, such as psychoeducation groups, are becoming more widespread for many reasons.

First, many more people need help than can be served simply by relying exclusively on individual counseling (Albee & Gulotta, 1997; Conyne, 2000, 2004; Romano & Hage, 2000). Groups provide an efficient way for counselors to reach out; one group leader can serve up to 12 members at once.

Second, groups also can tap naturally occurring therapeutic processes between people in social situations. Groups allow support and mutual helping to occur, they can quickly help members understand that they are not alone in dealing with a particular issue, and they provide multiple sources and opportunities for interpersonal learning (Yalom, 2005).

Third, groups provide educational and therapeutic settings where people can take control of their own lives by interacting with each other and with group leaders. To be helpful, the leader needs to be caring, help members attribute meaning to their experience, and establish an appropriately structured and stimulating environment (Lieberman, Yalom, & Miles, 1973).

Finally, groups are microcosms of life in general. As such, they offer members opportunities to participate in an interpersonal laboratory that not only encourages participants to behave as they generally would in life but also offers them a safe and supportive environment to try out new behaviors. All of these conditions of groups can provide a great impetus for learning and change, and they help account for why groups have become such an important educational and mental health resource today.

Yet, groups are complex and can be very challenging for beginning leaders. It is easy for a novice leader to get overwhelmed because there are so many factors to be aware of simultaneously. Beginning leaders often report feeling flooded by too many inputs, so many that they sometimes become nearly paralyzed with inaction. For example, in a counseling group of 10 members, there are 45 possible individual dyads, or groups of two, each of which will have its own individual relationship. How can a group leader fully understand the group's dynamic given all of these different relationships? And how can a group leader effectively lead such a group?

That is where this book comes in. We have written it to provide a working model to guide group leaders in choosing techniques and in using them effectively and ethically. We invite you to learn a way to make decisions that involves assessing a group situation using a set of six concepts and following a short series of decision-making steps to arrive at a technique that provides a "best fit" with the situation. This model for generating and selecting group techniques is based on certain ecological concepts—such as the importance of context and of the interdependence among group members—that mesh well with groups, and it can be used to support traditional counseling theories.

## Ecology and Group Work

Ecology and group work connect in interesting ways. The most obvious, perhaps, is that a group can be viewed as a system of interconnections, because any group is much more than the sum of its individual parts. Another way of thinking about this matter of interconnection is that a group is not simply a collection of individuals who occupy the same space to listen to a presentation. To be a group, it is necessary that the members communicate with each other, that some bonds begin to form among them, and that the members develop common goals or purposes.

Ecology suggests that everything is connected to everything else. For instance, consider this series of events. On Palm Sunday in many Christian churches millions of wax palm fronds are distributed as part of the worship service. The majority of these palm fronds have come from the rain forests of Colombia. The ecological problem is that when these fronds are cut from the young wax palms, the trees die or are stunted badly, thinning the palms. In turn, these palms are the only habitat of the indigenous yellow-eared parrot, of which there are said to be only 540 or so left in the world. The good news is that alternative environmentally sustainable palm fronds from Mexico and Guatemala are beginning to be used now in the Palm Sunday services, as a way to sustain both the wax palms and the yellow-eared parrot. This situation of the palms illustrates the interconnected balance existing within elements of a larger system. When one part is altered, it may affect other parts.

So, what does this ecological situation have to do with groups? In order for a group to work well and to sustain itself over time, several different parts need to emerge and fit together effectively. The number of members cannot be too large or too small (from 3 to 12 is a good size). The leader cannot be too centrally controlling or too laissez-faire in approach, and often it is beneficial to include a coleader, particularly if the group size is large. The group social system that is created should not be overly rigid and inflexible, nor should it be entirely loose and without direction. Members need to feel support but also they need to be challenged. An example may help.

In one group we have recently learned about, the leader failed to give adequate attention to developing the social system of the group. Rules, expectations, and goals were unaddressed. Without the guidance afforded by agreed-upon structure, members began missing sessions, coming late, or leaving early. These member behaviors indicated low commitment to each other and to the group itself. Midway through this group, the leader fell sick and was unable to continue with it (or with other work projects, either). Another leader stepped into this unusual circumstance.

One of the first actions taken by this new leader was to renegotiate what she termed "beginnings." That is, this new leader tried to reset the group from the start. She independently established one rule which was "No one comes late, leaves early, or misses sessions without a special circumstance." Group goals were discussed and clarified and the new leader helped each member develop personal goals that fit within the group goals and were realistic and attainable. Group rules were created mutually, surrounding confidentiality and attending to others. Specific attention, therefore, was given to creating a group foundation, with boundaries to guide the group and its members. This foundation had been missing before, and its absence then led to all kinds of unproductive and frustrating experiences. With this new foundation a clearer social system took root, allowing for members to get oriented and move ahead on developing a sense of purpose and a climate of safety. These gains, in turn, allowed for members to become more interactive, sharing personal information and giving and receiving feedback. This example shows how separate parts of a group influence other parts, much as how palm trees are necessary to sustain parrots in the previous ecological example.

Ecological concepts (Bemak & Conyne, 2004; Conyne & Bemak, 2004) are well suited to assessing groups and group leadership. We suggest that six ecological concepts are especially useful for assessing group functioning. These concepts, which are discussed later in the chapter, are:

- **Context:** External and group factors influencing the group and its members. For example, to begin a group in an elementary school, taking children out of class may be disallowed, so other approaches become necessary.
- **Interconnection:** Frequency and quality of member-to-member relationships. A group is dependent on intermember relationships and their connections or disconnections.
- **Collaboration:** Working together to move ahead. For instance, group rules and expectations become more accountable and reachable when all in the group are involved in setting them.
- **Social system maintenance:** Developing and continuing a group culture, including clarity and integrity of rules, norms, and expectations. A group involves creation and maintenance of a social system that has its own goals, rules, norms, and general culture.
- **Meaning making:** Creating meaning from experience. Although experiences and occurrences in the group are essential, what members learn from these events is at least as important.
- **Sustainability:** Transferring and generalizing learning and change. Group work, and all forms of helping, have been criticized when change is not carried forward outside the group. Applying learning and change to the "real world" is of high importance in group work.

Notice how these six concepts, which are italicized in the following paragraph, are woven into the text:

A group is a setting that is defined by its own particular *context,* including its purpose, developmental stage, and the resources available to it. For a group to function well, *interconnections* among members need to be positively formed, so that members do not function as isolated individuals. The leader(s) and members construct a *social system* with agreed-upon rules, norms, and expectations that allow their activities to proceed without either too much rigidity or too much fluidity. In a well-functioning group, the leader need not be the primary force who controls the action. Instead, members and the leader *collaborate* to mutually share responsibility and, over time, the leadership functions themselves. Productive interaction among members emerges, and is measured to a large degree by what *meaning* members assign to their experience as well as how aptly they will be able to apply and *sustain* outside the group the learning and changes that have taken place within the group.

These ecological concepts fit groups nicely and, therefore, are very useful in helping group leaders understand group events and guide their choice of techniques. However, the ecological concepts do not diminish the application of traditional counseling theory to group work. Indeed, any of these traditional theoretical bases (e.g., humanistic or behavioral) are important in group leadership. As with ecological counseling (Conyne & Cook, 2004), we see the ecological concepts in group leadership serving an overarching purpose, a metatheory, within which any other counseling theory can be used.

Let's pause to consider the "Reflection Points" that follow.

## Reflection Points
### (for individual analysis or group discussion)

1. Traditional classrooms have students' chairs arranged in rows and facing the teacher. How would rearranging the chairs and other physical resources impact students' interactions as well as learning? Can you describe other contextual factors that contribute to the way a group might function?

2. Describe a situation in which interconnections were important to the success of a group.

3. How does it feel to be part of a team in which the leaders approach others collaboratively versus giving orders?

4. Several college students get together twice a week and study accounting. In addition to performing well on the tests, they all notice that they are managing their personal finances with greater care. What are some other examples of sustainability that might result from groups?

Our purpose, though, is not to focus on the use of traditional counseling theory in group counseling. Many other excellent texts have done this before (e.g., Corey, 2004; Gladding, 2003; Yalom, 2005). Our intent is to provide a practical, decision-based, ecological approach to selecting and using group techniques that can be connected with existing theory—or, in many cases, that could stand alone as the primary source.

Group leaders need practical models that can help guide their selection of techniques. Armed with a model, or models, group leaders possess a resource for assessing group conditions and choosing the best course of action.

## *Metaphor of the Toolbox*

This book is intended to address the issue of group-leading competence by focusing on group techniques. Along with Trotzer (2004), we think that group leaders need a kind of basic "toolbox" at their disposal in order to feel ready and able to do their work with zest and effectiveness. Similar to how a carpenter, a decorator, a plumber, a Web site designer, or an artist enters a job site carrying a box of tools for the trade, so it is that a group leader needs to enter the group-leading context with a set of tools for that trade—that is, the group techniques that are available for use.

## Caution

Having just supported the need for group leaders to have a toolbox of techniques at the ready, we hasten to strongly advocate that a toolbox of techniques by itself is woefully insufficient for effective group leadership. Group techniques must be selected and used while being guided by an organizing conceptual system. The toolbox of techniques we make available in this book will be helpful and useful if its contents can be integrated within the guiding conceptual model we will describe (or some other credible model), the Purposeful Group Techniques Model (PGTM).

Examples of techniques within this toolbox are provided and described in Chapter 3. The complete toolbox is presented in the appendix of this book. It is important for group leaders to have access to a toolbox of group techniques, but only following a discussion of how to use them. Therefore, before discussing the contents of the toolbox, in this chapter we will lay a conceptual foundation for the effective use of group techniques and processes.

## What Are Group Techniques?

We use the term *techniques* very broadly. Rather than trying to differentiate among techniques, strategies, activities, structured experiences, and exercises, it is more fruitful to consider what leaders can do purposefully within their groups. Techniques is an umbrella term covering an array of intervention applications. More simply, techniques are the tools of the trade used by group leaders to influence growth and change.

We define techniques as follows:

*Techniques are intervention applications ("tools of the trade") that are used by group leaders—and sometimes by group members—to focus group processes, try out behavior, accentuate thoughts and feelings, and provide opportunities for learning.*

## Specific or Broad in Scope

Group techniques can be specific and concrete, or they can be broad and ambiguous in scope. An example of a specific and concrete technique is managing speaking time in the group by the speaker being required to possess the designated "speaking object," such as a ball. Without the object, a member may not speak. A broad and ambiguous technique is illustrated by the leader asking an open-ended, group-centered question to search for the level of understanding members may have about what has been discussed. For example, "I am wondering what sense you are making of our discussion."

## Ongoing Processes and Intentional Purposes

Whether a technique is specific or general, it needs to arise from ongoing group processes within the group and be used for intentional purposes. That is, techniques are connected directly to what is occurring in the group, and are chosen to fulfill clear needs. Leaders have been known to make mistakes by using a good group technique for the wrong reasons, maybe because they felt compelled to fill a silence in the group with something (anything), or perhaps because they had just experienced a "great" technique in a recent training experience and were highly motivated to try it out in their own group. So, for proper usage it is important that any technique fit the present circumstances of the group and be used purposefully.

## Planned or Unplanned

A last point we want to make about techniques is that they can be either planned in advance or be unplanned, the latter emerging naturally from the ongoing circumstances of group interaction (Corey & Corey, 2002; Corey, Corey, Callanan, & Russell, 2003; Howell, 1995; Jacobs, Masson, & Harvill, 2002; Kraus, 2003; Pfeiffer & Jones, 1980). Techniques can be selected and set within the overall session plan for a group and be implemented according to that plan. Although this sometimes occurs, more frequently group conditions fluctuate and are dynamic and leaders often have to adapt or improvise techniques. The ability to flexibly apply techniques evolves through training and supervised experience with group leading. As well, it can be very helpful if group leading techniques are guided by a model. As stated earlier, in this book we consider and use the Purposeful Group Techniques Model (PGTM), which is described in the next chapter.

## In Sum

In this chapter we set the stage for what is to come. We discussed why groups can be valuable and presented a set of ecological concepts that are well suited for understanding and working with groups. Group techniques were described as mechanisms, or tools of the trade, to move groups forward, whether these tools be otherwise thought of as activities, interventions, or exercises. The toolbox we will introduce you to contains a wide array of techniques that can be used by group leaders. The central point is that what group leaders do in groups needs to be germane to the group and its members and it needs to be integrally connected with a guiding framework.

Chapter 2 examines the guiding framework for the Purposeful Group Techniques Model (PGTM).

## References

Albee, G., & Gulotta, T. (Eds.). (1997). *Primary prevention works*. Thousand Oaks, CA: Sage.

Association for Specialists in Group Work. (1998). *Association for Specialists in Group Work best practice guidelines*. Retrieved from http://www.asgw.org

Bemak, F., & Conyne, R. (2004). Ecological group work. In R. Conyne & E. Cook (Eds.), *Ecological counseling:*

*An innovative approach to conceptualizing person– environment interaction* (pp. 195–218). Alexandria, VA: American Counseling Association.

Conyne, R. (2000). Prevention in counseling psychology: At long last: Has the time now come? *The Counseling Psychologist, 28,* 838–844.

Conyne, R. (2004). *Preventive counseling: Helping people to become empowered in systems and settings* (2nd ed.). New York: Brunner-Routledge.

Conyne, R., & Bemak, F. (2004). Teaching group work: An ecological perspective toward personal, social, and systemic change [Special issue]. *Journal for Specialists in Group Work, 29,* 7–18.

Conyne, R., & Cook, E. (Eds.). (2004). *Ecological counseling: An innovative approach to conceptualizing person– environment interaction.* Alexandria, VA: American Counseling Association.

Corey, G. (2004). *Theory and practice of group counseling* (6th ed.). Belmont, CA: Thomson Brooks/Cole.

Corey, G., Corey, M., Callanan, P., & Russell, J. M. (2003). *Group techniques* (3rd ed.). Pacific Grove, CA: Brooks/Cole.

Gladding, S. (2003). *Group work: A counseling specialty* (4th ed.). Upper Saddle River, NJ: Merrill/Prentice Hall.

Howell, J. (1995). *Tools for facilitating team meetings: Easy tools that help plan, organize, conduct, and evaluate team meetings.* Seattle, WA: Integrity.

Jacobs, E., Masson, R., & Harvill, R. (2002). *Group counseling: Strategies and skills.* Belmont, CA: Thomson Brooks/Cole.

Kraus, K. (2003). *Exercises in group work.* Upper Saddle River, NJ: Merrill/Prentice Hall.

Lieberman, M., Yalom, I., & Miles, M. (1973). *Encounter groups: First facts.* New York: Basic Books.

Marrow, A. (1969). *The practical theorist: The life and work of Kurt Lewin.* New York: Basic Books.

Pfeiffer, J., & Jones, J. (1980). *Structured experience kit.* La Jolla, CA: University Associates.

Romano, J., & Hage, S. (2000). Prevention and counseling psychology: Revitalizing Commitments for the 21st century. *The Counseling Psychologist, 28,* 733–763.

Trotzer, J. (2004). Conducting a group: Guidelines for choosing and using activities. In J. DeLucia-Waack, D. Gerrity, C. Kalodner, & M. Riva (Eds.), *Group counseling and psychotherapy* (pp. 76–90). Thousand Oaks, CA: Sage.

Yalom, I., Leszcz, M. (5th ed.). (2005). *The theory and practice of group psychotherapy.* New York: Basic Books.

2

# A Framework for Using Techniques: The Purposeful Group Techniques Model (PGTM)

**ADVANCE ORGANIZER**

This chapter covers the following material:

**The Purposeful Group Techniques Model (PGTM)**

**Step 1: Identify the Group Type and Purpose, Best Practice Area, and Developmental Stage**

*Developmental Stage*

**Step 2: Analyze the Presenting Situation by Applying Ecological Concepts**

*Context*　　　　　　　　*Social System Maintenance*
*Interconnection*　　　　*Meaning Making*
*Collaboration*　　　　　*Sustainability*

**Step 3: Review Possible Group Techniques, Considering Focus and Level**

**Step 4: Select a Best-Fit Technique**

**Step 5: Implement and Evaluate How Well the Technique Worked**

**In Sum**

Group leaders need techniques, but they also need a guiding framework to help them use these techniques effectively and appropriately. The Purposeful Group Techniques Model (PGTM) was developed to provide guidance for group leaders.

We have found the model to be helpful for leaders in many circumstances. Perhaps most important, it can help leaders consider and then select and use group techniques intentionally, rather than drawing from a set of techniques without careful thought, almost as if drawing from a grab bag. To use another metaphor, we are interested in group leaders and trainees learning a process for how to catch fish rather than providing them with fish already caught.

Leading groups is a challenging and exhilarating opportunity. To be effective, group leaders need to be able to assess situations and to choose techniques that will work. The PGTM is very practical, aimed at guiding group leaders to select techniques that will work.

## The Purposeful Group Techniques Model (PGTM)

The model is comprised of five interrelated steps that we introduce here (also see Table 2.1) and will discuss throughout the book. The five steps are aimed at helping group leaders move through a process for selecting appropriate techniques.

These five steps are defined as follows:

1. **Identify** the group type and purpose, the relevant best practice area, and the developmental stage it may be in at the present time.
2. **Analyze** the presenting group situation by applying ecological concepts of context, interconnection, collaboration, social system, meaning making, and sustainability.
3. **Review** possible group techniques (techniques contained in the toolbox may be helpful here), considering focus and level;
4. **Select** a best-fit technique for that situation that holds promise for success.
5. **Implement and evaluate** how well the technique worked.

---

**TABLE 2.1**

### Purposeful Group Techniques Model Steps

1. Identify
2. Analyze
3. Review
4. Select
5. Implement and evaluate

## Step 1: Identify the Group Type and Purpose, Best Practice Area, and Developmental Stage

**Group Type and Purpose** In order to select a technique, a group leader must first understand and keep in mind some basic information about the group. The most common types of groups for counselors are counseling groups and psychoeducation groups. These are what we focus on in this book. Other types also exist, including task and psychotherapy groups—which we discuss in Chapter 10. Each group type is unique, and each type has its own general purpose.

In one system of categorization (Association for Specialists in Group Work [ASGW], 2000), group types include task groups, psychoeducation groups, counseling groups, and psychotherapy groups. Other types include support groups, personal growth groups, process groups, T-groups, and self-directed groups, among others.

A brief definition of each group type (ASGW, 2000; Conyne, 1999) follows:

*Task Groups:* These groups are used to resolve or to enhance performance and production goals within a work group, through attention to team building, collaborative problem solving, and system change strategies.

*Psychoeducation Groups:* The purpose of psychoeducation groups is to educate members and develop their skills. Often they are geared to prevention of future problems. Leaders impart information and train in skills, within an interpersonal milieu.

*Counseling Groups:* These groups are used to help members improve their coping skills by focusing on interpersonal problem solving, feedback, and support within a here-and-now framework.

*Psychotherapy Groups:* Through psychotherapy groups, members learn how to reduce psychological and/or emotional dysfunction by focusing on bringing past history to the present and incorporating diagnosis and assessment within an interpersonal orientation.

Although most group techniques apply generally across all types of groups, some may be more relevant than others as a function of the group type. For instance, agenda setting and problem-solving techniques may match better with task groups, whereas self-disclosure techniques align more fully with counseling, psychotherapy, and psychoeducation groups. Note that any one technique could be used in a variety of ways, at different times, and for different purposes than how we may have categorized it. This is as it should be, because group leading is highly dependent on flexible and adaptive use that is consistent with the exercising of professional judgment.

In this book we concentrate on counseling and psychoeducational groups as the most frequently used by counselors and other helpers. Yet, we don't neglect task and psychotherapy groups, as they are very important and are being increasingly used. Task and psychotherapy groups are considered in Chapter 10.

**Relevant Best Practice Area** Best practice guidelines have been developed in many disciplines to help shape effective and ethical delivery of services. In the field of group leadership a good example of best practice guidelines was developed by the

Association for Specialists in Group Work (ASGW, 1998). These ethical guidelines were organized in relation to three important best practice areas of group leadership, colloquially known as the three P's: planning, performing, and processing. Group techniques are associated with each best practice area. A brief definition of each of these areas follows (Conyne, 1999; Rapin, 2004; Rapin & Conyne, 2006).

*Planning* involves all preliminary steps to conducting the first group session or meeting. These steps include assessing needs and context, designing the group, selecting resources and space, recruiting and selecting members (as appropriate to the group type), organizing a leadership plan, and many other important aspects. Another consideration that we think is crucial in successful planning is determining whether a solo group leader versus coleaders will be utilized.

*Performing* involves applying or modifying the plan through within-session transactions. In short, performing refers to actually leading the group. Some important elements of performing include delivering necessary group competencies, creating and nurturing therapeutic or learning conditions, being able to accurately observe group processes, effecting a decision-making process to select and implement best-fit techniques, behaving in an ethical manner, and many others. Continuing our discussion on the importance of a solo leader versus coleader, performing can at times be quite different with each model. Consider a critical incident occurring in a group, such as a sudden conflict between two members, that demands a leadership response. With two leaders, how is this managed? Coleaders need to agree how to handle such contingencies in advance.

*Processing* involves drawing meaning from group events and experiences. Processing occurs *within* sessions (thus also could be considered a subset of the performing phase) as well as *between* sessions or meetings when leaders review and reflect on their work. It is helpful to the group when the leader or leaders engage members in a discussion about how decisions are made. This discussion might occur at the time the decision is being made or could occur afterward. Processing of techniques is as important to success as is appropriate selection and implementation of techniques (DeLucia-Waack, 2004). For a comprehensive review of processing in group work, see Ward and Litchy (2004).

In general, most discussions of group techniques have been focused on the performing phase of group leadership. Of course, a cogent argument can easily be launched that performing is the most important practice area of all in group leadership. However, the other two areas of group leadership also are important and they influence, individually and collectively, how well performance can occur. In fact, the three P's are conceptualized as reciprocally influencing each other. That is, planning-performing-processing are interlinked within an overall cyclical system of group leadership. Graphically, the three P's system can be depicted as shown in Figure 2.1.

## Developmental Stage

There are over 100 published group developmental stage models (examples include Anderson, 1984; Corey & Corey, 2006; Gladding, 2003; Jones, 1973; Trotzer, 2006; Tuckman & Jensen, 1977). We have adopted a very simple model for use in this book: beginning, middle, and end. A group is subject to different forces and members

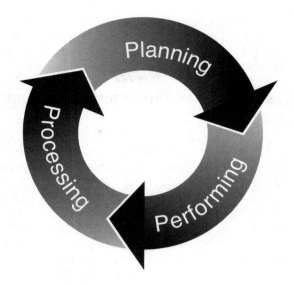

**Figure 2.1**
Three P's

behave qualitatively differently in each stage. Therefore, assessing the stage of development for a specific group yields important information about what kinds of leader techniques might be appropriate.

In the *beginning stage*, group members work on getting established and in transitioning toward a higher level of functioning. They tend to be dependent on the leader and external structure during this time, while needing to understand the goals and procedures that pertain. In the beginning stage of group, then, members seek to find their way, how they will fit, how the group will be helpful, and what is expected. As they move through this beginning stage and develop increased certainty about their place in the group, then they can begin to take more chances and to become more involved. In turn, they naturally influence the existing way that the group functions. This transition toward greater control on the part of members sometimes is experienced as tension and conflict, the nature of which can be subtle or intense. Its presence is a hallmark of moving from a very beginning stage toward a more productive stage.

In the *middle stage* of a group the members seek to be more connected and to become more productive. Having progressed through getting established and transitioning to enhanced and shared control, members are more open to each other and to considering how to collaborate in combining resources. These gains allow for a greater interdependence, a give-and-take of self-disclosure and feedback, both of which accelerate learning and change. This is the working stage of a group.

In the *ending stage* of development, group members consolidate their gains and forecast their future beyond the group's termination. They grapple with identifying what they have learned, with how they can apply and sustain their learning, and with saying goodbye to each other and moving on with their lives.

Thus, to summarize Step 1 of the PGTM, the leader or leaders need to be aware of important factors that serve to shape the kinds of techniques that could be most appropriate and effective. These factors involve what type of group is being led, what its purposes are, and what developmental stage best characterizes it currently.

## Step 2: Analyze the Presenting Situation by Applying Ecological Concepts

Next, the leader is asked to assess the group, beyond type and purpose, best practice area, and stage of group development. An ecological approach can be very helpful to guide this assessment.

The six ecological concepts that we suggest are important for group leaders to keep in mind as they select techniques. They can be viewed as complementary to Yalom's 11 therapeutic factors (Yalom, 1985), which generally are thought to be necessary for effective group psychotherapy. Several of these therapeutic conditions are included in the following discussion.

### Context

Group techniques should not appear out of a vacuum, nor should they be parachuted into the group. Rather, group techniques should be chosen that are consistent with the ongoing and evolving context of the group.

No group stands alone. All groups are part of a proximal and distal set of circumstances, conditions, and influences, and each group brings with it its own evolving set of contextual dynamics. Therefore, any group is part of a larger context, and group leaders frequently undervalue that reality. A counseling group offered by a mental health center is subject to such external contextual factors as the center's policies and procedures, its physical setting, community values and population needs, and managed care considerations. A task force commissioned within city government is subject to setting, policies and procedures, expectations for performance and goal accomplishment, deadlines, and so on. Moreover, all groups are influenced by macroexternal factors, such as national and international events, and the dominant cultural and political values inhabiting society. Within any group, the evolving developmental context sets the tone and influences presently occurring events and experiences. A group that has been characterized by inconsistent member attendance over its first three sessions affords a particular contextual history, different from another group whose member attendance has been stellar. Group leaders need to be aware of such external and internal contextual influences as they consider what group techniques to use in which situations.

The strategy "Conceptualize that context is everything" emerges from this concept.

### Interconnection

A group is comprised of interconnections among its members. There is no group without these interconnections; otherwise, the group is merely a collection of separate individuals occupying the same space and time.

Yalom and Leszcz (2005) pointed out that cohesion is a vitally important therapeutic factor in groups, serving as a necessary precursor for group productivity and interpersonal learning. Establishing and strengthening interconnections among members weaves a bond that promotes cohesion.

Clearly important for group counseling, group psychotherapy, and psychoeducation groups, interconnections also are needed within task groups. Interconnections foster "working together," a basic concept that cuts to the essence of group work— that is, how members relate to, work with, and learn from one another. Group techniques, therefore, need to promote the creation, maintenance, and strengthening of interconnections among members.

Group leaders need to help members make connections among themselves. One way to think of these interconnections is to imagine a network or a web. The denser the webbing among members, as evidenced by their nonverbal and verbal interactions, the more interconnected they can be—and the more potentially valuable the group experience can become.

The strategy "Forge interconnections among members" emerges from this concept.

## Collaboration

Group leaders should not foist their ideas and approaches on members. Although the group leaders are more trained and experienced in the theory and practice of group-work leadership, the members are more expert in their own experience and situation. Group leaders need to collaborate, or work with, members in all phases of group work, including the implementation of group techniques. Presenting a group technique idea tentatively, seeking to elicit member approval, usually is a desired approach to use. Rather than instructing a member to do something, the preferred style would be to ask the member if he or she might be willing to try it.

Lieberman, Yalom, and Miles (1973), in their classic research study involving group leadership, found that effective leaders did not dominate and did not completely turn over group operations to members. Rather, effective leaders provided enough—but not too much—structure (executive functioning), challenge (emotional stimulation), and support (caring) to help members move ahead constructively. Collaborating with members in this process is important.

Here is a very simple example of collaboration between leaders and members. Often in the first session of a group, a question will arise about whether there will be a bathroom or food break during sessions. One way to handle this question is for the leaders to decide about this issue in advance and make it known to the members. We do not advise that approach, in general. Deciding together about a break, without spending excessive time on it, can promote interaction and yield a decision that all can accept. Collaboration means working on important matters together whenever possible and, although it may take longer for decision making than does a leader-based decision, the outcomes can be substantially better.

The strategy "Do with, rather than do to" emerges from this concept.

## Social System Maintenance

A group leader is always trying to build a group culture characterized by systemic interconnections among all parties, and where rules and expectations are clear and fair. In fact, one way to think of a group leader is as a host or hostess of a social system. By this statement we mean that the leader seeks to work with group members to create a unique social system that includes mutually determined and clear expectations, goals, rules, norms, and patterns of behavior.

Developing a positive social system involves both clarity about rules and building expectations for change. In the groups we lead and supervise, we always encourage members to value that this particular collection of people, in this place, at this time is both unique in history and in their collective experience. Never again will this opportunity exist. Further, we point out that together they can create and sustain a novel and personally significant social system for accomplishing group and personal goals. So, we try to stimulate members to cherish the moment—that is, to learn to appreciate their experience as they live it and to recognize their role in shaping that experience.

Several of Yalom's therapeutic conditions are exercised during the creation of a positive social system. For example, we impress upon members that the group is a place where hope exists (instillation of hope factor) and where they can help one another improve (altruism factor). We tell them that they will find others in the group who may also be experiencing concerns similar to their own, that they are not alone in the world (universality factor). We work toward developing with members a culture of safety and risk taking where they will become increasingly able to self-disclose appropriately and to give and get feedback. Through doing so, Yalom's conditions of interpersonal learning and existential meaning can be realized.

The strategy "Create and maintain a functioning social system" emerges from this concept.

## Meaning Making

Group work needs to help members understand and derive meaning from their experience. Experiencing by itself is not enough. At one time, though, many leaders assumed that good group work could be measured by members who expressed emotion during group sessions, or by sessions that involved a high level of energy. But high or deep activity alone is insufficient for learning and change to occur and be sustained. It also is very important that members understand what the experience means.

Lieberman et al. (1973) pointed out that members need to learn from their experience. They referred to this process as meaning attribution. Constructivist approaches in counseling and psychology have elaborated the concept of meaning making as a central goal of the therapeutic compact (Conyne & Cook, 2004). Therefore, a very important group leader function is to help members draw meaning from their experience in the group and, also, for leaders to derive meaning from their work to both help the present group progress and evolve a leadership theory and style that has generalizability (Conyne, 1999).

The strategy "Connect experience with knowing" emerges from this concept.

## Sustainability

People participate in groups in order to learn or change. The ability of group members to apply and to sustain learning and changes they have made within the group to their ongoing lives over time is a critically important issue. Group leaders and members need to attend to the issue of sustainability of gains outside the group throughout the course of the group.

We have seen too many situations where group members learn how to communicate more directly and appropriately with other group members, but where no attention has been given to helping them carry out those new skills in their families, with their colleagues, or in the world in general. In such instances these new skills often will disappear over time. On the contrary, when leaders systematically assist members to plan and practice using new skills with specific people or in specific situations, the members stand a better chance of sustaining those skills.

Helping members practice skills within the group, accompanied by homework assignments in which they seek to apply these skills, can assist in promoting sustainability. So, for instance, if a member is attempting to improve her ability to communicate with others, role-plays can be conducted in the group, feedback provided, and plans made for the member to try out specific communication strategies with another person outside the group, with results brought back to the group for review and further work. Approaches such as this can foster continuation of change.

The strategy "Attend to changes lasting over time" emerges from this concept.

The foregoing underlying ecological concepts and strategies are organized in Table 2.2. For each concept and strategy an example group technique is provided. These exemplary techniques are drawn from the techniques Toolbox contained in the Appendix.

### TABLE 2.2

### Ecological Concepts, Strategies, and Exemplary Group Techniques

| Ecological Concepts to Support Group Technique | → | Strategies Associated With Ecological Concepts | → | Exemplary Group Techniques |
|---|---|---|---|---|
| Context | → | "Conceptualize that context is everything." | → | Seating (Toolbox #26, Performance) |
| Interconnection | → | "Forge interconnections among members." | → | String Activity (Toolbox #84, Performance) |
| Collaboration | → | "Do with, rather than do to." | → | Sharing Group Trepidations (Toolbox #1, Performance) |
| Social System | → | "Create and maintain a functioning social system." | → | Physiogram (Toolbox #54, Performance) |
| Meaning Making | → | "Connect experience with knowing." | → | My Learning (Toolbox #17, Processing—Within-Session) |
| Sustainability | → | "Attend to changes lasting over time." | → | Six-Month Reminders (Toolbox #30, Processing—Within-Session) |

## Step 3: Review Possible Group Techniques, Considering Focus and Level

In this part of the PGTM we define two dimensions (adapted from Cohen & Smith, 1976) that can help group leaders conceptually organize the hundreds of group techniques that are available for use. Important beyond this organizational value, the two dimensions also provide guidance about how to sort through and/or generate techniques that might be used in any group session or meeting.

The two guiding dimensions are:

1. *Group technique focus.* A group technique can be focused cognitively, affectively, behaviorally, and/or structurally. That is, techniques can help group members:

- think about their situation (cognitive, thinking): "List three reasons why this might be a bad idea."
- explore their feelings (affective, feeling): "How are you feeling about this option?"
- develop or practice interpersonal skills (behavioral, skills): "Try saying that now using 'I' statements."
- change the ongoing course of interaction (structural, direction of flow): "Can we shift now, to go back to an earlier point in our discussion?"

2. *Group technique level.* Group techniques can be aimed at varying levels within the group, ranging from the individual, to the interpersonal, to the group itself.

- At the individual level, a member is the focus of a technique. Here, a member may be led to speak about himself or herself or someone else may direct comments at the member. "I am feeling very happy right now, I've learned so much!" might reflect this level of involvement.
- At the interpersonal level, a technique is used to promote members to talk with one another. For example, the leader may ask Bill and Susan to listen to and paraphrase each other's communications.
- At the group level, the focus is on the group itself. A leader might ask "How are we doing today?" Or a member might refer to the group in this way: "We don't seem to be getting anywhere today, but I'm wondering how the rest of you see this."

In addition, in the PGTM trainees are schooled to consider contextual issues in the overall selection of a technique. That is, what has happened historically within this group, as well as what events immediately preceded the choice point in question are important for shaping the technique choice made by group leaders.

Twelve types of techniques (i.e., four levels of technique focus times three levels of technique level) can be produced through various combinations of these guiding dimensions. Table 2.3 summarizes two guiding dimensions for group techniques.

| **TABLE 2.3** |
|---|

## Two Guiding Dimensions for Group Techniques: The PGTM

| Technique Focus | Technique Level |
|---|---|
| Cognitive | Individual |
| Affective | Interpersonal |
| Behavioral | Group |
| Structural | |

# Step 4: Select a Best-Fit Technique

Selecting what technique to use in what situation for what purpose is a challenging and necessary task. There are many types of techniques and the situations and goals for their use also are complex. As we have observed, to avoid a grab-bag approach to technique selection, a coherent decision-making process is needed. A central tenet of our approach is that group leaders must learn a process they can use to purposefully consider and then select appropriate techniques for use in their groups. Highly functioning group leaders are able to choose an appropriate technique in real time as group interaction is transpiring (Cohen & Smith, 1976; Conyne, 1999; Conyne, Wilson, & Ward, 1997; Trotzer, 2004).

Selecting a best-fit technique includes the previous three steps we have discussed: (a) be aware of group type, purpose, best practices, and developmental stage; (b) analyze the presenting situation; and (c) review possible group techniques. In addition, decision-making steps are used to select the best-fit technique from all those that have been considered.

These decision-making steps ask the group leader to weigh the relative advantages and disadvantages of the techniques under consideration, finally estimating which one might be most likely to produce greatest advantages and fewest disadvantages. Professional judgment is necessary, which can be assisted by group leaders applying the following five evaluative criteria.

- **Appropriateness:** For example, which technique would best fit the culture of the group and its members?
- **Adequacy:** For example, which technique would be strong enough, but not too strong, to have the desired effect?
- **Effectiveness:** For example, which technique could most fully achieve the goal?
- **Efficiency:** For example, which technique would require the fewest resources?
- **Side Effects:** For example, which technique would minimize negative side effects while maximizing positive side effects?

All things considered, a technique meeting these criteria would possess many advantages and few disadvantages and would be worth selecting.

## Step 5: Implement and Evaluate How Well the Technique Worked

This final step moves beyond choosing a technique to evaluating the technique's value once it has been implemented. Group leaders learn from what they do. But, in order to maximize their learning, group leaders need to intentionally reflect on their work in the group—what works, what is not effective, how satisfied are the members, and other questions of importance. We will not focus on this step, as we are more interested in technique selection, but it is important to underscore that group leaders need to be concerned with the effectiveness of techniques that they apply.

Table 2.4 lists the decision-making steps used to select a technique.

---

**TABLE 2.4**

### Selecting a Technique Using Decision-Making Steps

- Review and identify relevant toolbox for technique possibilities (or develop your own techniques)
- Weigh advantages and disadvantages of each technique by applying evaluative criteria
- Select best-fit technique possessing greater advantages than disadvantages
- Implement and evaluate the choice

---

### Example of Joe, the Group Leader

#### Group Type

Joe leads a psychoeducation group that is curriculum based. Over the course of the 15 sessions he generally provides a 10- to 15-minute educational lecture to the group, followed by a structured activity that builds upon the lecture. The last hour of each session is then utilized for a group discussion in which all members are asked to participate.

#### Analysis of the Group Situation

The group is at a beginning stage of development. The third (of 12) sessions has just ended and Joe is wondering how to proceed in the next session. Joyce has monopolized the group's discussion time each session by talking for very long periods in ways that are often tangential to the topic. Joe realizes that he could easily use the educational component and structured activities as a way to help the group and the member learn and explore the implications when one member monopolizes the discussion time. Equally important, Joe is aware that the group is in the beginning stages of group development. Early development may lead members to feel uncomfortable about a member monopolizing the discussion time and they may be unsure of how to respond. As Joe continues to process and analyze this information, he is doing so to help guide him in selecting a possible group technique that will benefit the group.

### Ecological Issues

There usually are several ecological issues involved in group situations. The point is to determine which is most salient at the time. In this case, Joe determines that Joyce's tendency to monopolize disallows interconnections to develop among members, and he knows that the group members need to become more interdependent in order for progress to emerge.

### Review Possible Group Techniques

A range of possible group techniques usually is possible to work on any particular ecological issue. (Note that there frequently is no single "right" way. The leader tries to select a technique that is more potentially advantageous than disadvantageous, or that will be appropriate and effective.) Joe identified four possible techniques that might promote interconnections: (a) he might ask Joyce if she is interested in receiving feedback from others in the group (cognitive focus, individual/interpersonal level); (b) he might pay closer attention to the nonverbal behavior of other group members the next time Joyce launches into a long monologue to see if he might get some clues about their feelings (behavioral focus, individual level); (c) he might carefully design a series of structured activities that would block Joyce from taking center stage (structural focus, interpersonal level); or (d) he might interrupt Joyce and ask her if she could describe how she is feeling as she talks, in an effort to help her contributions become more therapeutic (affective focus, individual level).

### Select the Best-Fit Technique

The techniques under review now need to be subjected to a decision-making procedure that includes:

a. Review the toolbox to identify possible techniques that might be used to promote an ecological direction, in relation to their focus (cognitive, affective, behavioral, structural) and level (individual, interpersonal, group).
b. Weigh the advantages and disadvantages of each technique, considering how each meets the evaluative criteria of appropriateness, adequacy, effectiveness, efficiency, and side effects.
c. Select a technique with more advantages than disadvantages.
d. Implement and evaluate progress and success.

In considering these steps, Joe selected what he thought was the least intrusive one—observation of nonverbal behaviors of group members during monopolizing behavior of Joyce—and also reasoned that the data yielded from it might be important in choosing any additional techniques to use. When Joe tried this technique in the next session, he was amazed to find lots of valuable information: He noticed eye rolling by Jack, shifting in her seat by Harriet, and an occasional sighing by Frank. He realized that there was a lot of nonverbal interaction among members when Joyce was speaking and the task was to help the nonverbal become verbal in manageable ways. Armed with this new data, Joe then decided during the session to ask Joyce if she might be interested in hearing from others in the group about their thoughts and feelings during the last few minutes when she was speaking. She seemed somehow relieved by this, rather than put off, saying that this is why she was in the group in the first place. So, they were off and running in a different direction—one that seemed promising in increasing interconnected verbal interaction. Of course, the success of this technique needs to be monitored and evaluated.

Let's pause to consider the "Reflection Points" that follow.

## Reflection Points
### (for individual analysis or group discussion)

1. What do you make of how Joe moved through the steps?
2. What would help determine an appropriate technique? Can you provide an example?
3. Effective techniques are those that help members reach their goals. What might be some examples of goals within a counseling or psychoeducation group? How might you be able to tell if a selected technique is effective?
4. Refer back to Chart 2.2. Discuss the exemplary group techniques for each concept and strategy. Can you see how these fit together? What questions do you have, if any? Can you think of any other group techniques that might work?

## In Sum

Becoming an effective group leader involves more than simply learning about group techniques and how to use them. Although being aware of a range of techniques and their proper use is very important, it is essential that group techniques be placed within a guiding framework, as many have observed (e.g., Corey, Corey, Callanan, & Russell, 2004; Jacobs, Masson, & Harvill, 2002).

In this chapter we described the purposeful group techniques model, or PGTM. This model is based on taking an ecological approach to selecting group techniques, paying particular attention to the concepts of context, interconnection, collaboration, social system mainte- nance, meaning making, and sustainability. We then suggested a set of steps that can guide group leader selection of group techniques, involving a review of potential techniques, weighing the advantages and disadvantages of each technique, selecting the best-fit technique, implementing that choice, and then processing progress and success. In the next chapter, we show how the model can be applied in practice.

## References

Anderson, J. (1984). *Counseling through group process*. New York: Springer.

Association for Specialists in Group Work. (1998). *Association for Specialists in Group Work best practice guidelines*. Retrieved from http://www.asgw.org

Association for Specialists in Group Work. (2000). *Professional standards for the training of group workers*. Retrieved from http://www.asgw.org

Cohen, A., & Smith, R. (1976). *The critical incident in growth groups*. La Jolla, CA: University Associates.

Conyne, R. (1999). *Failures in group work: How we can learn from our mistakes*. Thousand Oaks, CA: Sage.

Conyne, R., & Cook, E. (Eds.). (2004). *Ecological counseling: An innovative approach to conceptualizing person– environment interaction*. Alexandria, VA: American Counseling Association.

Conyne, R., Wilson, F. R., & Ward, D. (1997). *Comprehensive group work: What it means & how to teach it*. Alexandria, VA: American Counseling Association.

Corey, M., & Corey, G. (2006). *Groups: Process and practice* (7th ed.). Pacific Grove, CA: Brooks/Cole.

Corey, G., Corey, M., Callanan, P., & Russell, J. M. (2004). *Group techniques* (3rd ed.). Pacific Grove, CA: Brooks/Cole.

DeLucia-Waack, J. (2004). Response: Inappropriate group activities: These will work! In L. Tyson, R. Perusse, & J. Whitledge (Eds.), *Critical incidents in group counseling* (pp. 59–64). Alexandria, VA: American Counseling Association.

Gladding, S. (2003). *Group work: A counseling specialty* (4th ed.). Upper Saddle River, NJ: Merrill/Prentice Hall.

Jacobs, E., Masson, R., & Harvill, R. (2002). *Group counseling: Strategies and skills*. Belmont, CA: Thomson Brooks/Cole.

Jones, J. (1973). A model of group development. In J. Jones & J. Pfeiffer (Eds.), *The 1973 annual handbook for group facilitators* (pp. 127–129). La Jolla, CA: University Associates.

Lieberman, M., Yalom, I., & Miles, M. (1973). *Encounter groups: First facts*. New York: Basic Books.

Rapin, L., & Conyne, R. (2006). Best practices in group work. In J. Trotzer, *The counselor and the group: Integration theory, training, and practice* (4th ed., pp. 291–318). Philadelphia: Routledge.

Rapin, L. (2004). Guidelines for ethical and legal practice in counseling and psychotherapy groups. In J. DeLucia-Waack, D. Gerrity, C. Kalodner, & M. Riva (Eds.), *Group counseling and group psychotherapy* (pp. 151–165). Thousand Oaks, CA: Sage.

Trotzer, J. (2004). Conducting a group: Guidelines for choosing and using activities. In J. DeLucia-Waack, D. Gerrity, C. Kalodner, & M. Riva (Eds.), *Group counseling and psychotherapy* (pp. 76–90). Thousand Oaks, CA: Sage.

Trotzer, J. (2006). *The counselor and the group: Integrating theory, training, and practice* (4th ed.). Philadelphia: Accelerated Development.

Tuckman, B., & Jensen, M. (1977). Stages of small group development revisited. *Group and Organizational Studies, 2*, 419–427.

Ward, D., & Litchy, M. (2004). The effective use of processing in groups. In J. DeLucia-Waack, D. Gerrity, C. Kalodner, & M. Riva (Eds.), *Group counseling and group psychotherapy* (pp. 104–119). Thousand Oaks, CA: Sage.

Yalom, I. (1985). *The theory and practice of group psychotherapy*. New York: Basic Books.

Yalom, I, and Leszcz, M. (5th ed.). (2005). *The theory and practice of group psychotherapy*. New York: Basic Books.

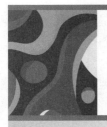

# How to Select and Use Techniques in Counseling or Psychoeducation Groups

**ADVANCE ORGANIZER**

This chapter contains the following material:

**Practical Application of the PGTM**
*Purpose of the Toolbox*
*How to Use the Toolbox*
*Caveat for Using the Techniques*
*Contents of the Toolbox: Examining a Prototype*

**Implementing the PGTM**

**Critical Incidents and Their Use**
*Coding*
*History*

**Critical Incident Format**

**Step 1: Identify the Group Type and Purpose, Best Practice Area, and Developmental Stage.**

**Step 2: Analyze the Presenting Situation by Applying Ecological Concepts.**

**Step 3: Review Possible Group Techniques Considering Focus and Level.**

**Step 4: Select a Best-Fit Technique and Then Provide a Rationale for Your Choice.**

**Step 5: Implement and Evaluate How Would Technique Worked and then Process Its Effectiveness.**

**Group Leadership and Its Techniques Are Personal**

**An Example of a Critical Incident**

**In Sum**

**Learning Activities**

Chapters 1 and 2 set the stage for using group techniques by stressing that leaders must select group techniques purposefully, being guided by a sound conceptual model, and not select them impulsively and without purpose. The Purposeful Group Techniques Model (PGTM) can help group leaders become more intentional about their selection and application of group techniques.

Now we turn to using this model to select and implement group techniques. In this chapter we focus on the training approach that is used throughout this book. The approach applies the model through use of a toolbox and critical incidents. These training applications and resources are described in the following sections.

## Practical Application of the PGTM

Certainly, tools are wonderful inventions for getting work done. The sewing machine has greatly eased the work of the tailor or seamstress and the chain saw helps both the logger and the "weekend warrior" accomplish work not otherwise possible. Technology has revolutionized our world. Without today's tools (computers, MP3s, cell phones, personal digital assistants [PDAs], etc.) many of us would be challenged. Tools can be great things, indeed!

Yet, we also know that tools can be misused. A hammer obviously is not the tool of choice for tightening a screw, and everyone has experienced the uncivil use of cell phones in public places where everyone in earshot has to endure someone else's soap drama. Yes, tools can be used inappropriately and ineffectively at times and they can sometimes be dangerous if not used with caution. Many personal insults or injuries have resulted from careless application.

Techniques are the "tools of the trade" for group leaders. We envision them as being contained in a toolbox, as we have said. The PGTM is intended to provide a guiding process and a resulting zone of safety for the use of these techniques.

## Purpose of the Toolbox

The toolbox is contained in the appendix and is organized according to the three practice areas of group leadership: planning, performing, and processing. It is important that group leaders have at their disposal techniques that span the entire range of group leadership, not being restricted to just the delivery of group leadership within sessions or meetings (i.e., performance). The toolbox provides group leaders and those learning to become group leaders with a way to readily identify some possibilities for action within each best practice area. Techniques contained in the toolbox are meant to be used as aids, serving the larger purpose of effective and appropriate group leadership

Whereas the techniques contained in the toolbox are useful ones, they represent just a sampling of all the techniques possible. Moreover, we do not mean to imply that leaders should use only techniques that are already developed and published. It is possible that leaders—usually advanced leaders—are able to invent their own techniques as well.

## How to Use the Toolbox

Techniques contained in the toolbox are intended generally to provide ideas for action. However, usage may differ, depending on experience level.

We suggest that those who are novices and just getting started with group leadership (beginning level) review the toolbox resources closely, looking for some concrete possibilities for consideration and potential adoption. On the other hand, for those who are more experienced (intermediate level), we suggest you scan the toolbox items with the intent of adapting the examples or to stimulate your own creative ideas. Last, for those who may be very experienced (advanced level), we suggest you first plumb your own thinking and experience and generate technique possibilities from your own resources, turning to the toolbox as a check.

## Caveat for Using the Techniques

We have already noted that the steps of planning, performing, and processing often blend together and that they do not—in practice—always exist discretely and independently. This is as it should be, but for instructional and training purposes it is helpful and convenient to organize these three P's separately.

The same situation exists for techniques contained in the toolbox. Although we have conveniently packaged certain techniques within either planning, or performing, or processing, it is, for example, entirely possible that a particular technique organized within the planning section might be appropriate for use within another best practice area, such as within-session processing. Or, for another example, that a technique we might describe for use with a psychoeducation group could, in some other context, be suitable for use with a counseling group. It is important to remember this caveat as you move through this book: Although organized models are important, flexibility and professional judgment are essential for proper use.

## Contents of the Toolbox: Examining a Prototype

As stated, techniques for planning, performing, and processing are contained in the toolbox appendix. That way, all the techniques are organized in one easy-to-reference location. In the following paragraphs we show how a technique appears in the toolbox within the best practice areas of planning, performing, and processing, along with a short discussion.

***Planning Technique Prototype*** The planning technique occurs at the beginning stage of a group and can be used for any type of group. The planning technique prototype shows the associated ecological concepts. Holding a preliminary group session provides a context for potential members and creates a model for a functioning social system. Although demonstrating the intention to be collaborative with members, the leader is also beginning to address all other ecological issues.

## Planning Technique Prototype

| Group Types | Best Practice PLANNING | Stage(s) | Ecological Concept(s) | Focus(i) | Level(s) |
|---|---|---|---|---|---|
| Psyed Couns | Hold a preliminary group session to orient potential members. | Begin | Context Collaboration Social system | Cognitive | Interpersonal Group |

*Performing Technique Prototype* In the performing technique prototype, a nonverbal technique is shown that can be used to promote listening skill development. In this example, careful listening skills are addressed by the degree of attention required for group members as they take turns passing an object, which basically functions as the "right to speak." This technique especially helps develop expectations and rules that are part of the social system. It is a structural intervention that also is focused on skill development (behavioral), and the technique is directed at developing behaviors and patterns of behavior at the individual, interpersonal, and group levels.

## Performing Technique Prototype

| Group Types | Best Practice PERFORMING | Stage(s) | Ecological Concept(s) | Focus(i) | Level(s) |
|---|---|---|---|---|---|
| Psyed Couns | Using any object, have the member who is speaking hold that object while all others are silent. She gives it to the next speaker who must address the very last thing said (careful listening skills). | Begin | Social system | Behavioral Structural | Individual Interpersonal Group |

*Processing Technique Prototype: Within-Session Processing* The within-session processing prototype is an example of processing that can take place during the group stages from middle to end. The assignment is to self-disclose, so it makes sense that it is not a beginning stage technique. Although there is an affective aspect to self-disclosure, the technique also is cognitively focused, as the leader may be asking for a type of check-in. This technique can be applied in any type of group. Meaning making is an ecological concept that often goes hand in hand with processing practices because leaders are usually intent on challenging members' thinking or behaviors in the group settings, while supporting them within the process. As members develop meaning they are in a better position to apply their learning, thus improving sustainability from the group to the real world.

## Processing Technique Prototype: Within-Session Processing

| Group Types | Best Practice PROCESSING Within Sessions | Stage(s) | Ecological Concept(s) | Focus(i) | Level(s) |
|---|---|---|---|---|---|
| Psyed Couns | "Imagine yourself as you are now— silent—and it is the last session. What have you gotten from the group? How do you feel about your level of participation? Share this with the group." | Mid End | Meaning making Sustainability | Cognitive Affective | Individual |

***Processing Technique Prototype: Between-Session Processing*** Between-session processing is illustrated through this last prototype. This technique is drawn from the deep processing model (Conyne, 1999), and is particularly useful for leader processing between sessions, either independently or with a coleader, supervisor, or colleague. Although simplified greatly in this toolbox, the technique affords a group leader the opportunity to reflect and consider potential courses of action. Deep processing is intended to improve meaning making and the sustainability of leader skills.

## Processing Technique Prototype: Between-Session Processing

| Group Types | Best Practice PROCESSING Within Sessions | Stage(s) | Ecological Concept(s) | Focus(i) | Level(s) |
|---|---|---|---|---|---|
| Psyed Couns | Deep processing model— 1. Transpose the group meeting by recording objective observations. 2. Reflect on your subjective awareness of the meeting. 3. Discover meaning through integration of objective and subjective awareness. 4. Apply increased awareness through action plan derived from evaluation. 5. Evolve as the plan grows with integration of best practices into an action plan. | Beg Mid End | Meaning making Sustainability | Cognitive Affective | Group |

Let's pause to consider the "Reflection Points" that follow.

## Reflection Points
### (for individual analysis or group discussion)

1. Have you ever been a member of a group that just did not work well? What did the leader do or not do that may have contributed?

2. Think of a time when you tried to solve a problem and you found just the right tools or methods to allow you to succeed. Why were you successful?

3. Think of a time when you tried to solve a problem and you could not find the proper tool or method to succeed. Why were you unsuccessful?

4. We maintain that techniques are important for planning, for performing, and for within and between processing. Why is this the case?

5. Go to the toolbox of techniques in the appendix. Randomly select one technique (left column) in planning, in performing, and in processing. Follow each across the columns to get a sense of how this works.

6. Think of your own critical incident. Go to the toolbox to find some possible techniques that might fit. Discuss them with a partner.

## Implementing the PGTM

Let's explore how the PGTM can be put into practice. In our teaching and training, critical incidents are used to provide concrete situations. Students or trainees consider the critical incident, which poses a challenge needing to be resolved through leader intervention, and then they follow steps of the PGTM to select the best-fit technique. They also are free to refer to the toolbox for assistance, if that is useful to them. In training situations, the learners also have the opportunity to compare and discuss their decision-making process and the technique they selected. Finally, training provides an opportunity to try out a technique, getting some feedback about how it is presented.

## Critical Incidents and Their Use

We have adapted the work of Cohen and Smith (1976) on critical incidents in growth groups as the primary format for learning about how to select and use group techniques, but we also have attended to critical incident work in task groups (Flanagan, 1954), group guidance (Gazda & Folds, 1968), group counseling (Tyson, Perusse, & Whitledge, 2004), and in group therapy (Donigian & Hulse-Killacky, 1999). We have set our critical incident scenarios within an ecological framework, as you have already noticed.

In the following chapters, you learn about techniques and their use through working with incidents drawn from group sessions. We present a situation for you to consider, following a consistent format to be described in the following text, leaving you at a choice point regarding what technique(s) you might select. You are then asked to review the toolbox, as appropriate, and to follow the PGTM steps to arrive at your choice. If you are involved with an educational or training session, you can try out your choice and obtain feedback from others. Our intent is to help you learn techniques within a decision-making structure that permits you to function effectively and appropriately as a group leader while developing your expertise in exercising professional judgment as a group leader.

The critical incident scenarios all follow the same educational and training format.

## Coding

Each critical incident scenario is introduced by a title, and is coded at the top left of the first page to indicate the best practice guideline (planning, performing, processing). The type of group being addressed, the best practice area, and the stage of group development also is indicated. This coding information will help orient you to the task at hand.

## History

Important background and influencing factors are provided for each critical incident. It is important that group leaders consider and select techniques while acknowledging the context of the group. Being aware of the group's evolving history and of salient events leading to the critical incident help identify the context.

## *Critical Incident Format*

The critical incident is presented. It is considered a critical incident because it is important to the members and the group and it requires professional judgment and action by the group leader(s).

Next, we ask: What technique do you choose? Work through the five steps of technique selection (identify, analyze, review, select, and implement and evaluate), individually or in small groups, jotting down or discussing several options for what technique you would use in the situation. What factors must be considered? For example:

**Step 1:   Identify the group type and purpose, best practice area, and developmental stage.**

**Step 2:   Analyze the presenting situation by applying ecological concepts. Ask: "Which of these concepts is relevant now? How are these concepts being expressed at this point?"**

*Context:* External and group factors influencing the group and its members

*Interconnection:* Frequency and quality of member-to-member relationships

*Collaboration:* Working together to move ahead

*Social system maintenance:* Group culture, including clarity and integrity of rules, norms, and expectations

*Meaning making:* Creating meaning from experience

*Sustainability:* Transferring and generalizing learning and change

**Step 3:   Review possible group techniques, considering focus (cognitive, affective, behavioral, structural) and level (individual, interpersonal, group).**

Closely review the relevant toolbox techniques and select one or more possibilities.

**Step 4:   Select a best-fit technique and then provide a rationale for your choice.**

After you have identified possible techniques, each needs to be reviewed and considered as you move toward selecting a best fit, where you are concerned with which technique might produce the most advantages and the fewest disadvantages. Selection involves a great deal of professional judgment on the part of the group leader, in addition to having available an array of possible techniques from which to choose. The evaluation criteria (Craig, 1978) discussed briefly in Chapter 2 can be of much help in this process. To review, the five criteria ask:

- *Appropriateness* potential: Which technique seems right, and meshes best with the values, culture, and history of the group and its members?
- *Adequacy* potential: Which technique will make the largest difference, produce the most growth, learning, or change?
- *Effectiveness* potential: Which technique has a better possibility of reaching the goal, of accomplishing what is needed?
- *Efficiency* potential: Which technique might be the least costly, the least elaborate, and the simplest?
- *Side effects* potential: Which technique would seem to spawn the fewest negative consequences?

Once you have determined what you consider to be the best technique, we present our thinking about what group technique might work well in the situation under "Steps Toward Selecting a Technique." Comparing your ideas with those we provide may further develop your learning. If you have the good fortune to be working with these critical incidents in a class or workshop, then we also encourage you to practice choices that have emerged, and then to process them.

**Step 5:   Implement and evaluate how well the technique worked (or estimate implementation) and then process the effectiveness of the technique.**

The "proof is in the pudding." How did the technique work? Was it useful? Did it help to move positively on the ecological issue of concern? Was it helpful for the members and the group? What did it lead to next? What would you change, if anything, for future use of this technique? To continue improving this group?

In reality, you would not have the opportunity to implement and then evaluate the technique's effectiveness. Do the next best thing: estimate. How do you think this technique would work in the circumstance provided? How effective do you think it might be?

---

### *Try This*

Pair up with another person and try out your choices. Give each other feedback. What might work? What might need to be changed? Compare your choices with those provided by the authors. Process your work: What have you learned? What are you learning about this process for selecting group techniques? What are you learning about yourself as a group leader? What might you be able to use the next time?

---

## *Group Leadership and Its Techniques Are Personal*

We have found that the PGTM provides a very helpful method to ground and guide how to identify and select techniques. However, we remind you of what is even more important than this or any other model: the "personhood" of group leaders (i.e., their personal values, sense of self, and how they are perceived by others) and the presence and interaction of the members themselves. Any technique is subservient to, and dependent on, the persons involved in its use.

After all, without the leader and the members there would be no group. Moreover, group work is a personal and interpersonal endeavor and all that is part of it is tied to people. Who the leader is, what values drive leader choices and behavior, and how the leader connects with other people in general and with the group members in particular are all essential contributors to overall group effectiveness. In terms of members, they can best be viewed as the authentic experts in their own lives; recognition of that perspective implies that group leaders need to establish collaborative working relationships with members, where both professional and personal expertise can be joined in the service of growth and productivity.

---

### *What Kind of a Person Are You?*

Given that the personhood of the group leader is the most important variable of all, think about yourself. What do you value? How do others perceive you? How are you with others in group situations? What are your strengths? What areas do you need to improve?

Write a five-page, double-spaced essay to reflect on your choice and use of group techniques.

## *An Example of a Critical Incident*

Here is a brief example to show how the PGTM might be applied within a psychoeducation group setting. Following the critical incident we present our views on the situation.

### *History*

This psychoeducation group consists of 10 counseling master's degree students. It is currently being conducted by two doctoral students (male and female) who have had advanced training and experience in group leading. Coleader supervision is provided by a faculty member who is an expert in group work. The group is approaching a working stage, midway through the fourth of 10 two-hour sessions.

The group has spent time forming, developing rules and expectations, building a collective understanding of confidentiality, and setting goals. The coleaders, Bill and Gail, are feeling good about this foundation, and that the time spent together by all members was effective. One member (Sam), though, has been much quieter than the others. Nonetheless, the coleaders entered session four expecting that the group was ready to move ahead.

### CRITICAL INCIDENT

Midway through session four Sam suddenly challenges the coleaders about how the group is going.

SAM:   I—or maybe anyone else in here—could have us working on *real* stuff by now, for sure! Can't you help us get going, instead of just spinning our wheels?

### WHAT TECHNIQUE DO YOU CHOOSE?

Work through the five steps of technique selection (identify, analyze, review, select, and implement and evaluate), individually or in small groups, jotting down or discussing several options for what technique you would use in the situation. What factors must be considered? (Use this space to write notes or ideas.)

### STEPS TOWARD SELECTING A GROUP TECHNIQUE

Here is our thinking:

### Step 1:   Identify the group type and purpose, best practice area, and developmental stage

Choice of group technique needs to match the type of group being used (counseling, psychoeducation, task, psychotherapy), the best practice area involved (planning, performing, processing), and the group's developmental stage (beginning, middle, end).

**Step 2:   Analyze the presenting situation by applying ecological concepts:**

Context

Interconnection

Collaboration

Social system maintenance

Meaning making

Sustainability

As in most group situations, several concepts may apply to any one situation. In this case, we might wonder about the concepts of *interconnection* (Sam seems to be outside the group looking in), of *social system maintenance* (Sam also is questioning how the group is doing and that it should be progressing faster), and of *meaning making* (Sam has made a particularly strong judgment about the group).

Also, the concept of *collaboration* might be especially salient. Sam is directly questioning leadership and control—how this group is being moved forward. The ecological issue of collaboration often raises these kinds of considerations. How are leaders and members negotiating the processes of decision making, power sharing and control, and leadership? Sam wants action, he proclaims. Bill and Gail are interested, we assume, in action, too, but action that results from a collaborative stance. In a collaborative approach, leaders work with members to resolve differences, to identify common areas of interest, and to find ways of working together to be productive.

**Step 3:   Review possible group techniques, considering focus and level**

Review the relevant toolbox section (refer to the appendix) that corresponds to the group's location in performing. As you are developing expertise, it may be advantageous for you to closely review the toolbox's contents for direct guidance, always realizing that only examples of possibilities are contained. Through this review, you might find a technique that fits your group situation very well or that could be readily adapted. More likely, your own ideas might be sparked, and you may find yourself generating your own possibilities. The more experience and confidence you develop with thinking about techniques, the less you may need to rely closely on the toolbox.

Focus and level are considered. Does the situation call for a technique that is focused on cognitive (thinking), affective (feeling), behavioral (doing), or structural (changing the flow of events) domains? At what level would the proper technique be aimed? At an individual level (such as Sam), member relationships between or among members, or at the group itself? From the techniques contained in the toolbox, what would be the best combination of technique focus and level to fit this situation?

As just one example (a variation of performing technique #82), such a technique might be:

*Focus:* Affective: "Sam, you seem to be urging us onward. . . . I've been wondering how things are going for you, about how you have been feeling about the group. . . . Can you say more about this?"

*Level:* Individual; the technique is directed at Sam and he is asked to respond. Others, or the group itself, are not included.

Here is another example, drawing from the same toolbox technique but implemented at a different focus and level:

*Focus:* Cognitive: "Thank you, Sam; I've been wondering how things are going for you and others in the group and what you have been thinking about the group? I wonder what others in the group might think about this."
*Level:* Group; the technique is aimed at the whole group, allowing for any member to respond.

### Step 4:   Select a best-fit technique and then provide a rationale for your choice

These two techniques differ in their focus (i.e., affective or cognitive) and level (individual or group). The choice point resides around whether the leader is interested in encouraging Sam to become feeling oriented or thinking oriented and, also, if he wishes to focus on Sam individually or to open responses to the group as a whole. This decision may stem from an assessment of Sam's readiness and his capability to manage thoughts and feelings, as well as an assessment of group development. The somewhat safer technique would be the cognitive focus provided at a group level. If the individual-level affective focus technique is selected, the leader might still want to follow up with a group-level intervention (assuming Sam is in agreement) to check Sam's perception with those of others. The job of the leaders at this point is to weigh the relative advantages and disadvantages of these techniques.

In terms of our evaluative criteria:

*Appropriateness:* Either technique seems appropriate for this kind of group, the developmental stage it is in, and the issue being faced.

*Adequacy:* The individual-level, affective focus technique might produce more intensity, if that is desired or needed.

*Effectiveness:* Each technique being considered could be effective.

*Efficiency:* Focusing on Sam directly at this point might yield increased efficiency.

*Side effects:* Generally, the more intense technique produces the most side effects, as risk increases. A possible side effect of the individual-level affective focus technique might be that more people would be led to interact more directly (positive side effect), or some members might feel increased pressure to directly participate (negative side effect).

### Step 5:   Implement and evaluate how well the technique worked

How did the choice work? Was it effective in reaching the goal set for it? Was it acceptable and appropriate for members? Did it fall short? What might be needed in the future to increase its overall benefits? These are the kinds of questions that group leaders might ask for when determining if techniques that they use are of value.

# In Sum

As the preface indicated, following this chapter the remainder of the book is organized by devoting a section to each of the best practice areas of planning, performing, and processing. Within each section, we will apply the purposeful group techniques model (PGTM), taking advantage of the toolbox and critical incidents drawn from the groups that counselors most often are asked to provide: psychoeducation groups and counseling groups. In a separate chapter (Chapter 10) we will consider techniques appropriate for two additional and important types of groups that counselors are asked to deliver: task groups and psychotherapy groups. The result is that you will learn a coherent way to consider and apply group techniques across the broad range of practice in group work.

To that end, the PGTM can be very helpful as an augmenter of existing personal and interpersonal forces and dynamics. But first and foremost we need to look at ourselves and each other as the primary sources to guide group techniques.

We have included some "Reflection Points" to consider and learning activities to complete before moving on to the next part.

---

## Reflection Points

1. Do you tend toward thinking, feeling, or doing? When in a group, do you find yourself attending more closely to individual members, to interactions between members, or the whole group itself? What are some implications for you as a group leader?

   Tendencies will give you some clues about the kinds of group techniques to which you might be drawn naturally. Take a moment to respond to the questions above. If you are in a situation to pair up with another, share your thinking.

2. A model for using group techniques and processes, the purposeful group techniques model, was discussed in this chapter, along with how to use techniques in the toolbox. You read the example involving Sam that focused on the process of decision making. Now, to get some practice in using the model, consider the following critical incident, review the decision-making steps, and apply the dimensions of the model to it.

---

# Learning Activities

## Critical Incident Example

Group members in the same personal growth group described earlier in the chapter, this time at session 8 (of 10), refuse to participate in an exercise suggested by the coleaders. They claim that the exercise is "too far removed" from what the group is supposed to be about, and some indicate that they are still confused about the group's purpose, anyway.

Complete the following in a time frame of 60 minutes.

(a) Join with others in a small discussion group.

(b) Consider the ecological concepts that apply.

(c) Scan the toolbox for examples of some possible group techniques to use or adapt. Consider the focus and level that might be needed. If you locate a technique that you like, fine. Otherwise, use the examples in the toolbox to stimulate your own ideas.

(d) Select or develop two or three alternative techniques.

(e) Discuss the advantages and disadvantages of each technique using the five evaluative criteria to assist you.

(f) Select the best-fit technique and discuss your rationale.

# References

Cohen, A., & Smith, R. (1976). *The critical incident in growth groups.* La Jolla, CA: University Associates.

Conyne, R. (1999). *Failures in group work: How we can learn from our mistakes.* Thousand Oaks, CA: Sage.

Craig, D. (1978). *HIP pocket guide to planning & evaluation.* Austin, TX: Learning Concepts.

Donigian, J., & Hulse-Killacky, D. (1999). *Critical incidents in group therapy (2nd ed.).* Belmont, CA: Thomson Brooks/Cole.

Flanagan, J. (1954). The critical incident technique. *Psychological Bulletin, 51,* 28–35.

Gazda, G., & Folds, J. (1968). *Group guidance: A critical incidents approach.* Woodridge, IL: Follett Educational Corporation.

Tyson, L., Perusse, R., & Whitledge, J. (2004). *Critical incidents in group counseling.* Alexandria, VA: American Counseling Association.

# Techniques in Planning Counseling and Psychoeducation Groups

Group leading today involves giving proper attention to what works in meetings and sessions but, also, to their planning and to making sense of their impact. Good group leading and the effective use of group techniques, therefore, begins with adequate planning of a group.

This part consists of one major chapter on planning. All groups require planning in order for leaders and members to have necessary direction. We will be guided by the Best Practice Guidelines in Planning that have been recommended by the Association for Specialists in Group Work (1998), as well as other sources as we consider appropriate techniques and how to use them.

The guidelines are summarized below:

## Best Practices in Planning

**Possesses awareness of professional context**
- Code of Ethics
- Compliance with licensure, certification, accreditation

**Possesses conceptual understanding**
- Understands value of group work
- Defines scope of practice
- Operates from a coherent conceptual framework

**Completes ecological assessment**
- Identifies and answers important assessment questions
- Matches group-work type (e.g., task, psychotherapy) to population

**Implements program development and evaluation**
- Identifies group purpose
- Defines group goals
- Complies with insurance and fee policies (if applicable)
- Secures necessary resources
- Makes leadership/coleadership decisions
- Secures suitable meeting space
- Completes marketing and recruitment plan, as needed
- Develops a professional disclosure statement, as needed

**Prepares the group and its members**
- Completes any required screening
- Provides informed consent, as needed
- Describes confidentiality and its limits
- Identifies and participates in relevant continuing education activities

**Possesses awareness of relevant trends and technology**
- Understands managed care impacts, as appropriate
- Understands client demographics
- Understands technology impacts

---

As we point out in the next chapter, techniques for planning a group involve attending to major, broad considerations about the nature of the group and how to get it formed, and also to details about how any one session or meeting might be conducted. Having a plan in hand is far preferable to "winging it," and we will discuss a number of techniques to assist in this effort.

So, a group plan is a good thing to have! Yet, it needs to be a kind of "living document," a plan that invites experience and is open to being modified appropriately. Improper use of a plan is to follow it slavishly, without considering how its implementation is going and with little or no attention to changing circumstances. Good group leaders, then, use their well-constructed plans adaptively, subject to what works and to changing conditions.

On the following pages, we discuss what proper planning of a group and its independent sessions or meetings involves. In each critical incident we introduce the toolbox that pertains to the relevant Best Practice area—in this case, Planning. The Planning section of the toolbox is helpful for beginning group leaders to use generating ideas for group techniques, and it also can assist more experienced group leaders to check out their own ideas about techniques.

# 4

## *Planning Techniques: Designing What Is to Be Done*

**ADVANCE ORGANIZER**

This chapter contains the following material:

**Assignment: Develop a Group Plan**

*Broad and Detailed Planning*
*Spontaneity Versus Planning*
*Plan Monitoring*
*Plan Adapting*
*Planning Versus Processing*
*Being Conscious of Setting, Population and Counselor Role*
*Groups as Multicultural Processes*

**Critical Incident Training in Planning**

**CRITICAL INCIDENTS**

CI 4.1: "The Representative Planning Group Surprise"
Group Type: *Generic planning group*
Best Practice Area: *Planning*
Group Developmental Stage: *Prior to Beginning Stage*

CI 4.2: "More Than Just the Facts, Ma'am"
Group Type: *Psychoeducation*
Best Practice Area: *Planning*
Group Developmental Stage: *Prior to Beginning Stage*

CI 4.3: "Details, Schmetails!"
Group Type: *Counseling*
Best Practice Area: *Planning*
Group Developmental Stage: *Prior to Beginning Stage*

CI 4.4: "The Stress-filled Residents"
Group Type: *Psychoeducation*
Best Practice Area: *Planning*
Group Developmental Stage: *Prior to Beginning Stage*

**In Sum**

## Assignment: Develop a Group Plan

Most group techniques texts center on the best practice area of performance, with less attention paid to the areas of planning and processing. Moreover, most of these texts address counseling groups, with little or no coverage of the other types of groups (i.e., task, psychoeducation, and psychotherapy groups). In this text we expand coverage of group techniques to include planning and processing as well as the major types of groups. In addition, as stated earlier, we anchor our discussion of group techniques within a purposeful decision-making model. We draw from three general references for guidance: (a) for planning, performing, and processing, the *Group Work Best Practice Guidelines* (ASGW, 1998; Rapin, 2004); (b) for group-work types, the *Professional Standards for the Training of Group Workers* (ASGW, 2000); and (c) for a purposeful decision-making model, the critical incident model of Cohen and Smith (1976).

This book's is approach intends to be comprehensive (see Conyne, Wilson, & Ward, 1997) by including all of these areas. Note that recommendations contained in the ASGW documents previously cited addressing Best Practice Guidelines and Training Standards are being used by other professional group-work associations, such as the Division of Group Psychology and Group Psychotherapy of the American Psychological Association (e.g., Barlow, 2004; Ridge, Barlow, Wiggins, Lee, & Money, 2004), and by a range of group-work journals (e.g., Conyne & Bemak, 2004; Klontz, 2004).

Planning is a major best practice area within group work. As Rapin and Conyne (1999) observed, planning is concerned with

> all steps that are preliminary to conducting the first session. This includes, but is not limited to designing the group, choosing appropriate meeting space, publicizing the group, and recruiting and selecting group members. (Quoted in Trotzer, 1999, p. 256)

A wide range of considerations, therefore, are involved with planning any group, whether it be a task, psychoeducation, counseling, or psychotherapy type. See the chart in the Part II introduction for a review of the Best Practice Planning Guidelines.

A number of group courses in counselor training programs now include an instructional component on planning a group. Several examples of planning regimens can be found in Conyne et al. (1997). Figure 4.1 on p. 45 shows a syllabus taken from the second required course in the University of Cincinnati group-work training strand titled Introduction to Group Leadership. This course follows a foundations course called Group Theory and Process. As part of this second course, taken by school counseling and mental health counseling students, students are required to develop a comprehensive plan for a group that they may offer in the future. The syllabus contains material that our colleague, Bob Wilson, and we think should be part of any group plan.

---

**Assignment: Develop a Group Plan**

One of the objectives of the course is for the student to develop a plan for a time-limited, theme-oriented group. To that end, readings have been provided which will guide the development of the student's group plan. Enclosed below is a suggested outline to help you organize your work. The outline is intended as a guide, and should not be interpreted as a restriction. Although the topics mentioned in the outline are important for any group plan, each group plan is likely to need individual modifications in order to faithfully convey the intentions of the leader for the group's members. It is suggested, therefore, that in your group plan you cover the following topics:

1. General Description of the Type of Group Proposed
2. General Outline of the Structured Group Experience Proposed
   a. Background and Rationale for the Group
      - What sort of group do you intend to run?
      - For what population is it intended?
      - What group developmental model will be used as reference?
   b. General Goals for the Group Experience
      - What general goals do you intend to achieve for this group? (e.g., consider using Lazarus' BASIC ID: *B*ehavior, *A*ffect, *S*ensation, *I*magery, *C*ognition— *I*nterpersonal relations, and need for *D*rugs (medications) as a framework for setting goals)
   c. Time Period for the Group
      - How many hours/session, sessions/week, number of weeks?
      - When does group occur in the cycle of the year (e.g., academic calendar)?
   d. Leaders
      - Who (solo, co-led), training and experience of each leader?
      - What is training and experience of leader(s)?
   e. Methods
      - What general topics will be covered?
      - What general methods or techniques will be used?
   f. Recruitment Screening (As appropriate for type of group)
      - How will members be recruited?
      - How will they be screened for inclusion?
   g. Evaluation
      - How will the group and member progress be evaluated to determine process and outcome effects?
3. Session by Session Description of Planned Events
   a. In each session, what goals do you intend to achieve?
   b. What strategy (strategies) do you plan to use to achieve each of the goals listed?
   c. How will you explore the process of your experience?

---

**Figure 4.1**
Syllabus for Group Theory and Process Course

The following is an example drawn from one student's proposal. You may use it, or some modification of this approach, in reporting your session by session plans.

**SESSION 1—Total time, two hours.**

Goal 1—To have members become acquainted.

*Member Tasks*—To learn each other's names and something about each member.

*Strategy*—(a) brief introduction by each member, (b) members interview in pairs and report to the group.

*Time Required*—Strategy (a): 20 min; strategy (b): 10 min per interview; processing 20 min.

*Physical Setting*—Members seated in a circle, except when dividing into pairs for interviews.

*Materials Needed*—None

*Method*—(a) for self-introductions, each member will be asked to give his or her name and a short statement of how he or she is feeling "right now," (b) for the paired interviews, each member chooses another member and then finds a spot to interview his/her partner for ten minutes [method is abbreviated for this example].

*Processing*—The group leader will invite discussion of feelings about introducing self, introducing others, being introduced by others . . . leading to a discussion of "self-presentation" and "stage-fright."

**SESSION 2—Total time, two hours.**

Goal 1—To identify feelings about being in this group.

*Member Tasks*—To identify greatest benefit and greatest fear about being in this group.

*Processing*—Each member will be asked to disclose how it felt to talk about his/her fears and expected benefits.

Goal 2—To disclose more personal feelings about being a returning adult female student.

*Member Tasks*—To talk about "how I decided to return to college after having been out of school for as long as I have."

*Processing*—Each member will be asked to disclose their reactions to hearing about other members' feelings and experience.

# Broad and Detailed Planning

As can be seen, planning a group includes considering broad overarching matters (such as the rationale for the group), and it includes paying close attention to detail (such as in session-by-session design). The issue for special consideration in this chapter is what techniques can be used in the planning process to assist with meeting both kinds of planning: (a) the broad sweep of planning, and (b) its close detail.

## Spontaneity Versus Planning

The planning step in group leadership is essential to effective performance. When group leading was beginning to emerge as a professional practice, planning considerations were given short shrift. In fact, group leadership training was focused nearly exclusively on what happened within sessions, often with a clear priority placed on being spontaneous, otherwise known somewhat facetiously as "flying by the seat of your pants."

Any recent text in group leadership, as well as the Best Practice Guidelines, attends to planning issues, and rightfully so. Although spontaneity remains an important aspect of group leadership, most theorists suggest that it cannot exist independently from purposeful intention. Planning the group prior to its implementation is an essential element of group leadership, as is attending to how the original plan holds up across the life of the group.

## Plan Monitoring

As just suggested, the original plan that was created needs to be monitored for its fit with actual events as they unfold. No matter how well researched and crafted, any initial plan cannot be expected to apply to ongoing events without adjustment and modification. Therefore, group leaders need to evaluate their session-by-session plans, noting what is working and what is not. Adjustments almost always must be made, sometimes in real time within a session or meeting, or in between sessions, as a result of between-session processing.

Here is one example of the need to modify a plan. Session three of a psychoeducation group on conflict skills for middle school students was planned in advance to focus on interpersonal problem-solving skills and their practice. However, surrounding the time of session three a major fire had occurred in the neighborhood community abutting the school, where several of the group members lived. Although all members arrived on time for the scheduled group session, the leader soon discovered that they were preoccupied with the fire and its effects, inhibiting their readiness to participate in the planned session. The leader appropriately altered the session to allow time for members to express and share their thoughts and feelings, setting aside the original plan for another day.

## Plan Adapting

The previous example also illustrates the importance of group leaders adaptively using their plans. The purpose of any group plan is to effectively and appropriately guide action, including the selection and use of group techniques. A group plan never should function as a rigid, immutable design existing independently from the group, the members, and its dynamic context. Leaders must learn how to flexibly adapt their predeveloped designs to fit with changing conditions.

## Planning Versus Processing

Interestingly, planning occurs not only before the initiation of the first group meeting but also throughout the life of the group. We suggest, for example, that leaders engage in between-session processing (see especially Chapter 9), where they meet face-to-face for reviewing, reflecting on, and evaluating the group's functioning. This process naturally produces opportunities for continuous improvement and for adjusting plans, as needed, to be more fully responsive to changing conditions.

## Being Conscious of Setting, Population and Counselor Role

Groups need to be planned with the setting, population and related counselor role being held carefully in mind. For counselors and other helpers, these three considerations often translate as follows: (a) Setting, whether school or community. (b) Population, ranging from children to frail adults, and (c) Role, whether school counselor or community/mental health counselor. In truth, there are far more commonalities across these dimensions than dissimilarities involved for counselors providing group work. However, a few important distinctions deserve mentioning.

**School or Community**. Schools provide numerous ongoing opportunities for group work (Conyne & Mazza, 2007; Crowell, 2007). Children and young adults, after all, attend them nearly every day of the school year. Yet, schools are highly regulated and it often is difficult to organize and deliver groups due to time constraints and jammed schedules. Schools also develop their own unique cultures and press, and sometimes can be detached from the larger community, which can serve as a positive or a negative force. At least in principle, schools are "hot houses" for learning, growth and change and this environment can be conducive to launching groups. Comprehensive developmental guidance programs provide ready avenues for group work.

Communities, by contrast, are far more diverse and unregulated, with freer flowing dynamics but with fewer clear options and supports for organizing and delivering groups. It is necessary for counselors to identify organizational opportunities, such as neighborhood centers and churches, through which groups might be offered (Conyne, 2004).

**Population range**. Groups for children need to be different than groups for adults. Much less empirical information is available about what groups work best for children, as compared with adults (Riva & Haub, 2004). It is known that groups for children generally need to be smaller in size, shorter in duration per meeting and number of meetings, and that they need to include structured activities rather than being mostly unstructured (Shechtman, 2004). In planning, therefore, it is important to design these features into children's groups. It is the case that this book is centered on groups for adolescents and adults, with less attention specifically to groups with children.

**Role, School Counselor or Community/Mental Health Counselor**. School counselor: As is pointed out in the four themes of the American School Counselor Association National Model (ASCA, 2003), school counselors need to engage in leadership, advocacy, collaboration and teaming, and systemic change as they become involved in school transformation initiatives. In schools, examples of such groups can include Individualized Educational Programs (IEPs), classrooms, local school decision-making groups, staff meetings, interdisciplinary curriculum development teams, psychoeducation groups, PTA meetings, parent workshops and instruction, classroom appraisal, peer mediation training, consultation and teaming, counseling groups, student clubs, and training workshops. Prevention groups aimed at helping students gain competencies to avoid negative life events and risk factors and to develop protective factors (e.g., life skills training groups) are of great importance (Conyne, 2004). School counselors lead, facilitate, consult, or advise any of these kinds of groups.

In community and/or mental health counseling, groups are becoming a staple service delivery method. Groups are important vehicles in the work place (Wheelan, 2004), with offenders and mandated clients (Morgan, 2004), in private practice (Cramer, 2004), in college and university counseling centers (Kincade & Kalodner, 2004), and mental health settings (Clifford, 2004), to name but a few setting applications. The nature of the group (e.g., prevention or remediation, its setting and population, and other factors) needs to be carefully considered in planning.

## Groups as Multicultural Processes

We observed earlier that all group work is multicultural. Planning any group needs to be premised on the understanding that ". . . one cannot undertake group work or group work training without considering the socioeconomic, political, and demographic trends in modern society" (Bemak & Chung, 2004, p. 34). The RAND Foundation (RAND, 1999) identified four developing conditions in the United States that portend significant societal implications: (a) increasingly complex ethnic diversity, with sometimes diverging and potentially competing interests, (b) emerging disparities across generations, such as the "digital divide," that could affect adult employment and training needs, (c) "graying" of the population, that may influence budget priorities and shift resources from education systems, and (d) potentially growing economic disparities tied to education levels, threatening to create a "have and have-not" society.

These changes lead our society to become much more diverse than it is at present, accompanied by many challenges and opportunities. Group leaders must be aware of these kinds of changes, be preparing to design groups that are responsive and anticipative, and ready themselves to be up to the task of working with people presenting broader diversity.

The latter point is particularly pertinent. Group leaders must become culturally competent themselves (see Association for Specialists in Group Work's Diversity Competency Training Principles, ASGW, 1999), in addition to all the other competencies that are needed. Therefore, in planning, group leaders should assess themselves for cultural competence and seek learning experiences to advance this critically important quality.

## Critical Incident Training in Planning

What do group leaders need to know and be able to do to effectively use planning techniques in their work? Following are a series of critical incidents (CIs) in planning. As we mentioned in the preface, group skills can be applied with many populations, in different settings, and for different purposes. CI 4.2, "More than Just the Facts, Ma'am," illustrates the broad scope of group work with its focus on a nurse and a nursing situation (you will be able to follow progress of this case again in Chapter 9).

As with the critical incidents that are presented throughout subsequent chapters, critical incidents are devoted to both psychoeducation and to counseling groups. In all cases the critical incidents are intended to provide concrete experience with applying the PGTM. Please refer to Chapters 2 and 3 if you may need a refresher. Now, let's turn to the first critical incident.

### CRITICAL INCIDENTS

#### PLANNING CI 4.1

Group Type: *Generic Planning Group*
Best Practice Area: *Planning*
Group Developmental Stage: *Prior to Beginning Stage*

### *The Representative Planning Group Surprise*

#### HISTORY

The William A. Henderson Middle School is located in the center of the most destitute neighborhood of the city. A public school, its 700 students are characterized by 30% living in poverty, 85% of whom receive free or reduced-cost lunches. Issues of particular concern in this school involve high dropout rates, poor academic performance, homeless student subpopulation, an unsafe surrounding neighborhood, high disciplinary and suspension rates, a large number of single-parent families, and significant mistrust of families toward the school and other forms of "establishment." As well, within the school teachers and staff tend to feel overwhelmed; disheartened; pressured by local, state, and national initiatives to increase academic performance indices; and burdened by few resources with which to work—including the absence of counselors due to state budget cuts 5 years ago.

The counseling program was successful in obtaining a 3-year federal grant aimed at improving academic performance and lowering the dropout rate at Henderson. A key component of planned grant activities involved use of various forms of small groups as a preferred form of both remedial and preventive intervention.

The questions are: "What kinds of groups does Henderson need, addressing which problems, with what participants?" Although the existing research literature contained a number of programs that had been successful in other locations, both group based and otherwise, program administrators considered it important to conduct a local ecological assessment to inform and guide the planning and implementation process.

They decided to recruit and form a "representative planning group." The intention was that this group would consist of members who reflected important constituencies of the school, of families, and of the community. Achieving this reality was not possible, despite considerable effort. For instance, although the community is 85% African American, the 15 members of the representative planning group contained but 3 African Americans; the remaining ethnic breakdown contained 10 White and 2 Hispanic members. The first meeting of this group, led by Sarah Johnson, is just about to start. Dr. Johnson is a White university professor who will serve as the grant director.

## CRITICAL INCIDENT

SARAH:  *(with warmth and enthusiasm)* Welcome to our planning group! We really are looking forward to learning from all of you what you see as the big needs facing our school and what services we should be providing.

JOHN:  *(a White service provider from the neighborhood mental health center)* This is terrific, so long overdue. Thanks for inviting our agency to participate!

SONJA:  *(a middle-age African American single parent of four children)* I've seen all this before and don't like the smell of it. Is this just going to be another case of all you university folk landing down here to get some research and then move on?

## WHAT TECHNIQUE DO YOU CHOOSE?

Individually or in small groups jot down or discuss several options for what technique you would use in this situation. What factors must be considered?

## STEPS TOWARD SELECTING A TECHNIQUE

Here is our thinking:

### Step 1:  Identify the group type and purpose, best practice area, and developmental stage

A representative planning group is an example of a task group that provides an important way to involve local people in the development of any kind of group, including counseling and psychoeducation groups. This is the reason it is included as a planning technique. A representative planning group can be an important means to collect the combined wisdom of people who represent the target population and those connected with it as planning proceeds. Such groups typically are conducted early in the planning process and, along with other data, provide a basis for program development.

### Step 2: Analyze the presenting situation by applying ecological concepts

Planning for any group or group-work program needs to be based on relevant ecological data—the needs, strengths, and deficits of prospective members; situational supports and constraints; resources available and unavailable; challenges and opportunities facing prospective members; perceptions about the "host institution"; and other factors. Members of a representative planning group, of course, need to reflect the target population and those who are associated with it. It is a large accomplishment when that condition is met successfully.

The representative planning group is premised on the ecological concepts of the importance of context, collaboration, and interconnection. It is formed to learn directly about the context of concern (in this case, Henderson middle school) from people who are in a genuine position to know. In addition, its formation documents a rejection of "doing things *to* people," while accepting the notion of "doing things *with* people."

As with any intention, however, actual implementation usually needs to navigate around challenges, both expected and unexpected. In the previous dialogue, although resistance is expected at some point in the process that needs to be positively addressed, it may have been unexpected that it would occur so quickly.

### Step 3: Review possible group techniques, considering focus and level

***Planning Toolbox #7,*** Representative Group. This overall planning technique is the representative planning group, which is a form of task group. In order for it to be successfully employed, the group leader or facilitator must be skilled in all the necessary areas of group work and be competent in applying a wide range of group techniques.

*Focus:* Structural.
*Level:* Group.

The representative planning group is a large structural intervention that is specially created to reflect important characteristics of the targeted setting and population. Because it is a group itself that is conducted during the planning phase, performance techniques are appropriate for use. The purpose of the representative planning group is to obtain ecologically valid information that can become part of the planning process.

***Planning Toolbox #20,*** Ask members to discuss something important. In this case, to talk about their feelings of anxiety, mistrust, insecurity, and so on with the group by asking if the members see any of their own concerns in other members.

*Focus:* Affective.
*Level:* Group.

Ordinarily, the group facilitator might start at a different point in the beginning of a group to discuss some context and general goals and procedures for the planning group, and then sponsor a go-round where members could begin to get acquainted. This session, though, unexpectedly has gotten off to a "fast start," where suspicions and mistrust immediately are expressed by one member. In such instances, group leaders need to be able to think and act quickly finding an appropriate technique to use.

Planning technique #20 provides a basis for how the facilitator might begin to respond. It seems important to acknowledge the feelings of the member and to find a way for others to talk about any thoughts and emotions they might have coming into the group.

***Planning Toolbox #6,*** Group Leader Goals. Here, the leader sets goals for the group.

Once members have had the opportunity to share their thoughts and feelings, the facilitator may want to focus on what the planning group's purpose is and to discuss with the members how best to move ahead together in working on those goals. In this case, the purpose of the group is to better understand the needs and conditions of the students at Henderson, so planning for the group and other forms of service can be based on that important information.

### Step 4:  Select a best-fit technique

This situation illustrates how a single technique often is insufficient to address ongoing events and experiences in a group. Frequently, there is so much occurring that multiple techniques are necessary.

The second and third technique just discussed might need to be used sequentially or, perhaps, be integrated—depending on how the members respond. Expression of thoughts and feelings should be encouraged first in this session (within boundaries), given what already has occurred. Then attention should be paid to the goals and procedures of the group. The group cannot be expected to be effective and efficient without a shared understanding of what it is all about and how the members are going to get there.

### Step 5:  Implement and evaluate how well the technique worked

SONJA:  I've seen all this before and don't like the smell of it. Is this just going to be another case of all you university folk landing down here to get some research and then move on?

SARAH:  Thank you, Sonja, for being honest about your concern. I will respond to that in just a moment, but I wonder if I might first ask others for any of your thoughts or feelings as you are coming into this planning group.

*(Some others respond, with various thoughts and feelings, some being positive.)*

SARAH:  Well, thanks to all of you. Different ideas here. I want to pick up with Sonja's, if I may, to say that I appreciate that you, and some others, might be somewhat suspicious of this group and the project coming in. I understand that. . . . That really is an important reason why we are forming this representative planning group and you are here . . . we want *you* to tell us what is important, what needs to be done, what your kids need—we want to work *together with you* in planning the services that are needed.

## If in a Class or Workshop, Then:

### *Practice the choice*

Pair up with another student and try out your choices. Give each other feedback. What might work? What might need to be changed? Compare your choices with those provided by the authors.

### *Process the choice*

What have you learned? What are you learning about this process for selecting group techniques? What are you learning about yourself as a group leader? What might you be able to use the next time?

PLANNING CI 4.2

Group Type: *Psychoeducation*
Best Practice Area: *Planning*
Group Developmental Stage: *Prior to Beginning Stage*

## More Than Just the Facts, Ma'am

## HISTORY

Nurse Joiner, one of three local parish nurses, has been visiting patients living in an old section of the city, which has begun to deteriorate physically. Many of the homes in the area are in poor repair and several of the businesses on the main road are boarded up. The nearest health care facility requires people dependent on public transportation to make two bus transfers on the metro bus line. Over the last three years, Nurse Joiner has noticed that there is an increasing number of adults diagnosed with adult onset diabetes. She wants to hold a psychoeducation group weekly for patients to provide information and support. Three members have said that they would come regularly, whereas three others have said only that they "would see."

Nurse Joiner just visited her third patient of the day, Mazie, who showed marked increases in blood sugar and was recently warned by a doctor that she may have to begin insulin treatments. Nurse Joiner talked to Mazie about how she will need a stronger commitment to maintaining her health by controlling her diet, and thereby controlling her diabetes without insulin. The frustration that Nurse Joiner feels is heightened by the knowledge she has about limitations her patients face with shopping and transportation, often leading to poor diets and poor food choices.

## CRITICAL INCIDENT

Three parish nurses meet for peer supervision once each week. Nurse Joiner shares with the others her frustration in getting her patients to commit to this group—which she believes they desperately need.

NURSE JOINER:   I just don't understand how Mazie can be so careless about her diet! She isn't thinking about how she has to watch what she eats. Then there's Carlo, who won't get up off the couch. Millie and Pete say that they will be coming to the group. I find myself wondering if starting this group is going to be worth it.

BARB:   (*one of the other parish nurses*) Your group could make a big difference for clients like Mazie and Carlo. I'm sure that there is something you can do to try to pull your group members together. Do you have any goals that you could share with them?

NURSE JOINER:   Well, I do have a couple of ideas. I have such high hopes that this group could be a real support system, but somehow I have to get Mazie and the others to "own" the group. I need something to get the members really involved.

## WHAT TECHNIQUE DO YOU CHOOSE?

Individually or in small groups jot down or discuss several options to what technique you would use in this situation. What factors must be considered?

## STEPS TOWARD SELECTING A TECHNIQUE

Here is our thinking:

### Step 1:   Identify the group type and purpose, best practice area, and developmental stage

A group such as this one, which intends to educate Nurse Joiner's patients about living with diabetes, is a good example of a psychoeducation group. This is a method that is helpful in disseminating important information, while also creating a social system in which patients with similar experiences are able to gain knowledge and develop a sense of support, in essence, from sharing their personal stories. In this planning stage, Nurse Joiner is struggling with her concerns about the patients and has sought advice from her colleagues.

### Step 2:   Analyze the presenting situation by applying ecological concepts

A variety of concepts seem applicable with respect to Nurse Joiner's group. Though she has identified a specific need in her community that can be effectively addressed in a group format, there is a question about the willingness of the potential members to commit to a group. It is not enough to have a good idea with good information, but it is necessary to engage the members and gain commitment on their parts. As a beginning leader Nurse Joiner wants to develop her skill in attending to group process and not just settle with her planning to date.

Nurse Joiner's idea is to forge interconnections among members and to create and maintain a social system that would benefit her patients in their ongoing health concerns. She questions whether her patients, because of their limited social activity, have the ability to form relationships within a group format. This is an important consideration. Her strategy in peer supervision, therefore, is analyzing the ability of the potential members to form a group and participate in it. She thinks about how she can "do with" rather than "do to," collaborating with the patients to obligate themselves to the group.

### Step 3:   Review possible group techniques, considering focus and level

***Planning Toolbox #3,*** Preliminary Session. Hold a preliminary group session to orient potential members.

*Focus:* Cognitive and behavioral.
*Level:* Individual, interpersonal, and group.

A preliminary group session is helpful to gather information from those people for which the group is intended. Providing an opportunity to gauge members' understanding of the group process and content can also determine for the leader to some degree who will actually act upon their intention to attend. The leader may set up the preliminary session to gain awareness of how potential members will interact with each other, and also have the chance to discover their individual understandings of what the group process will be like.

***Planning Toolbox #6,*** Group Leader Goals. The leader sets goals for the group.

*Focus:* Cognitive.
*Level:* Individual.

As a leader, Nurse Joiner is confident that her patients need this psychoeducation group to become informed about health issues. Setting goals for the group is an important leader function, which requires her to think broadly about the contextual factors operating in the lives of her patients. This technique also provides a natural assessment tool for the leader, as she can check the actual group development over time in relation to the goals set for the group from the outset.

### Step 4:   Select a best-fit technique

Nurse Joiner believes strongly in the potential of the group to become a support unit. She has established relationships with her patients in the comfort of their own homes, and as their nurse, has gained their trust. The group experience, however, puts her in a different role as a group leader. The important leadership skill of collaboration offers

Nurse Joiner an increased awareness of her patients in a different setting. She also values the opportunities to make connections for the group members about how commitment to the group's goals can mirror commitment to their personal health goals.

Opting to hold a preliminary orientation session with her potential group members seems like a good idea for several reasons. A discussion among all group members may hold each person accountable for expressing the value the group has for them, and not just what Nurse Joiner has told them is "good for them." Her own stake in leading this group for her patients is about her commitment to helping her patients learn, think about their behavior, and make changes that will enhance their quality of life. Getting the patients to think about this and express their beliefs and feelings has potential therapeutic value in and of itself.

Nurse Joiner is unclear about her patients' understanding of a group's objectives, but this can be addressed in a preliminary session. The psychoeducation subject matter, however, is critical to their survival, literally, and she believes strongly in the concept that a group can provide a social system of support for her patients. In the preliminary group her patients have the chance to discuss group membership and what that means. This way the psychoeducation nature of the group is enhanced and can be integrated into the discussion. Probably the most beneficial side effect of the group itself is the fact that it provides important education about the members' health issues. They have the opportunity to try their interpersonal skills in an open discussion format on a topic of which each member is the expert—themselves!

### Step 5:   Implement and evaluate how well the technique worked

NURSE JOINER:   Well, I do have a couple of ideas. I have such high hopes that this group can be a real support system, but somehow I have to get Mazie and the others to "own" the group. I need a plan to get the members really involved.

I have been thinking now that it might be most helpful if I try to get my patients into a group to discuss what it can be like. I could pose the question to them such as "How can this group benefit you?" or maybe I could ask "What do you see as the purpose and goals for holding this group in relation to your health concerns?"

NURSE HILL:   Or how about: "What part would you like to have in how this group runs?"

NURSE BLAIN:   I like that, too.

NURSE JOINER:   If I came up with a series of questions, I would be prepared to facilitate some good discussion about groups in general and then draw them into how that fits with their personal goals. I would appreciate you two listening to some of my ideas for questions.

## If in a Class or Workshop, Then:

### *Practice the choice*

Pair up with another student and try out your choices. Give each other feedback. What might work? What might need to be changed? Compare your choices with those provided by the authors.

### Process the choice

What have you learned? What are you learning about this process for selecting group techniques? What are you learning about yourself as a group leader? What might you be able to use the next time?

---

## Planning CI 4.3

Group Type: *Counseling*
Best Practice Area: *Planning*
Group Developmental Stage: *Prior to Beginning Stage*

## *Details, Schmetails!*

### HISTORY

Bea Gibbons has been asked by her agency director to develop a counseling group for clients who present with addictive behaviors. Bea is a full-time licensed mental health counselor, whose clients are mostly Appalachian, of modest income status, with many receiving subsidized health benefits. Her group leadership experience has been limited to psychoeducation groups. Over the past two years Bea has worked with many clients on a variety of substance abuse issues, which she believes would be better dealt with in a counseling group format. She also recently participated in a weekend training program offered by the Addictions Studies program at the local university.

Bea targeted this group to clients struggling with addictions. She posted flyers in the waiting area and on various bulletin boards throughout the agency, indicating the time and week night for the 20-session group, which is to begin in three weeks. In addition, she provided handouts to other counselors and at the front desk for distribution to potential group members. Phone calls have been referred to Bea from five clients expressing interest. Two referrals each have been made from two other counselors, totaling nine potential group members.

It has been two weeks since Bea posted the flyer in the waiting room and 1 week since the other counselors had referred their clients to her group. Bea just met with another counselor, Roger Stone, about the possibility of working together in leading this group. She is aware of Roger's experience as a leader with counseling groups. Bea believes that she and the clients can benefit greatly from his expertise. Roger also is a licensed chemical dependency counselor. About half of the group's potential members are dealing with addictions and chemical dependency issues.

### CRITICAL INCIDENT

The agency director questions Bea at the weekly staff meeting about her progress in developing the group to this point.

DIRECTOR MARSH:   Bea, how are you coming with that group? When do you get started?

BEA:   Well, I posted some flyers and received a couple of referrals from John and Roger. I also have notes about five phone calls. I guess I am ready to get started as soon as I contact each of the clients.

DIRECTOR MARSH:   Okay, so have you planned for your space? Are you clear about your focus for the group? Are you going to have a coleader?

BEA:   I was just talking to Roger about helping me with the group. I am collecting information about the referred clients' needs. I can have a report for you by next week. My idea was to start within the next two weeks if the clients can be here. At least, that is what I put on the flyer.

DIRECTOR MARSH:   Bea, it is vital to plan all the details in plenty of time for the clients and for our staff.

## WHAT TECHNIQUE DO YOU CHOOSE?

Individually or in small groups jot down or discuss several options for what technique you would use in this situation. What factors must be considered?

## STEPS TOWARD SELECTING A TECHNIQUE

Here is our thinking:

### Step 1:   Identify the group type and purpose, best practice area, and developmental stage

Bea is clearly in the planning stage of developing an addictions group, but seems unclear as to the number of details necessary to organize such a group. In her agency there are policies that must be followed for many purposes, including payment and insurance, confidentiality issues, and more. Although Bea actually does have a clear counseling group concept, her experience leans toward an education model. Obtaining the help of an experienced chemical dependency counselor as a coleader would be particularly helpful for the sake of the potential group clients, but also for Bea as she develops her own group-leading skills.

### Step 2:   Analyze the presenting situation by applying ecological concepts

It is important that Bea consider how the group will be grounded contextually from the outset. The group was advertised as appropriate for clients presenting with addictive behaviors, and she has learned that the behaviors of her interested clients include multiple types of addiction: drug addiction, alcohol abuse, and sex addiction. How will these different issues affect the potential interconnections necessary to forge a cohesive group? The ecological concept of meaning making will be a significant factor in the responses of the group members to creating a cohesive social system. In reality, forming interconnections among group members can be used as an effective "tool" in the group.

### Step 3:   Review possible group techniques, considering focus and level

Although Bea is a beginning leader with an addictions group, she has led other groups. Roger is an advanced leader in counseling groups. He has found that often the simplest techniques can work the best, and realizes he needs to help Bea in her planning.

***Planning Toolbox #12,*** Boundary Planning. Plan boundaries include logical, financial, authority, time, money, and other.

*Focus:* Structural.
*Level:* Group.

Because the leaders are planning many details necessary for a group to run in an agency, they have to consider specific details, which include agency directives, scope of practice, compliance with fee policies or insurance mandates, group leader and coleader selection, and meeting space and times. The director made a point to emphasize the importance of tending to these specific details and not just doing the broad, sweeping type of planning. Bea and Roger agree that there is important information to be gathered about the group from the agency's perspective. Roger tells Bea that he is confident about his ability to handle the details about time, space, and writing the objectives for the group plan. This would leave Bea to discover agency policies about insurance and fee policies. The planning from this standpoint could be done separately, with a follow-up meeting later for the leaders.

***Planning Toolbox #12,*** Boundary Planning. An adaptation of this technique is to hold a discussion of how the group will function and what roles members (and leaders) will have.

*Focus:* Cognitive.
*Level:* Interpersonal and group.

Negotiation between coleaders about how the two will function together with issues like authority for decisions, and what roles the two leaders will have from the outset will be essential to smooth functioning. Modeling such behavior for the group members will be one of the objectives in the group plan for those dealing with addictions, members who often have difficulties in their interpersonal relationships. This technique emphasizes group-level impact because the structure established at the outset will determine the ways in which the leaders and group members will interact once the group gets started.

### Step 4:   Select a best-fit technique

Planning boundaries makes sense to both leaders because it encompasses important detailed information that affects the agency as a whole, as well as the group coleaders and potential group members. Roger's experience with those who struggle with addictions informs him that careful planning about the functioning between coleaders, in particular, has significant value when they encounter clients who often have poor relationship skills. Bea agrees that from her own experience, the power of a group for all clients is the potential to develop these relational skills.

It is important for Bea and Roger to be clear about what information they need to plan appropriate boundaries. Defining these details certainly improves the awareness that the leaders have for how a group functions within an agency. Best practices inform Bea that she has to identify resources, such as a setting, privacy requirements, and the availability of a trained coleader. The fact that Bea has an available male coleader is a good choice for including both men and women in the group, for example. Addressing how coleaders work together and relate to each other also provides them with an opportunity to work out differing perspectives, and talk about what their leadership will look like to the group's members. A coleader can assist Bea in maintaining the group's focus, and can help watch for behaviors that affect the dynamics of the group as a whole. A potential negative side effect could emerge if Bea and Roger fail to manage their relative experience levels effectively; for instance, if Bea would appear to be less capable, whereas Roger always seemed in charge.

### Step 5:   Implement and evaluate how well the technique worked

DIRECTOR MARSH:   Bea, it is vital to plan all the details in plenty of time for the clients and for our staff.

BEA:   I know. I did want to let you know that the details for our group have been specific with regard to agency policy and the details that you recommended for the staff and for accounting.

DIRECTOR MARSH:   Though some of the potential group members are already clients of our agency, it is always helpful to be sure to plan your group and your orientation to include clarifying details, such as agency policies. It goes a long way toward creating a positive group experience. It also shows that you did your homework.

Later, Bea and Roger approach Director Marsh's office.

BEA:   Dr. Marsh, Roger and I have the details that you asked for. I have to admit that I just didn't realize how many other details there were. I realize now that it is not enough to look at the big picture, and the specific details are important too. Roger and I both agree that we have learned a lot in our collaboration, and yet we have made some important decisions specifically about how we will work together as coleaders.

DIRECTOR MARSH:   I believe that it will work out well, given the amount of attention you have given to this planning.

ROGER:              I think we both learned something new in this experience. It will probably make us better group coleaders!

## If in a Class or Workshop, Then:

### *Practice the choice*

Pair up with another student and try out your choices. Give each other feedback. What might work? What might need to be changed? Compare your choices with those provided by the authors.

### *Process the choice*

What have you learned? What are you learning about this process for selecting group techniques? What are you learning about yourself as a group leader? What might you be able to use the next time?

### PLANNING CI 4.4

Group Type: *Psychoeducation*
Best Practice Area: *Planning*
Group Developmental Stage: *Prior to Beginning Stage*

## *The Stressed-Out Residents*

### HISTORY

Brad is a licensed social worker and Christy is a licensed counselor. They have worked together many times, coleading a variety of psychoeducation groups. Specifically, they have developed a niche in coleading groups that help members develop stress management techniques to effectively cope with pressure-packed work settings.

### CRITICAL INCIDENT

Over a cup of coffee with the residency director of a major teaching hospital, Brad and Christy have the following conversation.

DR. NICHOLSON:     (*residency director*) *Looking intently at Brad and then Christy.* It's the kiss of death for a teaching hospital to have doctors quit the residency training program!

CHRISTY:            I understand that after completing 4 years of medical school, to be a full-fledged doctor an individual must complete a residency that

|  | lasts several years, but I'm not sure I understand. Don't a few people drop out along the way? |
|---|---|
| DR. NICHOLSON: | No! No! That's the point, they rarely drop out. These are very diligent and smart individuals who have already shown a lot of determination to make it through medical school. They just don't quit! |
| BRAD: | So, you've had a few drop out recently? |
| DR. NICHOLSON: | (*looking a bit embarrassed*) Yes. Last year we had two residents—fine doctors—quit. Because we haven't had a resident quit in almost eight years we thought it was just a blip on the radar and ignored it. But this year we've had two more residents unexpectedly quit and last week another came into my office and said she wanted to take an extended leave for personal reasons. |
| BRAD: | Uhmm, I think I'm beginning to see. |
| CHRISTY: | So, other than the loss of doctors to see patients and so forth, what other impact is this having? |
| DR. NICHOLSON: | It all becomes a vicious cycle. The truth of the matter is that word gets out to all the medical schools pretty quickly that something is going on at a hospital that can't fill its residency slots or keep the residents. When this happens medical students won't even consider such a place and it becomes a nightmare. So, if we don't fix things quickly, the long-term consequences are immense. The bottom line is that even though we provide a valuable service in training the residents to be fine doctors, we can't run a hospital without them. They work long, hard hours and are paid a fraction of what they will make once they complete residency. At the end of the day, that's just how many hospitals make it work. |

From the conversation, Brad and Christy also learn three additional pieces of information: (1) Budgetary constraints over the last few years have limited hiring new nurses, though the hospital has expanded. (2) A typical resident works 70+ hours per week. (3) A recent survey of the residents suggests that they are not coping with the stress as effectively as residents in other similar hospital settings throughout the region. As the conversation wraps up, Dr. Nicholson contracts with Brad and Christy to implement stress management groups that are intended to help the residents manage stress more effectively.

As they return to their cars, Brad says to Christy:

| BRAD: | This sounds good—and important. Stress seems so much involved with this problem. |
|---|---|
| CHRISTY: | Yes, it does. I'm excited about this one. Yet, how do we begin? We haven't worked with this population before. Could we first set a meeting time for next week? (*Brad nods.*) Bring some ideas. |
| BRAD: | Yeah, and let's both bring some ideas. |

## WHAT TECHNIQUE DO YOU CHOOSE?

Individually or in small groups jot down or discuss several options for what technique you would use in this situation. What factors must be considered?

## STEPS TOWARD SELECTING A TECHNIQUE

Here is our thinking:

### Step 1:  Identify the group type and purpose, best practice area, and developmental stage

Planning constitutes all the work that the coleaders, Brad and Christy, must accomplish prior to the first session of the stress management group. Typically, stress management groups are considered to be psychoeducational because there is an emphasis on at least four factors: (1) environmental context (e.g., the stressors in the hospital that may be impacting the residents' levels of stress); (2) here-and-now (e.g., the coleaders would encourage discussions around stress in the present, being not so concerned with past events); (3) prevention (e.g., learning skills to avoid unhealthy responses to future situations); and (4) targeting of high-risk situations and behaviors.

### Step 2:  Analyze the presenting situation by applying ecological concepts

This critical incident is a prime example of the importance of the ecological concept of context. Contextual factors emerge at several levels of analysis. At a macrolevel Dr. Nicholson clearly indicated that medical school administrators' perceptions about resident training programs are essential for achieving success in attracting good residents. Or to put it another way, in this situation contextual factors are of great importance in influencing the sustainability of a residency program. At a more proximal contextual level the shortage in nursing staff, even as the hospital is expanding services, suggests a tension that may be an important factor for Brad and Christy to consider in planning for this group. Brad and Christy are also thinking about the context in which the groups will occur. What are the costs and benefits of holding the group at the hospital or somewhere else? Last, Brad and Christy are interested in understanding the level of commitment to a group experience that the potential members will bring.

Brad and Christy are also considering the value in working collaboratively with the group. As Dr. Nicholson pointed out, the future group members are high achieving, smart and hardworking. In some ways, the members are likely more knowledgeable about the physiology of stress than the coleaders. Therefore, valuing member expertise as well as their present experiences is very important.

As Brad and Christy plan for this group they also spend time considering how to establish interconnections among the members that will lead to the reconstitution of a social system. That is, whereas it is likely that these residents have worked long hours together and have established relationships and even a culture, Brad and Christy are interested in helping them appreciate the unique opportunity that the group provides in working together as a cohesive unit. This will help them achieve their individual and collective goals.

### Step 3:   Review possible group techniques, considering focus and level

At this point, Brad and Christy do not know the individuals and are likely focusing their energy on planning for the entire group. Their focus in planning would likely consider a variety of foci: cognitive, behavioral, structural, and affective.

***Planning Toolbox #8,*** Attitude Assessment.

*Focus:* Affective.
*Level:* Individual.

Because the group has yet to begin, the level of assessment is necessarily at the individual level. Brad and Christy hypothesize that using this assessment technique might contribute to a developing mindset among members that assessment is appropriate and can be expected to occur in the future. For instance, the coleaders are also interested in understanding how potential members are feeling about the prospect of participating in a group, given the other events competing for their time. To obtain this data, another questionnaire might be administered.

***Planning Toolbox #16,*** Planning Consultation.

*Focus:* Cognitive.
*Level:* Individual.

Brad and Christy are experienced group leaders and experts in stress management. However, they realize their limited experience in working with medical doctors, especially in this setting. To help plan for a successful group, the coleaders decided to seek consultation from a professional knowledgeable about medical doctors and the demands they tend to face. Possible consultation might occur with key individuals from the hospital's human resources department, Dr. Nicholson, and others who have expertise in related areas. Also, consultation might precede the first group session or be an ongoing process throughout the life of the stress management groups.

### Step 4:   Select a best-fit technique

Often techniques are not mutually exclusive, but rather complementary. Perhaps this is all the more true in the planning stages of group work. Both techniques already described are suitable in planning for a group with potential members who are very busy and likely to be attending with significant needs and attitudes. Both techniques also are effective in helping guide the coleaders as they consider the unique constellation of members that will be working together to learn stress reduction techniques and about themselves in a specific context.

A possible side effect when seeking consultation is cost for the consultant's time. Another side effect in consulting with individuals that have a vested interest in the outcomes (e.g., Dr. Nicholson or hospital human resources) is that of dual relationships. Although dual relationships are sometimes unavoidable, ethical guidelines and careful consideration must be given to this process. A side effect that Brad and Christy will also want to consider when assessing group members is that assessments are typically limited to a specific point in time and may not reflect accurately the characteristics of the individual completing the instrument.

### Step 5:   Implement and evaluate how well the technique worked

CHRISTY:    Yes, it does. I'm excited about this one. Yet, how do we begin? We haven't worked with this population before. Could we first set a meeting time for next week? (*Brad nods.*) Bring some ideas.

BRAD:    Yeah, and let's both bring some ideas.

After some discussion, Brad and Christy decide that both techniques will help them in planning for the pending groups. In conducting an attitude assessment they are gaining valuable information about the individual members and what feelings they are likely bringing into a group. Also, Brad and Christy assume that consulting with medical experts and others in the field will support their efforts and help in planning for successful groups.

### If in a Class or Workshop, Then:

#### *Practice the choice*

Pair up with another student and try out your choices. Give each other feedback. What might work? What might need to be changed? Compare your choices with those provided by the authors.

#### *Process the choice*

What have you learned? What are you learning about this process for selecting group techniques? What are you learning about yourself as a group leader? What might you be able to use the next time?

## In Sum

Planning is a best practice area that has been articulated by the Association for Specialists in Group Work. The planning function is important for good group work to proceed, whether it occurs in schools or in communities. A group plan provides direction, which is necessary for all group leaders, but may be especially helpful for novice and intermediate group leaders.

This plan needs to be viewed as modifiable, contingent on events and experiences occurring within meetings and sessions. The plan set before the first session provides a great service of helping guide startup steps and provide a basic orientation for leaders and members alike. However, as the group evolves over time, the plan inevitably will require adjustments, so that a better fit results between what is envisioned and what it turns out is needed.

The critical incidents presented in this chapter introduced you to some examples of planning with counseling and psychoeducation group work, and with how to implement the Purposeful Group Techniques Model. The PGTM, along with techniques in the toolbox, can assist group leaders in moving ahead intentionally to consider and use techniques that present an especially good chance of working well.

Once a colleague recited to us a story from his days long ago in an army platoon. The sergeant instilled in soldiers the following, as the story goes: PPPPP: Prior Planning Produces Positive Performance. There also was a corollary, which we need not mention here, referring to what the absence of prior planning produces. In any case, elements of the PPPPP story also fit group leadership.

# References

American School Counselor Association. (2003). *The ASCA model: A framework for school counseling programs.* Alexandria, VA: Author.

Association for Specialists in Group Work. (1998). *Association for Specialists in Group Work best practice guidelines.* Retrieved from http://www.asgw.org

Association for Specialists in Group Work. (1999). Principles for Diversity-Competent Group Workers. *Journal for Specialists in Group Work, 24,* 7–14.

Association of Specialists in Group Work. (2000). *Association for Specialists in Group Work: Professional standards for the training of group workers.* Retrieved from http://www.asgw.org

Barlow, S. (2004). A strategic three-year plan to teach beginning, intermediate, and advanced group skills. *Journal for Specialists in Group Work, 29,* 113–126.

Bemak, F., & Chung, R. (2004). Teaching multicultural group counseling: Perspectives for a new era. *Journal for Specialists in Group Work, 29,* 31–41.

Clifford, M. (2004). Group counseling and group therapy in mental health settings and health maintenance organizations. In J. DeLucia-Waack, D. Gerrity, C. Kalodner, & M. Riva Eds.), *Handbook of group counseling and psychotherapy* (pp. 414–426). Thousand Oaks, CA: Sage.

Cohen, A., & Smith, R. (1976). *The critical incident in growth groups.* La Jolla, CA: University Associates.

Conyne, R., & Bemak, F. (Eds.). (2004). Teaching Group Work. Special issue: *Journal for Specialists in Group Work, 29,* 7–154.

Conyne, R., & Mazza, J. (2007). Ecological group work applied to schools. *Journal for Specialists in Group Work, 32,* pp. 19–29.

Conyne, R., Wilson, F. R., & Ward, D. (1997). *Comprehensive group work: What it means & how to teach it.* Alexandria, VA: American Counseling Association.

Cramer, D. (2004). Building the foundation for group counseling and psychotherapy in private practice. In J. DeLucia-Waack, D. Gerrity, C. Kalonder, & M. Riva (Eds.), *Handbook of group counseling and psychotherapy* (pp. 378–400). Thousand Oaks, CA: Sage.

Crowell, J. L (2007). An exploration of urban teachers' work from an ecological perspective. (Doctoral dissertaion, University of Cincinnati, 2007).

Kincade, E., & Kalodner, C. (2004). The use of groups in college and university counseling centers. In J. DeLucia-Waack, D. Gerrity, C. Kalodner, & M. Riva (Eds.), *Handbook of group counseling and psychotherapy* pp. 366–377. Thousand Oaks, CA: Sage.

Klontz, B. (2004). Ethical practice of group experiential psychotherapy. *Psychotherapy Research, Practice, and Training, 41,* 172–179.

RAND. (1999). Population Matters Research Brief RB5046. Demographic trends foreshadow major economic and social challenges. Retrieved from

http://www.rand.org/pubs/research_briefs/RB50
46/idex1

Rapin, L. (2004). Guidelines for ethical and legal practice in counseling and psychotherapy groups. In J. DeLucia-Waack, D. Gerrity, C. Kalodner, & M. Riva (Eds.), *Group counseling and group psychotherapy* (pp. 151–165). Thousand Oaks, CA: Sage.

Rapin, L. & Conyne, R. (1999). Best practices in group counseling. In J. Trotzer, *The counselor and the group: Integrating theory, training, and practice, (3rd ed.)*, pp. 253–276. Philadelphia: Accelerated Development.

Rapin, L., & Conyne, R. (2006). Best practice in group Work. In J. Trotzer, *The counselor and the group: Integrating theory, training, and practice, (3rd ed.)*, pp. 291–318. Philadelphia: Accelerated Development.

Ridge, N., Barlow, S., Wiggins, B., Lee, J., & Money, K. (2004, July 31). *Establishing postdoctoral training programs for group psychology and group psychotherapy*. Paper presented at the annual meeting of the American Psychological Association, Honolulu, Hawaii.

Riva, M., & Haub, A. (2004). Group counseling in the schools. In J. DeLucia-Waack, D. Gerrity, C. Kalodner, & M. Riva (Eds.), *Handbook of group counseling and psychotherapy* (pp. 309–321). Thousand Oaks, CA: Sage.

Shechtman, Z. (2004). Group counseling and psychotherapy with children and adolescents: Current practice and research. In J. DeLucia-Waack, D. Gerrity, C. Kalodner, & M. Riva (Eds.), *Handbook of group counseling and psychotherapy* (pp. 429–443). Thousand Oaks, CA: Sage.

Trotzer, J. (1999). *The counselor and the group: Integrating theory, training, and practice (3rd ed.)*. Philadelphia: Accelerated Development.

Wheelan, S. (2004). Groups in the workplace. In J. DeLucia-Waack, D. Gerrity, C. Kalodner, & M. Riva (Eds.), *Handbook of group counseling and psychotherapy* (pp. 401–413). Thousand Oaks, CA: Sage.

PART **III**

# Techniques in Performing Counseling and Psychoeducation Groups

Performance is the second best practice area in group leading. The so-called second P (following planning and preceding processing), performance is the area most people think of first when leading a group—and it is the primary topic of most group theory and techniques texts.

There is very good reason for this attention to performance. After all, performance is where the rubber meets the road (Conyne & Bemak, 2004, p. 11) in leading a group. It refers to what group leaders actually do within their group sessions. Whereas in planning a group leader is concerned with designing a future direction for the group, and in processing the group leader is focused on making sense of what has happened, in performing the leader is directly on the line, putting the plan into practice and helping a group and its members move ahead productively. In doing so, the group leader's performance is centered on within-group phenomena such as member interaction, member needs, therapeutic conditions, and the balance between content and process. Because groups are interpersonal and social systems, the entire web of interactive influences occurring within the group is important for leaders to be aware of and to exploit (Bemak & Conyne, 2004; Conyne & Bemak, 2004).

In addition, group leader performance also must take into account extra-group conditions and dynamics. That is, each group, regardless of type and purpose, is set within a larger context (Conyne & Cook, 2004). Task groups, such as a committee, function within and are influenced by the organization or community of which they are a part. A counseling group is provided within a particular setting, such as a school or mental health agency, and is subject to its physical environment, policies, procedures, resource allotments, and other factors. School counselors are keenly aware of how the ongoing regularities of the school day affect when groups can be offered, for example.

All groups also are influenced by macro and distal factors over which the leader and members have little or no control. We are all painfully aware of external and remote influences that affect daily living—for example, when the national safety alert is raised from yellow to orange.

In general, group leaders function as the nurturer of a developing ecological system—that is, of the group itself in relation to its external environment—leaders collaborate with the members to promote interdependence and interconnectivity, seeking to link them together in a kind of web. This web allows for energy to flow without the loss of member individuality.

Midori, the great Japanese violinist, conducts summer concerts in rural areas of Japan in which she seeks to use her music to reach people proactively as she tries to generate *Kizuna*, which means in English "human interconnection." Kizuna is very much what group leaders need to be concerned with—applying group techniques that will lead group members to become more closely and humanly interconnected within the group and in consonance with their external environment.

Summarized below are the best pratice performance guidelines that have been recommended by the Association for Specialists in Group Work (1998). As with the related guidelines for planning and processing, these performance guidelines offer sound recommendations for practice. What they omit, however, is sufficient attention to leaders viewing the group in the context of its proximal and distal environment.

## Best Practices in Performing

Possesses awareness of self

Possesses understanding and skill in necessary group competencies

Is able to adapt the group plan
- In relation to unique needs and conditions
- In relation to ongoing group progress
- In relation to ethical, professional, and social boundaries

Understands and is able to develop therapeutic dynamics
- Group development
- Process observation
- Therapeutic conditions

Helps members generate meaning from the group experience

Collaborates with members in developing goals

Includes process and outcome evaluation

Attends to diversity issues of a broad nature among members

Maintains ethical surveillance, consistent with codes of appropriate professional and regulatory bodies

In the next three chapters, we present exercises and information addressing how group leaders can deliver techniques that nurture the development of an interdependent social system and then can work with members to take advantage of that system to promote growth and development. The chapters are ordered sequentially in relation to a most basic group development model that is based on stages: dominant trends and qualitative differences that characterize the general evolution of a group. Then developmental stages are:

Connecting leader performance with the developmental stage of the group is important. Effective and appropriate leadership early in a group's development is qualitatively different from what it might be toward the group's middle point or at the end. These developmental themes are drawn carefully within each chapter, as well as the leader techniques that can yield productive groups.

# 5

## Performance Techniques at the Beginning Stage of Group Development: Getting Established and Transitioning

**ADVANCE ORGANIZER**

This chapter contains the following material:

**Various Perspectives on the Beginning Stage of Group Development**

**Our Language for the Beginning Stage: Getting Established and Transitioning**

**What Does "Getting Established and Transitioning" Mean?**

*The Group Leader Serves as a New Social System "Host/Hostess"*
*Transitioning to Productivity Through Conflict*

**Critical Incident Training in the Beginning Stage of Performing**

CRITICAL INCIDENTS

Introductory CI: "Two Generic Techniques"
Group Type: *Psychoeducation, Counseling*
Best Practice Area: *Performing*
Group Developmental Stage: *Any*

CI 5.1: "What Are We Doing Here?"
Group Type: *Psychoeducation*
Best Practice Area: *Performing*
Group Developmental Stage: *Beginning*

CI 5.2: "You're Not the Boss!"
Group Type: *Psychoeducation*
Best Practice Area: *Performing*
Group Developmental Stage: *Beginning*

CI 5.3: "Determinator"
Group Type: *Counseling*
Best Practice Area: *Performing*
Group Developmental Stage: *Beginning*

CI 5.4: "Yes, but . . ."
Group Type: *Counseling*
Best Practice Area: *Performing*
Group Developmental Stage: *Beginning*

**In Sum**

Group leaders need to be aware of many factors as they perform the leadership function. A primary one is determining as best as possible the developmental stage of the
group, for where a group is in its evolution helps generally predict what members
may be ready to experience and do—and what group techniques might be useful.

This idea is not dissimilar from individual life span human development. One person may be able to do certain tasks when a teenager, for example, and others when a
young child or a retiree. So it is with groups. A group in its earliest stage of development allows for conditions that support certain kinds of tasks but not so readily other
ones. It would be inappropriate, for instance, for a group leader to ask members of a
counseling group during the beginning of their first group session to reveal a deep
personal secret. On the other hand, it might fit during the middle working stage of the
group to ask members to share deeply personal material.

Therefore, leaders need to consider group developmental stage in relation to
developmental tasks to be expected and concomitant techniques that might be
used. For instance, open, unstructured group discussion—while often very useful
for adults—is outside the developmental scope of young students in schools. Trotzer
(2006) presents a particularly helpful schema in which he outlines a clear relationship between developmental stage and the developmental tasks to be generally
expected within each of the stages. Awareness of developmental stage is so important in relation to group techniques that we have organized our discussion of performance techniques by three broad-stroke stages of group development: beginning,
middle, and end. In this chapter, we focus on the beginning stage.

## Various Perspectives on the Beginning Stage of Group Development

What is going on in the beginning stage of group development that might affect group
leader techniques? Many authors have commented on this question (see Conyne,
1989). Forsyth (2006) cited over 100 group developmental life span models. These
models tend to emphasize similar yet different phenomena. Some examples follow.

Trotzer (1999) suggested that in the beginning stage (which roughly approxi-
mates his stages of security and acceptance), members need to become "warmed up"
interpersonally, learn what limits and boundaries apply, and "they are" seek trust formation. Jones (1973) posited that members at the beginning stage generally are
dependent on the leader and other external forces and seek orientation to what is to
be occurring. Schutz (1958) indicated that members tend to be especially sensitive to
inclusion–exclusion issues at the beginning stage of a group. Tuckman and Jensen
(1977) underscored the importance of formation and becoming oriented, followed by
a period of storming or conflict over control and power issues. Anderson (1984), in
his TACIT (Trust, Autonomy, Closeness, Interdependence, Termination) model,
viewed trust as a central beginning issue. Corey and Corey (2006) viewed the initial
stage of group development as centering around orientation and exploration.
Gladding (2003) emphasized that leaders in the beginning stage need to help
members deal with apprehension and that orienting them to each other and to operating goals and rules of the group can be helpful. Yalom (1985) identified powerful
therapeutic factors that contribute to healthy group functioning. From this

perspective, at a group's beginning stage members tend to look for hope, value learning they are not alone, and benefit from the provision of information about the experience they are entering.

## Our Language for the Beginning Stage: Getting Established and Transitioning

Drawing from these perspectives, our own language for the beginning stage of group development revolves around forming and getting established. Even in a group in which the members already know each other—for example, in a task force of a company—the group itself is a new entity, formed to accomplish particular purposes. As a new group, therefore, it takes on a life of its own. Its evolution is dependent on many factors, not the least of which are the members and how they form and get established to work together within the group. In a group that is comprised of strangers—for example, in a psychotherapy group where no one knows anyone else—there is a double sense of newness: the members are new to each other and to the group at the same time. In either example just given, forming and getting established are critically important.

## What Does "Getting Established and Transitioning" Mean?

### The Group Leader Serves as a New Social System "Host/Hostess"

At each stage of group development, two continuing sets of dynamics need to be addressed: task functions and personal relations (Jones, 1973). That is, there always are things that have to be accomplished (these are the "what's," or the task functions) and people who accomplish them (these are the "how's," or personal relations).

In the beginning stage, in order to form and get established successfully, the leader (or coleaders) needs to introduce members to the group and to each other. The group leader functions as a new social system "host or hostess," who helps members get oriented to the group's surroundings and to what is available. The leader helps members begin to get comfortable, communicates what the group's purpose is, and informs them on how the events and activities will proceed. This role is not to be confused with that of a host or hostess of a typical party event, although there no doubt are some similarities.

The leader's role in the beginning of the group is unique. As we mentioned, this role centers on helping members develop a new social system—this group—that never existed before and probably never will again. At this early group development stage members are especially sensitive to the leader. They look to the leader first, literally fastening their eyes and ears on him or her. Because members know much less about the group purposes and methods and are not trained in group leadership, they tend to ascribe power and control in the beginning to the designated leader. So, at the beginning stage of a group the leader holds more power, influence, and control than perhaps at any other stage. It is important to recognize that reality and to use that power appropriately to help members come together and figure out what they can do in this new setting.

## Transitioning to Productivity Through Conflict

As the beginning stage of the group evolves over a few sessions or meetings, another set of issues can emerge. This emergent set of issues focuses on transitioning between getting established and becoming productive. This transition frequently revolves around issues of control and power. Where at first the leader clearly was in a position of control, this level of control begins to shift as the group evolves, either by leader design or by the nature of member involvement itself. Decision making, power, and control now become diffused among leader and members. This diffusion process can occur intentionally and without much or any conflict, or it can occur as the result of explicit conflict between the leader and members. In any case, the shift is entirely to be expected and it is necessary in order for the middle stage of group development to emerge, which is focused on connecting and producing.

## *Critical Incident Training in the Beginning Stage of Performing*

What do group leaders need to know and be able to do to effectively use performing techniques in the beginning stage of a group? Following are a series of critical incidents in the beginning stage of performing for counseling and psychoeducation groups. As with the critical incidents that are presented throughout subsequent chapters, they are intended to provide concrete experience with applying the PGTM in the selection and use of group techniques within sessions and meetings. As we suggested before, please refer to Chapters 2 and 3 if you need a refresher.

We begin our focus on performing by presenting a very flexible approach to use in selecting a group technique. This approach, which we term "Two Generic Techniques," is applicable to any type of group and at any developmental stage. We start at this point because group leader adaptation and flexibility are essential qualities.

### CRITICAL INCIDENTS

#### INTRODUCTORY CI: FLEXIBLE USE OF A GROUP TECHNIQUE

Group Type: *Psychoeducation, Counseling*
Best Practice Area: *Performing*
Group Developmental Stage: *Any*

### *Two Generic Techniques*

## HISTORY

This introductory critical incident addresses core issues that transcend any one developmental stage within performing. We consider the techniques used to be essential to effective group-work leadership because they highlight needed group leader flexibility.

The group history is a simple one. Imagine any single session within a counseling or psychoeducation group, and any point at which a technique is being considered, and then used.

## CRITICAL INCIDENT

The critical incident format for these two techniques is a generalizable one across sessions whenever considering the introduction of a technique.

LEADER:    Would it be okay if . . . ? (*The leader describes what he or she has in mind. This is alternative one.*)

MEMBER(S):    (*providing consent*) Yes, it would; let's try it. (*If they do not agree, then the leader may launch a discussion to understand opposition, may just drop further pursuit of that technique, or may work with members to adapt the proposed technique to become acceptable.*)

LEADER:    (*if members have agreed to participate*) Introduces/applies the technique. (*It may be simple and direct, or more elaborate.*)

LEADER:    (following the technique's application) How did that go? What did you learn? How might any of this be applied in or outside our group? (*This is alternative two.*)

## WHAT TECHNIQUE DO YOU CHOOSE?

Individually or in small groups jot down or discuss several options for what technique you would use in this situation. What factors must be considered?

## STEPS TOWARD SELECTING A TECHNIQUE

Here is our thinking:

### Step 1:   Identify the group type and purpose, best practice area, and developmental stage

We present the two techniques ("Would it be okay?" and "What have you learned?") as essential bookends to nearly any technique to be used within a counseling or a psychoeducation group. Variations of word usage are entirely appropriate in order to keep from becoming rote and mechanistic.

### Step 2:   Analyze the presenting situation by applying ecological concepts

"Would it be okay?" seeks informed consent. The ethic of voluntary participation is a *sine qua non* of all group work. Leaders refrain from pressuring members to do anything that is outside their own free choosing. It is particularly challenging in groups to protect this individual right. From an ecological group work perspective, asking if it would be okay is fully consistent with collaboration, where leaders and members seek to chart their course together.

"How did it go, what did you learn, what can be applied?" is intended to engage members in their learning actively, causing them to reflect and draw meaning from their experience. These questions address the ecological group work concept of meaning making. Moreover, when members are asked to envision or even to plan what can be applied, the very essence of group work is stimulated. Members are involved with groups to help them learn and gain skills that they can then use effectively and appropriately in life situations outside the group. Leaders who consistently ask members to consider applying what they are learning are activating the ecological group work concept of sustainability—moving beyond the group milieu to life contexts in which the members find themselves on a regular basis.

### Step 3:   Review possible group techniques, considering focus and level

***Beginning/Any Stage Performance Toolbox #23,*** Permission. The leader asks, "Would it be okay?"

*Focus:* Cognitive.
*Level:* Individual and/or interpersonal—depending on its use.

***Beginning/Any Stage Performance Toolbox #82,*** How Did It Go? Secondary questions are "What did you learn?" and "What can be applied?"

*Focus:* Cognitive.
*Level:* individual and/or interpersonal—depending on its use.

These two techniques, including variations of phrasing them so they do not grow stale, are staples rather than choices. Group members need to be informed about options and collaborated with about directions. Also, evaluating how things went, what they have learned, and what might be transferred to real-life contexts is a prerequisite for group techniques.

### Step 4:   Select a best-fit technique

There is a kind of ethical elegance involved when leaders ask members for permission, when leaders provide members with a choice to do something or not. Providing these options allows members to actively engage and affords the opportunity for "buy in." It is the very essence of appropriateness. Leaders should not arbitrarily do things to members, except in certain cases when prompt, decisive action may be required. Generally, leaders function most effectively when they have found ways to connect and engage members in the process of growth and change. Of course, continually seeking the permission of members, asking "is this okay?" over and over again would wear thin and soon become a negative side effect. Again, professional judgment is necessary when using any technique.

The same comments apply to the leader actively pursuing with members how activities and events are going ("How did that go?"). Leaders should never assume they have the answers, that they know how members are experiencing group life. That is, effectiveness can never be independently assessed. Leaders always can ask, can probe, can set a norm where members volunteer how things are going. This kind of ongoing dialogue can keep a group focused on what is appropriate for members and on what works.

### Step 5:  Implement and evaluate how well the technique worked

Idiosyncratic implementation of the "formula" we have outlined will enhance the presentation of any technique. Again, the approach involves (with group leader variation):

LEADER:    "Would it be okay if . . . ?" (*The leader describes what he or she has in mind. This is an informal informed consent procedure. This is alternative one.*)

MEMBER(S):  (*providing consent*) Yes, it would; let's try it. (*If they do not agree, then the leader may launch a discussion to understand opposition, may just drop further pursuit of that technique, or may work with members to adapt the proposed technique to become acceptable.*)

LEADER:    (*if members have agreed to participate*) Introduces/applies the technique. (*It may be simple and direct, or more elaborate.*) Great, then let's try this: Draw a time line of your life where you show when major points of interest occurred . . .

LEADER:    (*following the technique's application*) How did that go? What did you learn? How might any of this be applied in or outside our group? (*This is alternative two.*)

## If in a Class or Workshop, Then:

### *Practice the choice*

Pair up with another student and try out your choices. Give each other feedback. What might work? What might need to be changed? Compare your choices with those provided by the authors.

### *Process the choice*

What have you learned? What are you learning about this process for selecting group techniques? What are you learning about yourself as a group leader? What might you be able to use the next time?

> Group Type: *Psychoeducation*
> Best Practice Area: *Performing*
> Group Developmental Stage: *Beginning*

## What Are We Doing Here?

### HISTORY

Each year the psychology training program requires its students to participate in a "learning group" for 12 clock hours over six, two-hour weekly sessions. Typically, this group includes both structured and unstructured experiences. These experiences are said to be aimed at helping members/trainees learn about what it's like to be a group member, to have an opportunity to self-disclose and to give and receive feedback, to participate in the here-and-now, and to observe group leadership being modeled by advanced group leaders. Members are told during a brief orientation meeting, also, that the group is not intended as a counseling, a psychotherapy, or a task group, and that it is a kind of adapted psychoeducation group.

### CRITICAL INCIDENT

It is the second session of this group (about hour 3.5). The first session seemed to go well, in general, with members becoming better acquainted and having worked together to create a set of ground rules, including confidentiality. There seems to be developing some anxiety about what the purpose is for the group; Susan and Felipe, the coleaders, are trying to address this concern:

FELIPE:   (*a coleader*) Yes, well as we have said, the purpose is intended to be somewhat ambiguous; but, we want us to stay focused on the present and for us to learn from each other what a group is all about.

ZACK:   (*Zack asks with some exasperation*) Yeah, I heard that . . . I know it probably *should* register with me, but it just doesn't, I'm afraid. You know, what does that mean, really? Anyone else with me on this, or am I just the odd person out here?

SUZANNE:   (*looking at the leaders*) No, well, yes, maybe! Oh, I don't know! I think we are just supposed to try stuff out and then learn from it, but I have no clue about how to do that. And, being a trainee here, no doubt I should know . . . I'm kind of embarrassed about this. Is it us, or is it that everything is all confused?

## WHAT TECHNIQUE DO YOU CHOOSE?

Individually or in small groups jot down or discuss several options for what technique you would use in this situation. What factors must be considered?

## STEPS TOWARD SELECTING A TECHNIQUE

Here is our thinking:

**Step 1:   Identify the group type and purpose, best practice area, and developmental stage**

This training group is described as a kind of psychoeducation group, and it is in its early stage of performing.

**Step 2:   Analyze the presenting situation by applying ecological concepts**

Context always is important for group work. In this example, group participation is required as part of a trainee's overall experience in the program. As well, the members are most likely all from the same training program. This situation engenders a unique context where members may feel, at some level, compelled to be involved while feeling somewhat hesitant to expose themselves to their fellow classmates. This context may present special forces in relation to how interconnected members may become both in and out of the group, how they may collaborate, the kind of social system they will develop, what meaning they may each derive from their experience, and how the sustainability of learning may affect future relationships. Thus, everything both within the group and within the larger program itself is intertwined. Such a level of mutuality can provide opportunities for positive learning, but it also can provide risks that could negatively influence subsequent interaction. Confusion among members may result from many sources. One likely possibility centers around goals, both in terms of what the overall group is intended to address and, within that, what individual goals might be feasible to accomplish. This level of analysis revolves around resolving the relationship between interconnection and individuality within the context at hand.

**Step 3:   Review possible group techniques, considering focus and level**

Following your analysis of the group's history, the critical incident, and the ecological concepts in play, exploring toolbox techniques may lead you to one or more highly feasible options.

Conversely, as you get more confident and more experienced as a group leader, you might wish to put off using the toolbox and, instead, search your own "internal toolbox." What might you come up with that could be helpful? What might you try? See what you come up with and move from there to next steps in this process. (You may want to compare the techniques that you devise with those in the toolbox.) At any rate, we encourage you to take advantage of the toolbox techniques as well as your own resources.

***Beginning Stage Performance Toolbox #80,*** Group Identification.

*Focus:* Structural.
*Level:* Group and individual.

Context is immensely important for group work, but it is especially salient in this particular critical incident; in addition, goal clarity is essential to obtain, both in general and within this critical incident. Therefore, we would ask the members to talk about the unique context of their group and how they feel about it. We would ask them, given that unique context and their feelings, to collaborate on developing their own definition of what the group's purpose is. Then, we would ask each member to define a personal goal to be addressed during the group's life, and how progress on it might be extended beyond the life of the group itself. Finally, we would ask members to discuss what they learned in this process of definition and application.

In a nutshell, the issues to be explored are:

1. Identify and discuss our unique context as a group.
2. Within that context, define our group's purpose.
3. Within that group purpose, what can be your purpose here?
4. How can you continue to work on that purpose outside the group?
5. What have you learned?

In terms of process, we would ask members to individually write their responses on a form that we prepared (10 minutes). Then we would ask them to pair up to discuss them (15 minutes). Finally, we would have the group as a whole interact in relation to what they have developed as individuals and within their pairings (30–45 minutes). The balance of time would be spent on action steps flowing from the preceding work.

## Step 4:  Select a best-fit technique

We want to illustrate that you and your coleaders can develop your own techniques as you gain increased expertise. You need not be tied inextricably to any toolbox or set of approaches that have been developed by others.

Further, we find the previously illustrated technique to be on target in helping members examine, individually and together, important contextual dynamics that may be affecting goals for the experience. We choose to face this interplay between context and goals directly but in such a way so as to provide some structure and safety net—after all, it is still early in this group's development and issues surrounding trust and security are relevant. This technique, which we call Identify Context and Purpose, seems appropriate to the group's level of functioning while being adequate to move it forward effectively once members examine how context and goals may be related and convert learning to action steps.

## Step 5:  Implement and evaluate how well the technique worked

SUZANNE:    (*looking at the leaders*) No, well, yes, maybe! Oh, I don't know! I think we are just supposed to try stuff out and then learn from it, but I have no clue about how to do that. And, being a trainee here, no doubt I should know . . . I'm kind of embarrassed about this. Is it us, or is it that everything is all confused?

FELIPE:     "Yep, I think you've hit something right on the head here . . . there may be a natural confusion from our situation and context and what we can do here in terms of goals.

JUANITA:    So, what might this mean? We really are a unique group, all from the same program, all trying to learn from our common time together. Maybe we could take a look at this directly and that may help. Bear with us here, we have a way—a technique—that may help us sort through some confusion and come out the other end.

FELIPE:     Yeah, we envision using a set of five brief questions that we each would respond to on paper (not to be turned in, or anything like that), then discuss with a partner, then as a total group—all about our group and our goals . . . whaddya think? Do-able? Want to try?

LUCY:       I'm all for trying to get out of this morass . . . Zack, Suzanne—what do you say?

SUZANNE:    Yes! I've been waiting for something like this, and I see Zack's there, too!

JUANITA:    Great, I take that as support . . . let's see what we can do.

## If in a Class or Workshop, Then:

### Practice the choice

Pair up with another student and try out your choices. Give each other feedback. What might work? What might need to be changed? Compare your choices with those provided by the authors.

### Process the choice

What have you learned? What are you learning about this process for selecting group techniques? What are you learning about yourself as a group leader? What might you be able to use the next time?

---

**PERFORMING (BEGINNING) CI 5.2**

Group Type: *Psychoeducation*[*]
Best Practice Area: *Performing*
Group Developmental Stage: *Beginning*
*Open group.

## *You're Not the Boss!*

## HISTORY

The attention deficit disorder (ADD) group at a local family agency consists of male and female adolescents 12–15 years of age, who meet once a week for an hour and a half to discuss issues. The group is open and continuous, though the size of the group is always capped at six members to one experienced leader. Each week an educational component is introduced as a theme, such as stress relief, communication skills, or skills related to academic performance. The rest of the time is spent usually discussing relationship issues.

The current group's members include two males and three females who have been together for three months, and one male who joined two weeks ago. At the beginning of each session each member is invited to check in and the rules are reviewed. Tonight the new male member, Jeremy, arrived 10 minutes late. He walked in just as the group was finishing the rules review. The leader nodded at him but continued to talk with a member, Julie, about the difference between keeping secrets and maintaining confidentiality.

## CRITICAL INCIDENT

Julie looked at Jeremy and paused. She slumped into her chair and looked down at the floor. The leader paused and waited to see if Julie wanted to continue the discussion or if other members wanted to remark. Jeremy appeared very restless and uncomfortable, shifting from side to side and popping one of his fingers against his pants leg. He did not look at the leader, but glanced at Julie. Only about 3 minutes passed when one of the girls blurted out a remark.

ANDREA:    Can we have a treat tonight?

JULIE:    (*snapping angrily*) Jeremy shouldn't have a treat. He was late!

(*The leader sits quietly observing Jeremy's reaction.*)

JEREMY:    (*snapping back*) You're not the boss!

JULIE:    It was rude to interrupt me!

LEADER:    (*looking at Julie*) Is there more that you want to say, perhaps without yelling at him?

JULIE:    Never mind! (*She slumps back into the chair and crosses her arms.*)

ANDREA:    (*chiming in*) I didn't mean to start something!

JEREMY:    It's none of your business! What is your problem anyway?

## WHAT TECHNIQUE DO YOU CHOOSE?

Individually or in small groups jot down or discuss several options for what technique you would use in this situation. What factors must be considered?

## STEPS TOWARD SELECTING A TECHNIQUE

Here is our thinking:

### Step 1:  Identify the group type and purpose, best practice area, and developmental stage

This agency group is psychoeducational by design, to provide skills training while also dealing with emotional issues. One of the group members is relatively new, but the other members and the leader are not. As an open group, a little more time is often needed to settle into relationships due to the ongoing potential for new members, often without notice to the group members. An open group, therefore, goes through cycles of developmental stages as members experience beginning stage issues and closure issues when new members join the group and other members leave.

### Step 2:  Analyze the presenting situation by applying ecological concepts

This group leader was surrounded by a room of separate individuals occupying the same space, unlike the more desirable interconnected group members who work together cohesively. The leader's desire to create a well-functioning social system is an important ecological concept that is continuously tested in an open group due to member turnover. Still, rules, norms, and expectations need to be addressed and the leader has an increased responsibility to help members define the unique context with each member change. How members make meaning from their experience can influence their future participation in the group.

The opportunities that arise for teaching relationship skills are of key importance in a psychoeducation group. What appear to be underlying negative feelings dividing the members of this group at the outset of the evening may be harnessed and reframed by the group leader to build a teachable moment. The sustainability of the group depends on the degree to which the leader and members can integrate each new member into the ongoing and often dynamic social system.

### Step 3:  Review possible group techniques, considering focus and level

The leader is interested in approaching the behaviors manifested in this group in a nonconfrontational way, expecting that developmentally in the early stage of this group the reactions from young adolescents will be to either withdraw or become defensive. This tendency already has been demonstrated by one member. The leader hypothesizes that, by using a technique allowing for expression of feelings about the group, the members may be able to engage in some processing that is not directed at any one person, but at the behavior that was manifested.

***Performing Toolbox #37,*** Toys in Concert. Give each member Tinker Toys or Legos and ask him or her to build a representation of what group cohesion looks like.

*Focus:* Cognitive and behavioral.
*Level:* Indiv1idual and interpersonal.

This is an opportunity to engage the members creatively by asking them to make meaning from the manipulation of toys to resemble ideal group member behavior. By asking them to create an individual representation, and perhaps by observing the work of others, members can gain some interpersonal understanding of other members, while also realizing that other viewpoints or perspectives exist for the same issue.

The leader likes this technique for several reasons, including the use of manipulatives. She is aware of the adaptability of the technique, mainly in considering the degree to which she can encourage the group to have a discussion about the meaning their symbols have now and for the future of the group. The leader also considers this technique to be nonthreatening for members, while still challenging them to think and learn about each other and themselves.

**Performing Toolbox #39,** Out with the Trash. Have all members sit in a tight circle around the room's garbage can. Have them all talk at once about what is most on their minds. Leader calls "Stop" at some point and the group can process the experience.

*Focus:* Cognitive and behavioral.
*Level:* Group.

The leader knows that students who struggle with ADD often benefit from behavioral techniques that require action. Such concrete activities can help students move about while working on their issues. This technique emphasizes the leader's desire to intervene with all members of the group, rather than singling out anyone.

### Step 4: Select a best-fit technique

The group members are young adolescents, who may or may not have a good "feelings" vocabulary and are lacking in many social skills. The garbage can technique is simple, the resource (garbage can) is readily available, and it uses a visible object with adolescents who often have trouble focusing on the task before them. The expression of thoughts and feelings aimed at a neutral object, such as the garbage can, is also symbolic (dumping one's personal "garbage") and can prompt interesting discussion. Though the technique does have the propensity to escalate, if properly managed it can be minimally intrusive if the group members speak only about their own feelings without attacking others. The leader's desire to allow time for group processing helped her decide that she could monitor this technique by limiting the time for talking at the can and being explicit in her directions. She chose to have the members go around taking turns to say an "I" statement with a feelings word until they could not think of any more words. She believes that this technique will prompt the group's members to own their own feelings and learn a valuable skill in communicating them.

### Step 5: Implement and evaluate how well the technique worked

JEREMY: It's none of your business! What is your problem anyway?

LEADER: (*standing up to draw attention to herself*) I would like you all to bring your chairs over here and sit in a circle around this garbage can, facing the can.

JULIE: Are we going to pick something out of the garbage can?

LEADER: No, I want you to put something into the garbage can. I would like you to "dump your garbage."

JEREMY: Do what?

ANDREA: I get it. You mean like stuff we don't want in here.

LEADER:  Well, yes, something like that. There are rules, though, so I want you all to listen carefully to my signals. When I tell you to start, I want you all to talk to the can, telling it all of your troubles of the day, of the week, whatever is on your mind. *But* you must use an "I" statement and as many feelings words as you can think of. For example, "I felt frustrated when I forgot my lunch." If there is something that is keeping you from participating well in the group tonight, think about putting it verbally in the garbage can. Then when I shout "Stop," I want you to be very quiet and listen. Understand?

ANDREA AND JEREMY:   (*at the same time*) Yes.

OTHERS:  Yes.

## If in a Class or Workshop, Then:

### *Practice the choice*

Pair up with another student and try out your choices. Give each other feedback. What might work? What might need to be changed? Compare your choices with those provided by the authors.

### *Process the choice*

What have you learned? What are you learning about this process for selecting group techniques? What are you learning about yourself as a group leader? What might you be able to use the next time?

---

### PERFORMING (BEGINNING) CI 5.3

Group Type: *Counseling*
Best Practice Area: *Performing*
Group Developmental Stage: *Beginning*

## *Determinator*

## HISTORY

Bea Gibbons has been running a group for individuals with addictions at her agency for three weeks with a coleader, Roger Stone. Designed as a 20-session group program, the leaders have been pleased so far that attendance in the group has been good, with only one of the nine members missing one session. Participation, however, has been variable. One particular member, Brad, talks significantly more than any other member, offering opinions and comments on any of the issues or topics presented to the group by the leaders or by the other members. Bea and Roger have noted the amount of attention drawn by Brad, and have observed various reactions by other group members in relation to his need to be heard. One of the other men in the group appears very annoyed and turns himself sideways in his chair most of the time, away from Brad. The other male members just seem to watch, while the three women make occasional comments only when asked to speak directly. It is difficult to gauge the level of engagement of the group members, other than Brad, because there have been so few sessions under their belts. Overall, it seems that Brad is determined to dominate the group's participation time.

## CRITICAL INCIDENT

In the last two sessions the members have focused discussion on their abilities (or lack thereof) to express their emotions and their ability (or inability) to communicate their needs to others. As the group members gathered in their conference room it was with some obvious apprehension: a severe storm warning was just announced over the television in the waiting area and on the local radio stations. Brad was already talking at length about the forecast for the next two days.

Bea tried to start the group's check-in routine, but Brad would not stop talking about the weather. Roger sat next to Brad in order to "run interference" if needed.

ROGER:    (*putting his hand on Brad's shoulder*) Brad, you seem to be quite concerned about the weather. How about if we give the other group members a chance to say how they feel tonight?

BRAD:    Well, sure, but they never say anything. I'm the one who always has to get things going.

MARY:    You seem to want to get things going and decide when to get things ended, too!

BRAD:    (*responding quickly*) Your point is? *You* say something then!

ROGER:    In all fairness, Brad, you have been very willing to be open and willing to participate in all of our discussions. I'd like you to hold that thought for just a moment. Mary, you may have had something to say, which you have not said, in the past or tonight. Perhaps each one of you can take a moment and consider where you stand with regard to sharing your ideas with the group.

## WHAT TECHNIQUE DO YOU CHOOSE?

Individually or in small groups jot down or discuss several options for what technique you would use in this situation. What factors must be considered?

## STEPS TOWARD SELECTING A TECHNIQUE

Here is our thinking:

### Step 1:   Identify the group type and purpose, best practice area, and developmental stage

Bea and Roger are running a counseling group, designed to give clients opportunities to focus on a variety of issues involved in their addictive behaviors. At the third of 20 sessions, this group is in its beginning stage. The group is having a difficult time getting started for this session, so the leaders will need to be more direct in helping the group members engage more fully in the discussions. Increased participation will enable all members to do more of the therapeutic work that the group is intended to support.

### Step 2:   Analyze the presenting situation by applying ecological concepts

Within the context of a counseling group, leaders must seek a balance between challenge and support for all group members, particularly difficult with a domineering group member like Brad. Bea and Roger consider many concepts with great sensitivity. Both leaders are concerned about the social system that has been created and is being maintained so far, with Brad as the determined dominator. Bea and Roger are equally determined to provide "free space" for interconnections among all of the group's members, without negating the needs of any one member, even Brad. In order to allow for personal growth and development for all group members, focusing the members on the context of the group and the process by which they all should be engaged, the leaders believe that the balance they seek can be achieved.

### Step 3:   Review possible group techniques, considering focus and level

There are multiple options for techniques as Bea and Roger see it, but their choice is about whether to be direct or indirect. There is the possibility, however, of ostracizing Brad if they are too confrontational in the beginning stage of the group.

***Performing Toolbox #30,*** Direct Feedback. Bea is inclined toward a somewhat direct approach of offering feedback about the troublesome behavior.

*Focus:* Cognitive and affective.
*Level:* Individual, interpersonal, and group.

Specifically directed to Brad, the leaders' confrontation with his individual and yet troublesome behavior would require him to think about the effects of his behavior on other group members, including the leaders. At an interpersonal level, this is a way for the leaders to model assertive communication to all members of the group, with the hope that through processing together, all members can learn a valuable new skill. How the group members experience that interaction is difficult to gauge, however, and would have the potential for positive and negative affective side effects.

The leaders are in agreement that a cognitive focus is important because all of the group members can benefit from some communication skills training. The degree to which they are considering an affective focus is a point of discussion for the two leaders. Again, the sensitivity that the leaders have for the group members will help determine at what level they choose to intervene. This technique offers potential benefits at all levels of the group's performance, from individual to group.

***Performing Toolbox #21,*** Time Tokens. Roger leans toward the indirect approach of using time tokens to limit the amount of time any one group member interjects into the group's conversations.

*Focus:* Cognitive and behavioral.
*Level:* Individual, interpersonal, and group.

This example of a simple technique can have a powerful effect if reinforced consistently. Each member focuses on his or her own level of participation and chooses when to use the time tokens. Because members are aware of how often they can talk with their number of tokens, they must make some decisions about who they will verbally respond to and when. Because the leaders are attempting to seek balance in the members' participation, the tokens will encourage more participation from some and less from other group members.

## Step 4:   Select a best-fit technique

In either option members are being asked to think about their own behavior as related to other group members. The choice of the leaders is to use a behavioral technique. This choice includes the leaders' assumptions about what they believe other group members are experiencing with this domineering member. Thinking about the group's developmental stage, Bea and Roger are concerned about how much benefit to members there is with a direct approach at this point. Besides, there is potential benefit to all group members with what can be thought of as a training aid, of sorts—the time tokens. All members will be able to think about how they will use their own time, providing self-monitoring, while also encouraging other members to take some responsibility for the monitoring of their own time. This has the potential of increasing interconnections among the group's members, and ownership of the group.

It is important for the leaders to assure all group members that their rights are important too. Directly confronting Brad about his behavior is an important way to demonstrate such skills as assertiveness and communication, but because it appears that this may be Brad's modus operandi, it will probably take more than one session to help him gain an awareness about the behavior and then to work on changing it. The token technique has the potential for more member buy-in, particularly over a longer period. It could become a part of the group's routine process, and also can allow for modifications by collaborating with the group members in case someone needs more time than his or her tokens allot.

One benefit of coleadership is the increased ability to be watchful about group maintenance tasks, such as facilitating communication, encouraging members to participate successfully, and providing help to them. Brad could feel dismissed or diminished personally and could quit the group if he does not have his needs met. The leaders hope that he will see the experience as a learning opportunity and not as a punishment. There is great sensitivity needed to convey support that is caring and yet firm at the same time, a concept that can be connected to other areas of their lives. There are many ways to talk about addictions, many of which focus on clients gaining increased self-awareness, particularly in the area of relationships.

Their support systems are often as dysfunctional as their addictive behavior, but encouraging personal growth and change is one way a counseling group can offer hope of recovery and improved mental and physical health and well-being.

**Step 5:   Implement and evaluate how well the technique worked**

ROGER:   In all fairness, Brad, you have been very willing to be open and willing to participate in all of our discussions. I'd like you to hold that thought for just a moment. Mary, you may have had something to say, which you have not said, in the past or tonight. Perhaps each one of you can take a moment and consider where you stand with regard to sharing your ideas with the group.

BEA:   It's very interesting that Brad has the perception that he must carry the conversation for the rest of the group members. I wonder how you all would feel about using a technique to try to balance out that responsibility for participating in the group's discussions.

BRAD:   Of course! Sure, fine by me.

ONE WOMAN MEMBER:   What is this technique you are talking about?

BEA:   I am going to give each of you a set of time tokens. If you want to have time to talk, you must use a token. When you run out, you must hold your discussion until another time. How does that sound?

ROGER:   We can decide together how many tokens you get. If you like the system, we can keep it; if you don't, we can scrap it. I would like to hear from each of you at this point. How about starting with you, Drew, and we'll go around until we finish with Brad.

## If in a Class or Workshop, Then:

### *Practice the choice*

Pair up with another student and try out your choices. Give each other feedback. What might work? What might need to be changed? Compare your choices with those provided by the authors.

### *Process the choice*

What have you learned? What are you learning about this process for selecting group techniques? What are you learning about yourself as a group leader? What might you be able to use the next time?

---

### PERFORMING (BEGINNING) CI 5.4

Group Type: *Counseling*
Best Practice Area: *Performing*
Group Developmental Stage: *Beginning*

## *Yes, But . . .*

## HISTORY

Gail was recently referred to the Lincoln County Community Mental Health Clinic by her priest, Father Samuel. Gail was very close to her older sister, who suddenly died in an accident. The accident was over a year ago and Gail seems unable to move beyond the tragedy. She reports feeling "stuck," frequently utilizing her vacation days to stay in bed and avoid going to work.

Upon completing the initial intake session, Gail agreed to join a group for other individuals also dealing with grief around the loss of a close friend or family member. The group is being co-led by Maria and Leonard, two hospice counselors who recognized the need a few years ago to provide grief support groups. Each summer they volunteer their time to run this grief support group that meets two evenings per week for six weeks.

To allow each member ample opportunity to work on personal goals, Maria and Leonard had discovered that eight members is the maximum size. In carefully planning for the current group, especially the first and second sessions, they purposefully crafted activities to facilitate members establishing some basic rules concerning appropriate ways to provide feedback, the importance of being open and fully participating in the sessions, and respecting differences. As well, the leaders planned two structured activities that guide the members toward building cohesion and a sense of working together. At the conclusion of the first session, all seemed to be going as planned, but both Maria and Leonard made mental notes about Gail's approach-avoidance style of interaction.

## CRITICAL INCIDENT

In the second session Maria and Leonard open with a structured activity that helped group members develop a personal goal that they wanted to realize as a result of participating in the grief group. Initially, Gail eagerly participated in the activity. However, during the go-around portion, in which members were invited to share their personal goal, the leaders observed that Gail's goal was immediately followed by a lengthy discourse as to why her goal was unobtainable. In fact, this was somewhat startling to the coleaders because prior to this, Gail seemed helpful to other group members, often asking clarifying questions and encouraging the others in a supportive manner.

VERONICA:    After Gerald died of brain cancer in March I haven't been able to sort through his clothes in the closet . . . or any of his belongings. A goal that I wrote down a few minutes ago, and would like to share with everyone, is to be able to begin sorting through his things and not feel ashamed or so damn awful about doing it.

GAIL:    Veronica, thanks for being so honest. I, too, hope that we can help you work on this.

*(After a few seconds of quietness in the group, the coleaders scan the group, making eye contact with each member. Maria then asks the group a question.)*

MARIA:    Has everyone had an opportunity to share their goal?

GAIL:    Well, I guess I'm the last one. Like Veronica I have a lot of my sister's belongings that I've been holding onto. But, what I wrote down for a goal is finding someone that I can eventually say is my best friend. It was always Angie my older sister. But, I just feel like allowing myself to be close to someone else is just a setup to get hurt. I know it's important to make close friends, but honestly, what's the point?

(*Group members, seeming to sense the importance of the moment, offer Gail encouragement and support—just as they had received from her. However, each group member's attempts to be supportive were deflected by Gail. "Yes, I agree, but . . ." was her response to each group member's feedback. Finally, Veronica and Gail engage in the following exchange.*)

VERONICA:    I hope you reach your goal in finding someone else to be close with. I know I need people in my life. That's why I'm here. I loved my husband, but if I don't learn to continue on, I'll surely become an awful person to be around.

GAIL:    Yes, I agree, but what's the real point! So, I get over my sister's death and eventually become close to someone else. Eventually we all die. Besides, I'm falling behind in my work. I don't have time to work on this emotional stuff until I catch up on my duties at work.

VERONICA:    (*turning red in the face, looking directly at Gail, and saying loudly*), I'm not sure you belong in this group. What's the point? You don't want to get close to anyone and according to you we're all going to die anyway!

(*The group members seem stunned by Gail's excuses and Veronica's bold pronouncement.*)

## WHAT TECHNIQUE DO YOU CHOOSE?

Individually or in small groups got down or discuss several options for what technique you would use in this situation. What factors must be considered?

## STEPS TOWARD SELECTING A TECHNIQUE

Here is our thinking:

### Step 1:   Identify the group type and purpose, best practice area, and developmental stage

Maria and Leonard are coleading a counseling group to help the members cope with personal grief that has resulted from the death of a family member or close friend. It is the second session of a 12-session group. To help the members establish rules and a sense of direction, the coleaders have been purposeful in leading the group through a series of structured activities. This approach is often helpful for group leaders to use, especially in the early stages of group development. In counseling groups, this kind of leader involvement can be thought of as helping promote the conditions whereby the group may progress from beginning stages of group development to the middle or working stage of group development.

### Step 2:  Analyze the presenting situation by applying ecological concepts

Groups of all sorts present leaders and coleaders with novel and frequently complex challenges. Regardless of the planning and preparation prior to a session, Maria and Leonard (or any group leaders) are not always able to accurately predict how a group session will unfold or how members will respond individually or as a collective unit. In prizing the ecological concept of interconnections among the members, the coleaders planned and implemented an activity for the group that helped individual members share openly a personal goal they sought to work on over the 12 weeks. This sharing seemed to be happening, as members were supportive, talking to each other and seemingly learning from one another. However, Gail's "Yes, but . . ." approach seemed to challenge the work taking place. Another way to think about what is occurring within the group is that Veronica perceives that the group's developing social system may be under attack.

### Step 3:  Review possible group techniques, considering focus and level

Two techniques that emerge as possible ways for Maria and Leonard to proceed are: Toolbox #85, Thank You. I'm Wondering If We Could Hear from Others and #81, Revisit Group Rules and Expectations. Notice that the coleaders have selected two techniques that are at a group level. What is important at this juncture of group development is to involve the group in what is occurring. The coleaders also have selected two techniques that ask the group to work in different ways (i.e., behavioral and cognitive).

***Performing Toolbox #85,*** Thank You. I'm Wondering If We Could Hear from Others.

*Focus:* Behavioral.
*Level:* Group.

In this technique, all members are asked to value the unique experience by also contributing to the discussion. It is likely that others are experiencing the group and Gail's situation in a way that is similar and/or dissimilar to Veronica's feedback. Either way, Veronica and Gail might greatly benefit from a technique that allows others to contribute to what is occurring. The coleaders may need to repeat this technique a few times to encourage the group to establish a norm in which seeking other members' opinions and feelings is more commonplace.

***Performing Toolbox #81,*** Revisit Group Rules and Expectations.

*Focus:* Cognitive.
*Level:* Group.

In this technique the coleaders break from the emotionally charged situation that is occurring and ask the members to review prior agreed-upon group rules.

Sometimes group leaders ask group members to actually create a written list of rules and they review it frequently. In one group that Leonard once facilitated he asked the group to begin every session by stating the rules, which had the effect of helping members easily bring up concerns when the rules were not being followed. Maria and Leonard believe that reviewing the rules could facilitate a discussion regarding how feedback is occurring and what impact is being experienced by the group as one member is reluctant and expressing ambivalence.

### Step 4:  Select a best-fit technique

Both techniques are easily put into practice and suitable to what is happening. As Maria and Leonard consider which technique to select they conclude that the first technique—Thank You. I'm Wondering If We Could Hear from Others—is more in keeping with the natural flow of the group discussion. That is, encouraging group members to increase their participation in the current discussion may have fewer side effects than a topic shift, which is required in revisiting the prior established rules. Also, making a simple statement is much more efficient than using the second technique and may seem less tangential to the group members.

### Step 5:  Implement and evaluate how well the technique worked

VERONICA: (*turning red in the face, looking directly at Gail and saying loudly*) I'm not sure you belong in this group. What's the point? You don't want to get close to anyone and according to you we're all going to die anyway!

(*The group members seem stunned by Gail's excuses and Veronica's bold pronouncement.*)

MARIA: Thank you, Veronica. I'm wondering if it might be helpful at this point to turn to the rest of the group. I'm wondering if we could hear from others.

BRENT: I'm not sure exactly how to say what I'm thinking.

LEONARD: Try your best. Perhaps if it doesn't come out as perfect as you might like it to, others will be able to help.

BRENT: Okay, I'll try. When Gail first started talking I thought, wow she's got it all together, but the more I listened, the more I heard her saying out loud the way I feel on the inside. I want desperately to get over the death of my wife, but I've got 101 excuses why tomorrow will always be better to start.

LEONARD: So, even though you could see through the excuses Gail was making, you also felt as if you understood her and how those excuses might coexist with a desire to also work through your grief.

BRENT: Bingo! But, I also completely understand Veronica's frustration because when Gail was talking I was thinking the same thing that Veronica snapped at her about. What on earth is Gail doing in this group? It was made abundantly clear to each one of us that we need to develop trust among us. I was thinking, Gail doesn't want to be here so how can we trust her. But the truth is, a part of me doesn't want to be here and do what might be asked of me. (*looking at the group*) Does anyone else feel this way?

## If in a Class or Workshop, Then:

### *Practice the choice*

Pair up with another student and try out your choices. Give each other feedback. What might work? What might need to be changed? Compare your choices with those provided by the authors.

### *Process the choice*

What have you learned? What are you learning about this process for selecting group techniques? What are you learning about yourself as a group leader? What might you be able to use the next time?

# In Sum

The challenges of group leadership at the beginning stage are substantial. So is the exhilaration involved with getting started, beginning to organize a new social system, meeting new people or, on the other hand, working with those already known, but in a new way.

The techniques most appropriate for the beginning stage of performing revolve around different expressions of establishing and transitioning in order to develop trust and a productive working environment. The group members are in a fragile state at this point, are dependent on the designated leader(s), seek to become oriented, and try to work out a way to proceed. For most, security and safety are real issues. Thus, leaders need to be aware of this incipient stage of development when they consider and select group techniques from all those available.

Following the steps of the PGTM no doubt seems somewhat laborious right now. Yet, as you practice them, they will become more familiar and should even begin to provide some welcomed direction. Remember, we are trying to teach a method for choosing techniques, just as much as we are trying to provide you with a set of technique possibilities.

Of course, the toolbox provided for the beginning stage of group development contains an impressive assortment of possibilities for you to consider. Here, as in those choice points to come in later chapters, we encourage you to stretch your comfort zone, to consider trying new tools, as well as the more familiar ones. As we all know, a hammer is a tool well suited for some tasks, but not for all.

# 6

## Performance Techniques at the Middle Stage of Group Development: Connecting and Producing

**ADVANCE ORGANIZER**

This chapter contains the following material:

**Various Perspectives on the Middle Stage of Group Development**

**Our Language for the Middle Stage: Connecting and Producing**

**The Group Leader Serves as a Facilitative Guide**

**Critical Incident Training in Middle Stage of Performing**

**CRITICAL INCIDENTS**

CI 6.1: What Time does this 10 A.M. Group Start?
    Group Type: *Psychoeducation*
    Best Practice Area: *Performing*
    Group Developmental Stage: *Middle*

CI 6.2: "Let's Notice our Strengths"
    Group Type: *Counseling*
    Best Practice Area: *Performing*
    Group Developmental Stage: *Middle*

CI 6.3: "What is Our Place in this Group?"
    Group Type: *Psychoeducation*
    Best Practice Area: *Performing*
    Group Developmental Stage: *Middle*

CI 6.4: "The Table"
    Group Type: *Counseling*
    Best Practice Area: *Performing*
    Group Developmental Stage: *Middle*

**In Sum**

Recall from Chapter 5 that a useful way to think of group leaders at the beginning stage is as a special kind of host or hostess of a newly forming social system. As this social system, the group, evolves over several sessions or meetings the leader's role shifts to that of a "facilitative guide." While still attending to nurturing and strengthening the emergent social system and its members, leaders now need to concern themselves with supporting forces and dynamics aimed at productive work. If group development is proceeding in accord with general expectations, group leaders can use techniques that allow them to facilitate and promote the energy that already is present.

## *Various Perspectives on the Middle Stage of Group Development*

The middle stage of group development is when leaders generally might expect that productive work should occur. The relationship between content and process theoretically, at least, reaches its peak during the middle stage, allowing for action to occur more readily and fully (Hulse-Killacky, Killacky, & Donigian, 2001). As Jones (1973) put it, personal relations have begun to become more cohesive, permitting ampler "data flow" to happen.

The middle stage of group development has been referred to by many theorists (e.g., Corey & Corey, 2006; Gladding, 2003; Trotzer, 2006; Yalom & Leszcz 2005) as the "working" period, where higher levels of information sharing, personal disclosure, feedback, and interpersonal problem solving emerge. As Gladding (2003) has observed, group members often remember the working stage of a group experience with fondness and pride.

Yet, it would be a mistake to assume that any one group will naturally progress into the working stage or even, if it seems to have arrived, that it will move through the stage full speed ahead. Group development theory predicts the general case; the life history of any single group may deviate considerably. Stages, including the middle stage, may be more properly thought of as recycling phases, where there is an ebb and flow. Leaders need to be aware that elements and processes of the beginning stage may become salient in the middle stage, as the group and its members cycle back and forth. Generally, though, when you stand back and examine groups, general tendencies can be identified; these we refer to as stages. The middle stage is characterized by productivity.

## *Our Language for the Middle Stage: Connecting and Producing*

We view the middle stage very consistently with others who have written about group development, including those previously cited. It is a period in which higher amounts of on-task, personally oriented work can be expected. Our terminology for this stage centers around "connecting and producing." That is, as group members move through the beginning stage issues of getting established and transitioning from mistrust to trust, they then are more able to form interconnections. They can now relate more easily and openly to each other. In short, with regard to personal relations functions, they become more highly connected. As they become more interlacing, they also are able to produce more information, more data, and more personal and interpersonal disclosure and feedback. In short, with regard to task functions, they become more productive.

When considering the group leader at the middle stage, the metaphor of a network is an apt one. Think of the old telephone system, where a central switchboard operator physically managed all connections; everything literally went through her (there were only women operators at the time). This "central switchboard" approach does not work so well when trying to forge and maintain interconnections. The newer "network" model is more suitable, where a group leader seeks to promote, support, and reinforce communications and interactions emerging between and among members.

## The Group Leader Serves as a Facilitative Guide

The role of a facilitative guide can be very useful as group leaders function within this network image. In many instances, being a facilitative guide means that the group leader becomes less obvious in the group. In the beginning stage, leaders need to be more involved and members expect them to be, too. At that point they tend to proactively assist members to become oriented, to help define a common sense of purpose, and to collaborate on creating rules and expectations—among other important tasks. They also may use structured exercises at times to help members become better acquainted on the way toward developing increased trust and security. In fact, more events and activities "go through them" at the beginning, similar to the switchboard model.

However, as the group moves into the middle stage, leaders try to protect against group members becoming centered on them. Instead, leaders prefer that leadership functions gradually become distributed across members over time. To assist with this intention, leaders encourage and support members to not only become increasingly involved in group interaction but also to take on increased responsibility. Events and interactions increasingly occur directly between and among members, with the leader helping these to occur. Sometimes, this may mean not getting in the way. That's right! A very important group leader technique can be just that.

This increased level of member activity needs to be "knitted together," or interconnected. The facilitator as guide becomes a "networker," helping members make connections and maintain them. Group leaders always are trying to foster productivity that is interdependent, and the middle stage of group development is when this unique kind of interaction can flourish.

What kinds of techniques might group leaders use during the middle stage of group development? Let's move to the critical incidents for this stage to discover how to select some useful techniques.

## Critical Incident Training in the Middle Stage of Performing

**CRITICAL INCIDENTS**

PERFORMING (MIDDLE) CI 6.1

Group Type: *Psychoeducation*
Best Practice Area: *Performing*
Group Developmental Stage: *Middle*

### What Time Does This 10 A.M. Group Start?

#### HISTORY

Manny is a counselor working in a large urban hospital. One of the responsibilities that he greatly enjoys is leading the 15-week psychoeducation group for people who have been newly diagnosed as HIV positive. He has been leading these groups for almost 3 years and has developed a curriculum that he believes is flexible, but also keeps the group members moving at a pace that will allow them to explore all the major aspects of living with the HIV virus.

At the beginning of each new group Manny works diligently to help group members develop a very important set of rules and expectations, such as confidentiality, trust, and promptness to meetings. Still, every group is unique and most groups struggle to be consistent in all these areas. In fact, the group that Manny is currently leading is in the ninth session and has been plagued by inconsistent attendance and tardiness for the last two sessions. With these particular psychoeducation groups it is not uncommon for one member, or occasionally two of the 12 members, to miss a weekly session or drop out altogether. Since session six, group attendance has been poor and of those who do attend, three or more members have started showing up 10–30 minutes late. As expected, the lateness of group members interrupts events already under way and delays the timely start, as Manny attempts to wait for late arrivals.

In response to this situation, Manny openly addressed attendance and tardiness by asking members to discuss how these events impact the group. Group members seemed to appreciate his approach in bringing up the subject for an open discussion. In response, members candidly talked about life events that made attendance and promptness an issue. Several members were even able to talk candidly and conjecture how these events might be avoidant behaviors and be related to denial issues around their HIV-positive diagnosis. Agreement was reached that attendance and promptness were important for the remaining sessions. Manny was pleased with the group discussion and was supportive of their idea to use the first 10 minutes of the meeting as an informal time for members to arrive, get a cup of coffee, greet and connect with others, and in general get situated. Then, the group session would start promptly at 10:10 a.m., with everyone being present and ready to work.

## CRITICAL INCIDENT

What happened at the next group session caught Manny by surprise. Instead of members arriving by 10:00 a.m., and using the 10-minute buffer time to get situated and for those who may be running late, half of the members did not arrive until almost 10:10 a.m. At 10:15, Manny began the meeting. At approximately 10:30 two more members arrived. Manny and other group members spent several minutes repeating the previously discussed topic of medication management. As if events could not worsen, at approximately 10:35 the last member arrived. Manny's assessment was that the situation regarding punctuality had worsened. He decided that now is the time is to do something.

SHAWN:   Hey guys, sorry for being late. I missed my ride and had to call some friends to give me a lift.

MANNY:   Thanks for making it. Others have struggled to get here, too. But, I'm not sure what to make of all this, given our agreement at our last session.

SHAWN:   What do you mean? It just sounds to me like it's been a rough day for everyone to get here.

## WHAT TECHNIQUE DO YOU USE?

Individually or in small groups jot down or discuss several options for what technique you would use in this situation. What factors must be considered?

## STEPS TOWARD SELECTING A TECHNIQUE

Here is our thinking:

### Step 1:  Identify the group type and purpose, best practice area, and developmental stage

Life is complex! We are all members of multiple systems (family, work, community, and religious institutions, just to name a few). Even beyond these various roles that compete for our attention, being diagnosed with a serious chronic health condition can be overwhelming. This psychoeducation group for those diagnosed as HIV positive is developmentally in the middle stages of performing.

### Step 2:  Analyze the presenting situation by applying ecological concepts

It is more likely that this group, or at a minimum a subgroup of it, is "in flight," that is, some members are running away from contact with each other. In an attempt to try and respond to the situation, Manny has focused on the content (i.e., attendance and punctuality). He initiated a group discussion in which the members renegotiated how to start each session, but talk and discussion has failed to convert to group member action. Manny is faced with an interesting challenge as sustainability of the new group rules failed to occur.

Although there is a temptation to imagine that a diagnosis of HIV might make for a very homogeneous group, this thinking is likely a hasty generalization. Nonetheless, the group seems to be operating as a whole and attendance and punctuality appear to be a pattern of group behavior (social system). As Manny considers the various group members, he might benefit from appreciating how each member is making sense (meaning making) out of being recently diagnosed with HIV. What meaning does this hold for each member and how might this impact attendance and punctuality? Manny might also want to explore how these recent behaviors over the last few sessions are impacting each member's sense of belonging and connectivity (interconnection). Manny has been working from a collaborative approach in renegotiating the time to start the group. Though he might have a tendency to say that this approach was unsuccessful and that a more authoritative leader role might be more effective, at this juncture we would advise Manny to continue to prize the ecological concept of collaboration or a working together approach.

### Step 3:   Review possible group techniques, considering focus and level

Because group attendance and punctuality are largely individual concerns, we would ask Manny to consider group techniques that help members at the individual level. Moreover, there is an argument to be made that attendance and punctuality problems transcend what is happening at the individual level, in which case Manny might want to explore group-level techniques. We wonder about this possibility because the continuation of poor attendance and punctuality seems to be a group happening, not isolated to a few. Because last session's talking (cognitive focus) was ineffective in translating into improved attendance and punctuality (behavioral focus), we would encourage Manny to examine group techniques that would help members from an affective, behavioral, and/or structural focus. Therefore, two techniques that Manny might consider would be Toolbox #57, Role Reversal, or Toolbox #70, Johari Window.

***Middle Performance Toolbox #57,*** Role Reversal. Members switch roles with other members or with the leader.

*Focus:* Structural.
*Level:* Individual.

In this technique, members are encouraged to step outside of their present role and assume the responsibilities of the leader. In doing so they might experience the challenges Manny is facing. This might be difficult, because members may not possess the skills and educational resources that Manny has developed to lead a psychoeducation group. Therefore, we recommend a variation on this technique, such as Manny assigning duties and tasks to members that would require them to be on time and present. Because the members are in the middle stage of group development, this strategy would seem to fit. Manny might assign dyads to be responsible for arranging the chairs prior to the meeting, another dyad to greet people as they arrive, and another to keep time and help start the meeting.

***Middle Performance Toolbox #70:*** Johari Window. Have members do a Johari Window and share in the group.

*Focus:* Affective.

*Level:* Individual and interpersonal.

In this technique, members are encouraged to explore awareness in interpersonal relationships. When done in a group setting in which sharing is encouraged, this technique provides an opportunity for group members and the group as a whole to explore blind spots in individual group members as well as the group. This technique asks the group to create a four-paned window for each member. Pane one is labeled "Open" and asks members to list qualities that they know about themselves (e.g., friendly, defensive, shy, etc.). In short, this window pane is all about self-awareness. The second window pane, labeled "blind," includes characteristics that others in the group may be aware of about members, but about which the members lack awareness (e.g., bad breath, hesitation in voice when nervous, etc.). The third pane is the "hidden" pane and is used to list and describe things that members know about themselves, but that others do not know (e.g., hesitant to open up to others, scared about living with HIV, etc.). Last is the "unknown" pane that represents the things that individual group members, as well as the entire group, are unaware of.

### Step 4:   Select a best-fit technique

The group is at a pivotal point in its development. Manny's original approach to his punctuality and attendance concerns was to work collaboratively and mainly examined the content (i.e., being late or absent from group sessions). Although members did seem to connect the content with process at the time of discussion, the results that Manny had expected did not occur. Perhaps a more appropriate technique would take "dead aim" at process and levels of awareness.

Both techniques we have discussed are geared toward this purpose, though very differently. Of the two, we have selected the Johari Window because it challenges group members to understand their blind spots that others are aware of and to process hidden areas of the self. This is certainly a developmentally appropriate technique for a group working in the middle stage of development. Likewise, it is a parsimonious technique in that it can be readily implemented with little preparation other than paper and pencil. One clear side effect of this technique is that the wealth of individual and group exploration might move the group more into a counseling mode and away from a psychoeducation group. Time might also become a critical factor using the Johari Window approach.

### Step 5:   Implement and evaluate how well the technique worked

SHAWN:   What do you mean? It just sounds to me like it's been a rough day for everyone to get here.

MANNY:   Shawn, you might very well be correct. It could be that today's difficulties in getting the group started on time are just attributable to a bad day. But, because we have about an hour and a half left, I'm wondering if you and the group might be willing to explore this area more closely . . . in a way that could be helpful to us all? I'm personally troubled that the commitment we made last week, which seemed to fall by the wayside today, might be suggesting something else is going on. To find out, I would like to propose exploring the topic, but perhaps in a different sort of way than we have before.

LOUISA: Yeah, I was thinking about this too. But what do you mean by "explore in a different way?"

MANNY: Well, we would use paper and pencil and write some things about ourselves, share them with others in the group, and then let others share additional things about us that they are aware of. I won't kid you, this can be intense, but also may really help us understand ourselves and what's going on in and with the group.

LOUISA: (*looking around the group*) Hmmm, may be worth a shot. I'd try it if others would too.

MANNY: Okay, then. How about the rest . . . what is your inclination?

SHAWN: I'm nervous about this because I wasn't even going to come today, because I'm afraid to learn any more about HIV. But I guess there's nothing to lose. Let's do it! (*The others nod in agreement, and so they begin.*)

### If in a Class or Workshop, Then:

#### *Practice the choice*

Pair up with another student and try out your choices. Give each other feedback. What might work? What might need to be changed? Compare your choices with those provided by the authors.

#### *Process the choice*

What have you learned? What are you learning about this process for selecting group techniques? What are you learning about yourself as a group leader? What might you be able to use the next time?

## PERFORMING (MIDDLE) CI 6.2

Group Type: *Counseling*
Best Practice Area: *Performing*
Group Developmental Stage: *Middle*

## *Let's Notice Our Strengths*

### HISTORY

This counseling group is for couples who are in a committed relationship. It is a 10-session experience, where each session is 1.5 hours. Session six is occurring now and it follows sessions that Grace, the group's leader, thinks have been lacking attention to members' strengths. Despite her efforts to encourage the couples, and the group as a whole, to discuss what works as well as what does not, the emphasis has been largely on deficits. She would like to introduce an exercise within this counseling group that might help members focus on their positive attributes and skills. What led her to this direction can be found in the final minutes of the previous session.

## CRITICAL INCIDENT

GRETA: (*to her partner, Jack*) It's the same thing in here, really, as at home, Jack. You just don't listen!

JACK: I guess I've heard that one before . . . (*turning to the other members*) Does any of this sound familiar to any of you, especially to you guys?

What follows are several comments from group members addressing "deficits," such as: Men just don't listen; it's genetic with them.

GRACE: The clock says we have to go, but I'm wondering now what you may see as going well in your relationships and in the group. Are there strengths? Let's pick this up next session, okay?

## WHAT TECHNIQUE DO YOU CHOOSE?

Individually or in small groups jot down or discuss several options for what technique you would use in this situation. What factors must be considered?

## STEPS TOWARD SELECTING A TECHNIQUE

Here is our thinking:

### Step 1:  Identify the group type and purpose, best practice area, and developmental stage

This is a counseling group in the sixth (middle stage of performing) of ten 1.5 hour sessions. It is aimed at improving couples' communication.

### Step 2:  Analyze the presenting situation by applying ecological concepts

Grace has asked the members to make meaning of their relationships and of their experience in the group itself by peering through the lens of "strengths." This strength-based approach represents an important way to promote meaning making, involving such considerations as "What sense are they making of their interactions, both in and out of the group? What is working? What assets may exist?" The leader also is working on the ecological concept of interconnection. She asks members to examine the positive ties that may exist within each couple and between the couples.

### Step 3:   Review possible group techniques, considering focus and level

***Middle Stage Performance Toolbox #59,*** Strength Bombardment.

In this structured technique, the leader asks each couple to step to the center of the group and to provide each other with nothing but positive feedback. The recipient cannot reply, but is placed in a listening/accepting mode. Processing follows. Then, the couple asks the group members for positive feedback related to the couple's participation in the group. Again, no response is allowed during this phase. Following its completion, a period of processing is held.

*Focus:* Structural.
*Level:* Interpersonal.

***Middle Stage Performing Toolbox #36,*** Brainstorm. Members initiate ideas in a nonjudgmental manner.

*Focus:* Structural.
*Level:* Group.

This structured technique can be used in many situations where production of large numbers of nonjudged, nonevaluated ideas are needed. Members are instructed in the "rules" of brainstorming (sometimes it is called "idea generation"). These rules include producing a quantity of ideas, not discussing items, piggybacking on one another's contributions, not judging, not evaluating, operating within a short time period of about 10 minutes, and using a recorder. Once the group is through with listing ideas, the members discuss them. Together, they prepare a report for the group. Regarding the critical incident being considered, the brainstorming might address "Brainstorm all positive aspects of our group."

### Step 4:   Select a best-fit technique

Frequently, counseling groups can take on a deficit-oriented focus. Although correcting deficits through interpersonal problem solving is an important goal in group counseling, it is a mistake to ignore or to minimize assets that exist. In fact, a hallmark of the counseling profession is to incorporate a strength-based approach, that is, identifying and using existing assets as a way to increase capacity. Often, this kind of approach also reduces deficiencies.

The best-fit issue in this critical incident revolves around whether to place the strength focus on others or on oneself. Each technique presented involves structure; it is the level that varies. Because this group is centered around relationships between couples and relationships within the group, however, it would seem more appropriate to select the other-centered exercise Strength Bombardment. Its relationship orientation would provide a more direct and efficient route to yielding success in the interconnectedness between couples and members.

### Step 5:   Implement and evaluate how well the technique worked

GRACE:   The clock says we have to go, but I'm wondering now what you may see as going well in your relationships and in the group. Are there strengths? Let's pick this up next session, okay?

(*At the start of next week's session:*)

GRACE:   It's good to see everyone again! I wonder if you have been mulling over my suggestion about strengths. Do you recall that?

GRETA:   Yeah, Jack and I actually did discuss that, kind of like homework, almost. It's interesting because we don't talk about these kinds of things.

GRACE:   Well, that's not too surprising. I wonder if you all might like to try an exercise that I think will help us focus on our strengths. It's called Strength Bombardment. Are you game to try?

(*The group moves into the exercise.*)

## If in a Class or Workshop, Then:

### *Practice the choice*

Pair up with another student and try out your choices. Give each other feedback. What might work? What might need to be changed? Compare your choices with those provided by the authors.

### *Process the choice*

What have you learned? What are you learning about this process for selecting group techniques? What are you learning about yourself as a group leader? What might you be able to use the next time?

---

### PERFORMING (MIDDLE) CI 6.3

Group Type: *Psychoeducation*
Best Practice Area: *Performing*
Group Developmental Stage: *Middle*

## *What Is Our Place in This Group?*

### HISTORY

Five of 12 sessions have been completed in this psychoeducation group focused on fostering increased multicultural understanding and improved multicultural relationships. Sponsored by the Urban League, this group is comprised of six African Americans (four females, two males), three Whites (two females, one male), and three Hispanics (two females, one male). All participants are young professionals, ranging in age from 22 to 30. They have volunteered to participate, responding to an invitation that was part of an intense citywide effort aimed at advancing interracial relationships. The coleaders of this group, Avanta Jefferson (African American female) and Jose Gonzales, (Latino male), also have volunteered for this assignment. They work together at Crossroads, a local mental health center. The leaders each have considerable group experience.

The group seems to be at a point where members are opening up to each other and making progress. There is a developing interest in gaining feedback, but lack of clarity and some hesitancy about how to proceed. In their between-session processing meeting the leaders have selected a structured exercise to assist with producing interpersonal feedback.

## CRITICAL INCIDENT

Midway through session seven, as members are struggling with the issue of giving and receiving feedback, the following events occur:

JOSE:    Avanta and I have been thinking of a way to maybe help us move ahead with this whole important feedback matter. It is a way of helping us become more aware of how each of us is viewed in the group, of our place here, and it can provide a way to talk about our relationships. It will involve us moving around the room some and then talking about what we find. Kind of ambiguous, I guess, but we wonder if you might be willing to try this out?

FREDA:    (*a group member*) Well, the different activities we've tried in here so far, I think, have been good, so I'd like to go with it.

AVANTA:    (*looking around the group*) Any opposition?

(*Head nods confirm that the group is willing to try the new technique.*)

JOSE:    OK, here is how we can move ahead. This exercise is called a Physiogram. Imagine the center of our room to be exactly in the center of our group. Each of us is asked to stand somewhere in relation to that center and central point. The closer to it, the more central to the group you would be, in your judgment. The farther from that center point, the more removed you feel that you are. Once in position, look around. Are you comfortable where you are as you see where others are located? If you would like to move, go ahead. Then we will discuss our place in the group and how we are located in relation to others. We want to focus especially on any interracial implications, as that is the main purpose for us being here. Okay, that's it, any questions? Good, then let's start.

(*The members place themselves in relation to the center of the room and each other.*)

AVANTA:    Okay, look around. Any observations to make?

SAM:    (*a group member*) I see clumps of skin color together.

## WHAT TECHNIQUE DO YOU CHOOSE?

Individually or in small groups jot down or discuss several options for what technique you would use in this situation. What factors must be considered?

## STEPS TOWARD SELECTING A TECHNIQUE

Here is our thinking:

### Step 1: Identify the group type and purpose, best practice area, and developmental stage

With this critical incident, we are considering a psychoeducation group whose purpose is to improve interracial understanding. This group is in the middle stage of performance.

It always is important to keep in mind the overall context of the group. What type of group is it (counseling, psychoeducation)? What best practice area is relevant (planning, performing, processing)? Within performing, what developmental stage seems to characterize the group at this point (beginning, middle, end)? "Locking in" the group in relation to these points grounds the technique selection process.

### Step 2: Analyze the presenting situation by applying ecological concepts

This group is dealing with potentially sensitive and certainly challenging material—improving interracial understanding and relationships. It is to be expected that the members, even though they have volunteered for this experience, may feel conflicted or are somewhat hesitant to move ahead at times. Thus, although they may wish to obtain and to provide feedback related to interracial matters, becoming actively involved in this process might be anxiety provoking.

Feeling a sense of group cohesion with interpersonal support would promote taking such risks. From an ecological perspective, the strength of member interconnection and the degree to which the group's social system is coherent and clear are important factors in attaining and maintaining cohesion. The leaders need to find a way to support members as they reach out in their interracial feedback efforts.

### Step 3: Review possible group techniques, considering focus and level

*Middle Stage Performance Toolbox #54,* Physiogram.

*Focus:* Structural.
*Level:* Individual, interpersonal, and group.

The leaders had decided to try the Physiogram activity, if the members agreed. (Steps in conducting a Physiogram are contained in the critical incident itself, already described.) They decided to use this technique because its structure fit with the ongoing use of structured exercises in the psychoeducation group and because they wanted to illuminate interracial dynamics concretely. The skill in using the Physiogram, as with most group techniques, depends on effective examination and discussion of what is revealed by the activity; with this technique, it means once members place themselves "in space."

*Physiogram follow-up:* During discussion, the leaders have two distinct, but nonexclusive, choices for follow-up to member observations.

*Strategy A:* Empower members, after initial discussion, to feel free to move themselves and/or to suggest that others move to another "more representative" location.
*Focus:* Structural.
*Level:* Interpersonal; and/or

*Strategy B:* Continue with discussion, involving no further physical movement

*Focus:* Cognitive.s
*Level:* Interpersonal.

### Step 4:   Select a best-fit technique

The Physiogram fits well within the ongoing group type, culture, and purpose. During the middle stage of performance a group generally can be expected to handle this kind of exercise. Exposing concrete manifestations of each other's place in the group affords an efficient way to reveal interrelationships and, in this case, to allow for an interracial perspective to be observed and discussed. Stimulating such a focused way to explore interracial associations is directly in support of the group's overall purpose. Negative side effects can be minimized through adequate discussion and processing of the thoughts and feelings that are generated through the exercise.

### Step 5:   Implement and evaluate how well the technique worked

SAM:      (*a group member*) I see clumps of skin color together.

AVANTA:   Okay, any other comments from others?

(*Others offer various similar viewpoints.*)

AVANTA:   Here's a wrinkle on this exercise we can try . . . how might we be if our "clumps," as we seem to be calling them, are changed some? Let's try breaking up these clumps and then discussing what we have. Can you all begin to shift closer to others who are not of your skin color?

(*They begin to move, showing some eagerness to do so.*)

AVANTA:   That's it; let's see what we have now.

## If in a Class or Workshop, Then:

### *Practice the choice*

Pair up with another student and try out your choices. Give each other feedback. What might work? What might need to be changed? Compare your choices with those provided by the authors.

### *Process the choice*

What have you learned? What are you learning about this process for selecting group techniques? What are you learning about yourself as a group leader? What might you be able to use the next time?

---

### PERFORMING (MIDDLE) CI 6.4

Group Type: *Counseling*
Best Practice Area: *Performing*
Group Developmental Stage: *Middle*

## *The Table*

## HISTORY

As helping professionals, sometimes we find ourselves taking on new and novel roles. Perhaps this happens because of a job change or organizational restructuring. Whatever the case, we find ourselves thrust into existing groups. This is what has happened to Annette, a licensed counselor. At her supervisor's request, Annette agreed to shift her duties away from an intake coordinator position to a counseling role for a women's long-term residential substance abuse treatment facility. An important role in her new job is leading the daily 2.5 hours counseling group in which members work together in exploring sobriety. Because the women of this treatment program have been together for several months, Annette is well aware that though she is to lead the group, she is an outsider attempting to gain the acceptance and trust of the 10 group members.

It is the end of week three. Annette's prior group experiences have served her well as she respected the existing social system by working from a collaborative team approach. Careful to seek consensus from the group in various tasks, the members have responded by readily accepting her as a member and leader of the counseling group. However, Annette has been concerned about the physical setting in which the counseling group meets. The group meets around a large rectangular table. Annette suspects that the table serves as a hindrance to interpersonal communication. She believes the table keeps members distant and inhibits the women from taking risks to talk about themselves as well as give feedback to the group and/or specific members. During the one occasion when Annette suggested that the table might restrain interconnectivity, group members expressed ambivalence.

The following critical incident concerns Annette's attempt to help the group consider the role the table may be serving in limiting the group.

## CRITICAL INCIDENT

ANNETTE:    I noticed during yesterday's meeting, that when I suggested we might consider the advantages and disadvantages of a table between us, everyone became silent. Would anyone like to take a stab at what the silence might have indicated?

BREE:       I don't see what the big deal is! Personally, I like having a place to set my coffee or just rest against.

(*All group members nod approval to Bree's comment.*)

SHANDA:     Yeah, what's the big deal?

## WHAT TECHNIQUE DO YOU CHOOSE?

Individually or in small groups jot down or discuss several options for what technique you would use in this situation. What factors must be considered?

## STEPS TOWARD SELECTING A TECHNIQUE

Here is our thinking:

### Step 1:  Identify the group type and purpose, best practice area, and developmental stage

To review, Annette is the new leader of an existing women's counseling group of 10 members in a long-term residential treatment center for substance abuse. It is near the end of the third week when Annette points out to the group members that the table around which the sessions occur may be functioning as a roadblock and is inhibiting group processes.

### Step 2:  Analyze the presenting situation by applying ecological concepts

Typically in counseling groups, individual members' goals are emphasized. Even so, other factors are important, such as a circumstance in which group members might benefit from learning how to better communicate or express feelings. Although it is clear that the group members have developed a social system with rules and norms, Annette is concluding that the table represents a contextual factor that is not optimizing the functioning of the group's ability to achieve valuable interconnections. This is not an uncommon observation, and it arises from the realization that the environment influences those inhabiting it (and vice versa). Physical elements of an environment, such as lighting, physical space, and furniture arrangement, can influence members' quality of group participation.

Annette is encountering a level of ambivalence from the members about the table. However, because Annette has been successful in working from a collaborative approach with group members so far, she has this foundation from which to draw.

### Step 3:  Review possible group techniques, considering focus and level

Annette wants to help the group members maximize the group experience by attending to environmental factors that could be influencing growth and development. There are a variety of group leader techniques that would likely aid this process. Two potential techniques are Toolbox #26, Seating, and #84, the String Activity.

Annette wants to help the group members take full advantage of the counseling group experience. The goal is to help members maximize their interactions within the group and to make meaning of how contextual factors influence their behaviors. Annette is interested in helping the women of this group be able to sustain this kind of evaluation and processing beyond the counseling group and into the broader contexts in which they will certainly find themselves once they leave treatment.

***Middle Performance Toolbox #26,*** Seating.

*Focus:* Structural.
*Level:* Interpersonal and group.

In selecting this technique the group leader is attempting to help members grapple with contextual factors firsthand. From Annette's perspective, talking about the table could be profitable, but perhaps not as beneficial as asking the members to work as a group in constructing an arrangement that is optimal to the group and then follow this exercise with a process discussion (e.g., "What happened and how did it work?"). This can be a powerful technique as group members are given the responsibility for the group, an approach that should be used only when a group has reached the middle stage of group development.

An advantage of this technique is that it is simple to implement and does not require additional planning or equipment. In implementing this technique, Annette might guide the discussion by saying, "Bree and Shanda, these are great comments. Thanks for this input." Annette scans the group and continues, "Perhaps a good way for me to help express what I'm trying to communicate would be to ask if all of you would participate in an experience that will probably take several minutes, after which we can talk about it. Would this be okay?"

***Middle Performing Toolbox #84,*** String Activity.

Other techniques that group leaders might use involve more structure, are more complex, and require more time. This is the case with the String Activity, which requires string (we suggest kite string) and scissors.

*Focus:* Structural and behavioral.
*Level:* Interpersonal and group.

As with the other technique, the string activity is intended to highlight how context (i.e., the table) might be impacting communication and interpersonal and group connectivity. In asking the group members to use string to portray all the possible communication links in the 11-member group, the members will be confronted with physical objects that impede the process. The string activity can be used to provide members with a concrete example of how members' behaviors are influenced by the surroundings.

With the string activity, members are provided a spool of string and one pair of scissors. The goal of this exercise is for members to work together in using the string to connect to each person in a way that reflects all the possible patterns of communication that are possible. In a group of 10 members and a leader, this will involve a large web of string and may even require a second spool, though it is our inclination to limit the activity to one spool and encourage the members to work to resolve this or other obstacles. Not including end-of-activity processing time, a minimum of 15–20 minutes should be allotted for this activity. In implementing this technique, Annette might say, "Bree and Shanda, thanks for your insights." As Annette scans the group she continues, "Yes, a table can be comfortable and not necessarily a hindrance. Still, I'm wondering if you and the others might be willing to participate in an activity that I think will help you understand where I'm coming from."

### Step 4:  Select a best-fit technique

Of course, there is no single right or wrong technique to use in this critical incident or in any other. As we have pointed out before, the professional judgment of the group leader, set within the present context, is most important. What technique best fits the ongoing culture of the group, how much time is available, is a direct or an indirect approach desirable for this group, what side effects could be anticipated? In short, what would work well with no harm? For example, in a group of professional men, it may be more acceptable to use a simpler rather than a more complex technique, one that is more direct. On the other hand, the particular context needs to be considered always in making such determinations.

### Step 5:   Implement and evaluate how well the technique worked

BREE:   I don't see what the big deal is! Personally, I like having a place to set my coffee or just rest against.

(*All group members nod approval to Bree's comment.*)

SHANDA:   Yeah, what's the big deal?

ANNETTE:   Bree and Shanda, thanks for your thoughts and feelings. I see some other body language from others that suggests they view things in a similar light. I think what I'm trying to say is that there's no doubt that good things are happening as a result of our group efforts. However, as a counselor and leader of the group, one of my goals is to see you take full advantage of this time and get everything out of the experience that you can. I'm wondering if the group would be willing to participate in an activity that I believe might help you understand what I'm trying to get at.

BREE:   I guess, but does this activity mean that afterward we're going to get rid of the table?

ANNETTE:   Heaven's no! What I would like to see happen is that after the activity we spend time discussing what went on during the activity. Then as a group we work together in determining any actions we want to act on regarding the table.

SHANDA:   That sounds fair to me. I'm willing to try the activity.

## If in a Class or Workshop, Then:

### *Practice the choice*

Pair up with another student and try out your choices. Give each other feedback. What might work? What might need to be changed? Compare your choices with those provided by the authors.

### *Process the choice*

What have you learned? What are you learning about this process for selecting group techniques? What are you learning about yourself as a group leader? What might you be able to use the next time?

# In Sum

Connecting and producing, characteristics of the middle stage of performing, are the high-water mark of any group. Members more freely interact. They tend to initiate and respond more directly. They are better able to give feedback, to share information, to work together in solving problems.

Sadly, not all groups make it to this point. Some disband, not being able to successfully evolve through the beginning stage. Some get to the middle stage but, again sadly, the group culture still is such that members are hiding more than they are revealing, and their interconnections remain only weakly developed.

Leaders at the middle stage of a group's development employ techniques aimed at strengthening existing connections among members so that they can become increasingly productive. As leaders are able to make gains in this domain, they can choose to diminish the extent of their active leadership somewhat to allow members to step forward.

We have shown through selected critical incidents, though, that even when a group is moving ahead positively there always are challenges and bumps in the road. All leaders, including highly experienced ones, can fully expect to be jarred from time to time. Do not fear, this is all part of the evolving process of working in groups! Another hallmark of the middle stage of group development is that these challenges can be managed and resolved, and members can learn and grow through these experiences.

As the group matures through this stage it is on course for its final one—ending. This is the subject of Chapter 7, which is next on the horizon.

# References

Anderson, J. (1984). *Counseling through group process*. New York: Springer.

Association for Specialists in Group Work (1998). *Association for Specialists in Group Work Best Practice Guidelines*. Retrieved from http://www.asgw.org

Bemak, F., & Conyne, R. (2004). Ecological group work. In R. Conyne & E. Cook (Eds). *Ecological counseling: An innovative approach to conceptualizing person–environment interaction*. Alexandria, VA: American Counseling Association.

Conyne, R. (1989). *How personal growth and task groups work*. Newbury Park, CA: Sage.

Conyne, R., & Bemak, F. (2004). Teaching group work from an ecological perspective. *Journal for Specialists in Group Work, 29*, 7–18.

Corey, M. & Corey, G. (2006). *Groups: Process and practice* (7th ed.). Pacific Grove, CA: Brooks/Cole. (Eds.), *Critical incidents in group couseling* (pp. 59–64). Alexandria, VA: American Counseling Association.

Forsyth, D. (2006). *Group dynamics* (4th ed.). Belmont, CA: Thomson.

Gladding, S. (2003). (4th ed.) *Group work: A counseling specialty*. Upper Saddle River, NJ: Merrill Prentice Hall.

Hulse-Killacky, D., Killacky, J., & Donigian, J. (2001). *Making task groups work in your world*. Upper Saddle River, New Jersey: Merrill Prentice Hall.

Jones, J. (1973). A model of group development. In J. Jones & J. Pfeiffer (Eds.), *The 1973 handbook for group facilitators* (pp. 127–129). LaJolla, CA: University Associates.

Schutz, W. (1958). *FIRO: A three-dimensional theory of interpersonal behavior*. New York: Rinehart.

Trotzer, J. (1999). *The counselor and the group: Integrating theory, training, and practice* (3rd ed). Philadelphia, PA: Accelerated Development.

Trotzer, J. (2006). *The counselor and the group: Integrating theroy, training, and practice* (4th ed.). Philadelphia, PA: Accelerated Development.

Tuckman, B., & Jensen, M. (1977). Stages of small group development revisited. *Group and Organizational Studies, 2*, 419–427.

Yalom, I. (1985). *The theory and practice of group psychotherapy*. New York: Basic Books.

Yalom, I., & Leszcz, M. (2005). *The theory and practice of group psychotherapy*. New York: Basic Books.

# 7

# Performance Techniques at the Ending Stage of Group Development: Consolidating and Forecasting

**ADVANCE ORGANIZER**

This chapter contains the following material:

**Various Perspectives on the Ending Stage of Group Development**

**Our Language for the Ending Stage: Consolidating and Forecasting**

**Critical Incident Training in the Ending Stage of Performing**

CRITICAL INCIDENTS

CI 7.1 "End of the Search"
  Group Type *: Psychoeducation*
  Best Practice Area: *Performing*
  Group Developmental Stage: *Ending*

CI 7.2 "Graded"
  Group Type: *Counseling*
  Best Practice Area: *Performing*
  Group Developmental Stage: *Ending*

CI 7.3 "Now That We Know"
  Group Type: *Psychoeducation*
  Best Practice Area: *Performing*
  Group Developmental Stage: *Ending*

CI 7.4 "Done"
  Group Type: *Counseling*
  Best Practice Area: *Performing*
  Group Developmental Stage: *Ending*

**In Sum**

Just as in a group, we are progressing in this book along a developmental path. In this chapter we examine group leader techniques that can be used to help a group and its members wind down and finally conclude its life. Of course, as in the other group developmental stages we already have considered, the challenges and opportunities are both similar and unique, calling for particular group leader applications.

At the close of a group, the leader needs to be concerned with the historical path both the group and its members have walked, while also peering into the future and determining what members can take with them. These directions differ, of course, from the group's beginning and middle stages of development. In the beginning stage, leaders are focused on getting the group established and orienting the members, then on traversing somewhat rocky shoals, at times, through a transition to the middle stage. During middle-stage development, members can become more interconnected and productive. This is the stage where new business can be generated and addressed, sometimes yielding new and exciting products—whether those are in the form of personal and interpersonal insights, new skills, or ideas and reports—just to name a few possibilities.

## Various Perspectives on the Ending Stage of Group Development

Endings are difficult for many people. Whereas saying hello can have its own anxieties, especially for shy people, saying goodbye seems challenging for almost everyone. In Bennis and Slater's (1968) *The Temporary Society,* they combined dual anxieties associated with bidding adieu and with the increasing call of accelerated change and temporary relationships. The authors predicted that American citizens would experience an unrelenting crescendo of brief, temporary relationships and communal arrangements of various kinds. This prediction has come to pass. Terminating relationships has assumed an increasing level of importance in general and, for our particular interest, in the ending stage of group work.

Group work theorists have identified a number of other important aspects of the ending stage of development. Gladding (2003) lists the following steps as being important: (a) reflecting about past experiences, (b) processing memories, (c) acknowledging feelings of ambivalence, and (d) participating in cognitive decision making. Lieberman, Yalom, and Miles's (1973) research demonstrated the importance of helping members integrate and apply their learning and make sense of it. Trotzer (2006) added the significance of affirming and confirming growth and of attending to follow-up. Corey and Corey (2006), in observing that the beginning and ending of groups are its most important phases, stressed that the ending is where members can consolidate their learning and can make concrete action plans for the future. There is much at stake at the end and being able to draw from and use effective leader techniques is essential.

## Our Language for the Ending Stage: Consolidating and Forecasting

Once again, our perspective is in agreement with that of other theorists. Indeed, the ending stage is important and is especially challenging. There is so much wrapped up in ending any experience. The intense learning experience characterizing any group that makes its way to the designated end point complicates the task.

It is helpful to organize the complexity of the ending stage into two large categories: (a) consolidation of learning from what has transpired, which involves reflecting on past events and experiences that occurred within the group; and (b) forecasting the future—that is, looking ahead to develop a plan of action that will show how learning from the group can be applied from now on. A kind of two-headed Janus emerges, where the group leader needs to use techniques that help members look both backward and forward at the same time.

Certainly, time needs to be planned for and allotted to the ending stage. We have seen far too many groups where ending is not even discussed or, if it is, it is left to the last session alone. "Oops, we're ending" definitely is not a best practice! Reminding members that termination of the group is approaching, and doing this two or three sessions or meetings before the scheduled final meeting, is strongly encouraged. Sometimes, leaders worry that mentioning the upcoming ending will cause members to relax or to avoid additional work. We generally have found this to be untrue, if the leader also provides a context for the approaching closing. We encourage leaders to frame the future ending as follows: "You know, our final session is in three weeks, just a reminder. Of course, this means that we have very little time left together and so much still to do. Let's keep our 'pedal to the metal' and move on" (or something like that).

Other ideas will emerge as we discuss the critical incidents contained in this chapter. So, on to the first of these critical incidents.

## Critical Incident Training in the Ending Stage of Performing

### CRITICAL INCIDENTS

### PERFORMING (ENDING) CI 7.1

Group Type: *Psychoeducation*
Best Practice Area: *Performing*
Group Developmental Stage: *Ending*

### End of the Search

### HISTORY

Valerie Fields, a licensed mental health counselor working in a school, was an integral part of starting a leadership academy within two local high schools. Five students from each school were chosen by their homeroom teachers to meet weekly to develop their leadership skills. With increasing incidents of violence in many of the local schools, this group of students has been working to learn about prevention and conflict resolution. Valerie has found that though the students are hardworking and reliable in their attendance, they rarely speak about their own feelings. Her coleader, Mike Goodfellow, is a football and track coach and has been a good collaborator, offering valuable reflections on issues the students were reporting. With 12 sessions together so far, Valerie had planned an overnight retreat for a closure activity, followed by quarterly meetings in the future.

Upon arriving to the retreat meeting Valerie saw that two male students huddled closely with her coleader, Mike, talking in low voices, and sitting apart from the other group members. Valerie noticed that the other group members were looking in their direction with a rather suspicious stare, and became aware of her own momentary feelings of awkwardness. She called to Mike in greeting, which he returned with a wave of his hand, but continued to talk to the two male students. Valerie then made a general call to the group to move their chairs into a circle. The room became quiet and glances were shared all around. Mike then greeted a few of the other students as they moved their chairs.

## CRITICAL INCIDENT

VALERIE:     So far in this training group we have talked a lot about violence in the schools, problems that students have with teachers or their friends, family issues that affect students, and how we can make a difference in preventing violent incidents at school.

JOSH:     Man, I don't think we'll *ever* have enough time to talk about all that!

MIKE:     You are probably right, Josh, but we are doing important work here.

NAJWA:     Every time I leave here I think of one more thing that I heard about or something that affects kids in school and at home that I know we haven't talked about yet.

PETER:     Seriously, what difference can we make anyway?

VALERIE:     Ah, Peter, here you've been our group's "cheerleader" all along! What's up?

PETER:     Nothin'. Just been thinking too much, I guess, and searching for a way to make sense of it all.

CHRISTINA:     (*huffing, arms crossed*) So is that why you and Josh were huddled in the corner with Mike, or are you getting ready for football camp?

JOSH:     We weren't huddled in the corner!

NAJWA:     Well, you were, actually, and everyone noticed.

CHRISTINA:     What is this . . . a guys' thing and a girls' thing? I thought we were supposed to all work together.

MIKE:     Ouch! I didn't mean for it to look secretive. Sorry!

## WHAT TECHNIQUE DO YOU CHOOSE?

Individually or in small groups jot down or discuss several options for what technique you would use in this situations. What factors be cosidered?

## STEPS TOWARD SELECTING A TECHNIQUE

Here is our thinking:

### Step 1:  Identify the group type and purpose, best practice area, and developmental stage

The purpose of a psychoeducation group, particularly in a school, is to provide an educational opportunity for students, which often includes skill development training. The most successful groups also reflect the needs of the students and the immediate community. This group's purpose is to develop student leaders while working to create programming about school violence, with this particular group of students acting as future peer mediators.

The expectations of the ending stage include encouraging members to reflect on their experiences and processing their memories. The group is reaching closure in its ending stage and one of the group leaders, Valerie, is sensitive to the fact that these students have spent a long stretch of time together. Though there will be regular check-in meetings, their work will continue in a different way in the future. Valerie has been thinking about the lack of feelings expression from these students until now, which will affect their level of processing and reflection. The apparent attitude of mistrust has not surfaced before, but is being expressed by the students verbally and nonverbally. Valerie's own confusion about the subgrouping incident tells her that they need to address it in order to move toward a satisfactory transition into the next form of interaction. She is also aware that her communication (or lack of communication) with her coleader may have been a real problem.

### Step 2:  Analyze the presenting situation by applying ecological concepts

The ecological concept of context is very important in this incident, because Valerie has to be mindful of the type of group it is—a psychoeducation group and not a counseling group—and the fact that it is held as part of a school system's desire to engage students in the managing of its resources. In fact, students are part of the resources! The social system created in this group seems to include some expectations about mutual sharing and open communication, for both leaders and members, though perhaps it has never been stated. Christina's response appears to show that some expectation has just been violated.

Coleader collaboration enhances the experience for all group members. In this incident two members have apparently raised suspicion by their seemingly covert actions, which is difficult to deal with late in the group's development. What do the group members understand is the group's purpose and how will the relationships of the members affect that purpose? The group's training in conflict resolution will be helpful in the school setting in the future, but it certainly needs to be able to influence the members' behavior in the group now! Peter's injection of "searching for a way to make sense of it all" also tells Valerie that as a leader she has some responsibility for helping these students make meaning of the group experience. Her desire is to make that opportunity available in the work during this retreat.

**Step 3:   Review possible group techniques, considering focus and level**

Valerie is cognizant of the group's focus on leadership development. One of the most important qualities in leadership is the ability to communicate well to others. In addition, she values the important skills of preparation and planning. These aspects of leadership development and personal growth are on her mind as she is considering possible group techniques. She intends to process the possible subgrouping incident with Mike later.

***Performing Toolbox #81,*** Revisit Group Rules and Expectations. Rechecking what has been decided can be helpful and necessary.

*Focus:* Cognitive.
*Level:* Individual and group.

Valerie and Mike have an unusually long period of time to wrap up the group process using a retreat for a closure activity. This allows for some processing in the group that may actually engage the students in affective reactions to their past work or to comments made by other students. Revisiting the rules and expectations functions as a review and may indirectly address the private conversation that the two boys had, which sparked a response from at least one of the other students, and Valerie.

***Performing Toolbox #75,*** Feelings Faces. Ask members to form pairs. Using pictures of feelings faces, have members choose a feeling and share a time when they experienced that feeling. Change faces (feelings) and change the person who shares.

*Focus:* Cognitive, affective, and structural.
*Level:* Individual and interpersonal.

The types of feelings faces from which members can choose (i.e., caricatures are more lighthearted than realistic faces) determine to what degree this technique is seen as fun or serious. Valerie thought originally that this would be a good activity to have the students move around and explore their perceptions about their experiences as group members.

**Step 4:   Select a best-fit technique**

Valerie considers both techniques to be good options and with the amount of time left in the retreat, the group actually could do both. There are other important planning steps that need to happen during the retreat, however, for the group's work in the future. Valerie wants to be sure that the students feel comfortable in their new roles as leaders first and foremost. Therefore, in choosing one technique she is sure to be able to use, Valerie considers technique #81 for revisiting the rules and expectations. Once again, as a counselor in the schools, Valerie has expectations she must consider in line with her responsibility in the students' training, to follow the school's initiative as closely as possible in order to deliver the desired outcomes. Certainly students are familiar with review of material, much like an exam review, so going back to the beginning to reexamine what they originally set out to do, and how, is simple, effective, and appropriate. Her concern is that the technique is not adequate in getting to the feelings she believes these students have yet to share.

The second technique described (#75) using feelings faces is appropriate for addressing exactly that—the students' feelings. As an activity it could be perceived as fun and energizing to the students, offering a tool that is useful for saying more about themselves. There is an opportunity for the discussions to deepen and to engage the group in communicating personal perceptions and misperceptions. Unfortunately, it is not as predictable a technique in terms of adequately dealing with all of the issues that superficial group talk might suggest. With high school students it is possible that such a technique can become too lighthearted and not achieve its desired results.

After a few moments, Valerie decides the most efficient way to address her concerns is to quickly address Mike to seek his approval for a technique for revisiting the rules and expectations, and why. It is an efficient and effective technique that needs no materials, though posting large sheets of paper on the wall to write the rules being discussed would be a more active approach to the technique.

### Step 5:  Implement and evaluate how well the technique worked

MIKE:  My bad! I didn't mean for it to look secretive. Sorry!

VALERIE:  Mike and I have a plan for discussing some very important things as we start our retreat. He and I need to touch base for a few minutes while all of you get something to write on and something to write with.

(*As the students move to get their pens and paper, Valerie and Mike speak privately and then return to the group.*)

VALERIE:  I must say that I was curious about Mike and the guys talking separately over there, too. I wonder if it *is* anything to be curious about, so I would like to discuss our expectations for this group. We need to talk about things that make us feel uncomfortable sometimes; it will impact how well we work together as we decide what the future holds for this group.

MIKE:  I agree! Actually, I would like to start. Is that okay with everyone?

(*Everyone nods or says um-hum.*)

MIKE:  One of the things I have learned from this group is just how perceptive you all are at this age, and how much it matters to you when adults honor their word. I think the guys will agree that we can tell you what that little conversation was about, and I apologize for sitting apart. Kevin, how about you sharing what we were talking about.

KEVIN:  Okay . . . might as well.

## If in a Class or Workshop, Then:

### Practice the choice

Pair up with another student and try out your choices. Give each other feedback. What might work? What might need to be changed? Compare your choices with those provided by the authors.

### Process the choice

What have you learned? What are you learning about this process for selecting group techniques? What are you learning about yourself as a group leader? What might you be able to use the next time?

---

## PERFORMING (ENDING) CI 7.2

Group Type: *Counseling*
Best Practice Area: *Performing*
Group Developmental Stage: *Ending*

## Graded

### HISTORY

A group of second-year students at the university meet biweekly in a closed group with two master's students from the counseling program to talk about their academic struggles and transition into college course work. All seven student members are on academic probation after their first semester and risk failing out of the university. There are three females (Erin, Jen, and Shawna) and four males (Eric, Sean, Tyrone, and Nick). Their advisors encouraged them to set up tutoring sessions with the math and/or reading centers, while the counseling graduate students hope to provide a supportive environment for these students. Tension and emotions often run high with frustration, confusion, and other feelings that tend to be self-defeating. With only two weeks left in the semester the group is aware of more tension than usual.

One of the students, Eric, showed up late to the session. One of the leaders just introduced a handout dealing with physical stress. She is in the middle of her explanation about the practice of relaxation techniques the group will be using in this session.

### CRITICAL INCIDENT

SEAN:      Hey, man! You're late again!

ERIC:      Back off, Sean. I had to pick up a book from the math tutor. I didn't mean to be late; sorry!

ERIN:          It's okay, Eric. Sean is just in a bad mood it seems. I guess we all are.

LEADER #1:     That's an interesting observation. What's going on?

SEAN:          What do you think?! We have no life! We have to come to this group, go to tutors, go to work and class. I thought we were supposed to be having fun in college!

LEADER #2:     Well, if that is the main reason to go to college, it will be very disappointing. I know some students come here thinking that way. College can be fun, but in a way you need to think of it as your job.

SEAN:          It sucks!

TYRONE:        Why don't you get in the group thing and tell us what you really think!

LEADER #1:     Sean, why don't you start the regular check-in and we can try some of these stress exercises, which I expect will help all of you.

SEAN:          No, I don't want to do the regular thing. I don't even want to be here.

## WHAT TECHNIQUE DO YOU CHOOSE?

Individually or in small groups jot down or discuss several options for what technique you would use in this situations. What factors be cosidered?

## STEPS TOWARD SELECTING A TECHNIQUE

Here is our thinking:

### Step 1:   Identify the group type and purpose, best practice area, and developmental stage

This counseling group was created to provide support to students who are on academic probation. Its focus is to address whatever issues caused the members' poor performance in the first place.

The graduate student leaders have just reminded the group members that there are only two weeks left in the semester and thus only two remaining sessions—making this the ending stage. Performing as a best practice area requires paying attention to group dynamics in obvious and subtle ways in order to facilitate growth and movement.

### Step 2:   Analyze the presenting situation by applying ecological concepts

It seems evident that the group has a social system that allows for fairly open communication by what the members have said so far. It is not unusual to expect that emotions run high within this complicated context. There are numerous potential reasons for why these students are in academic trouble, including poor time management, weak study skills, too much partying, missing class, and so on. The fact remains that they are required to attend the group in addition to using academic support services. The leaders hope that the students can take away some meaningful insights in order to improve their academic behaviors.

### Step 3:   Review possible group techniques, considering focus and level

The leaders are torn between addressing an individual member's issue and addressing the group members' reactions to it and to one another.

***Performing Toolbox #29,*** Outer Circle. When a forced client does not want to participate, have him create an outer circle where participation is not required.

*Focus:* Cognitive, affective, and structural.
*Level:* Individual, interpersonal, and group.

Sean seems pretty agitated and his behavior is considered resistant to the group, both in being late and in saying outright that he does not want to be present. A technique like Outer Circle is a powerful way to demonstrate what it is like for the member to be excluded.

***Performing Toolbox #69,*** Epitaphs. Have members write their own epitaph and then invite sharing.

*Focus:* Cognitive and affective.
*Level:* Individual.

This technique has the ability to be modified in various ways. It, too, is a powerful tool for clarifying values driving specific behavior.

### Step 4:   Select a best-fit technique

The leaders consider both techniques to be effective in addressing the group's strong reaction today. Aware of the ending stage in which this resistance is manifesting itself, care needs to be taken to ignite the fewest side effects. Both techniques are more than adequate in prompting the group to face resistance from even one member, as well as confront each individual member's ability to understand what part he or she plays as a part of the whole. Side effects for the Outer Circle could include Sean "checking out" completely, while it may heighten his particular sense of frustration even more. However, one option is to modify the Epitaph technique to consist of not what is said if they died, but rather what is said if they were no longer part of the group. It could have a positive side effect for the group members to experience what others have learned about them or what they brought to the group simply by being who they are. Careful directions need to be given to guide the members to learn about applying new skills they have learned, such as consolidating what they have learned in the past and how to make that reflect in their future behavior.

### Step 5:   Implement and evaluate how well the technique worked

SEAN:        No, I don't want to do the regular thing. I don't even want to be here.

LEADER #2:    It is understandable that this group has a unique context. Yes, you are told to participate and you have. This is a good thing. You can be proud of how you followed through with something that wasn't even your idea.

SEAN:         Hey, man! I'm sorry I went off on you.

JEN:          You might as well make the best of it, since we all have to be here.

LEADER #1:    I want to ask you to do something that requires sensitivity. You know how we've been working on all those great listening skills!

(*Several group members chuckle.*)

LEADER #1:    Okay, so I want you to think quietly for a moment about what it would have been like over the past 13 weeks if any one of you had not been here. We are going to write our epitaph of sorts. Not in the case of our death, but in the sense that this group happened and we had to leave suddenly. What would someone write about you? What did you bring to the group with your ideas, your presence, your hopes, or whatever?

## If in a Class or Workshop, Then:

### *Practice the choice*

Pair up with another student and try out your choices. Give each other feedback. What might work? What might need to be changed? Compare your choices with those provided by the authors.

### *Process the choice*

What have you learned? What are you learning about this process for selecting group techniques? What are you learning about yourself as a group leader? What might you be able to use the next time?

PERFORMING (ENDING) CI 7.3

Group Type: *Psychoeducation*
Best Practice Area: *Performing*
Group Developmental Stage: *Ending*

## *Now That We Know*

### HISTORY

The psychology training program's Learning Group has met now for five of its six 2-hour weekly sessions. Though somewhat difficult to get going, the group became engaged in the use of both structured and unstructured experiences. The results so far seem to be helping the group members and trainees learn about what it is like to be a group member, to have an opportunity to self-disclose and to give and receive feedback, to participate in the here-and-now, and to observe group leadership being modeled by advanced group leaders.

In today's last session the group leaders feel uncertain about their group plan, which was written before the group work ever started. Now that they are well acquainted with the group members, they had considered just "going with the flow" and letting the termination happen naturally. As advanced leaders, however, they know that they must carry a plan, just in case things do not work out as they expect.

## CRITICAL INCIDENT

FELIPE:      (*coleader*) It is hard to believe that this is our last meeting. Though we said the purpose of the group was intended to be somewhat ambiguous, it seems like the group found its focus and has done really good work.

ZACK:        Okay! I was one of the ones who took awhile to get the whole thing. The way I see it is we finally get the idea and now we have to stop. I don't like that very much.

JULIANNE:    Oh, I don't know! I think we are ready. If we start something else now we could go on and on forever! For me, I would like to try leading a group now.

SUSAN:       (*coleader*) I expect that you all are experiencing different reactions to this experience. We have only this one session left, however, so we need to make some decisions about what to do in closing.

## WHAT TECHNIQUE DO YOU CHOOSE?

Individually or in small groups jot down or discuss several options for what technique you would use in this situation. What factors must be considered?

## STEPS TOWARD SELECTING A TECHNIQUE

Here is our thinking:

### Step 1:  Identify the group type and purpose, best practice area, and developmental stage

This training group has been described as a type of psychoeducation group, and has been reported by the leaders to have done a good job overall in its earlier stages of performing. The current meeting is the group's last, so terminating is a very important stage for the members to go through, specifically for the purpose of experiencing the full group process in their training as future group leaders.

### Step 2:   Analyze the presenting situation by applying ecological concepts

Context in this case includes the mandatory nature of the group experience. As trainees, the members are learning a great deal about internal and external resources with a heightened awareness of the overall group process. The members have been involved at a personal level, but this does not mean that they were totally comfortable with exposing themselves the way they would in a nontraining group. The fact that the group consists of their fellow classmates affects the degree of interconnection the members may have experienced. Resolving the relationship between interconnection and individuality is difficult in most groups, but in this case, there are multiple layers of social systems interacting (i.e., getting to know classmates, being members of a group, being students in a course, etc.).

The sustainability of learning was a significant factor in the group leaders' plans. Confusion among members at one point centered around goals, both in terms of what the overall group was intended to address and what individual goals would be accomplished. Once resolved the confusion seems to be present again, this time in how much the group experience had meaning for each member.

### Step 3:   Review possible group techniques, considering focus and level

What might you try as a group leader? Remember that the coleaders have a plan but also have discussed the idea of being free to deviate if the situation seems appropriate.

***Performing Toolbox #82,*** How Did It Go? Simple and direct questions asked at appropriate times during a session can promote reflective participation.

*Focus:* Cognitive.
*Level:* Individual.
*Reminder:* Earlier we identified the issues to be explored:

1. Identify and discuss our unique context as a group.
2. Within that context, define our group's purpose.
3. Within that group purpose, what can be your purpose here?
4. How can you continue to work on that purpose outside the group?
5. What have you learned?

Keeping these issues in mind, the leaders believe that this simple technique would elicit the type of discussions they had originally planned for. It still seems like a good technique, perhaps modifying the list of questions.

***Performing Toolbox #83,*** Systems-Centered Subgrouping. Members are encouraged to identify subgroups within the group as a way of exploring interconnections and meaning.

*Focus:* Cognitive and affective.
*Level:* Interpersonal and group.

As graduate students in training, the leaders have a rich group of student members who expect to gain some knowledge from the group experience. The ability of the group members to perform such an analysis offers an opportunity to try a deep and engaging technique that seems suitable, particularly with the intention of helping the students discover meaning for themselves.

### Step 4:   Select a best-fit technique

The first technique identified, "How Did It Go?", is simple and yet is able to directly address specific issues if tailored to this particular group. There is no real limit on the number of questions and they can be modified. The point is to promote group member reflection. The group leaders chose this technique for their group plan because it is so adaptable. Not knowing what the student trainees would be like prior to the actual meetings, they wanted to have some flexibility.

Graduate students these days are incredibly diverse as a group, with a wide age range and differing ethnicities, cultural backgrounds, marital status, children, or lack of, and years of work experience. Depending on their educational training some students also have experience with reflection and some do not have much experience at all. A training group is an excellent medium in which to try such a technique.

The subgrouping technique is more limited in its use, as it calls for group members or leaders to label subgroups, which as you might imagine could be divisive depending on the context. With a training group, though, the potential for exploring some identified element in the process of termination offers these group members the opportunity to find clarity. The technique is meant to explore interconnections and meaning. Especially with students who are learning about group process, both of these ecological concepts are significant in understanding most of what their mandatory group is all about.

Felipe and Susan feel torn between the two techniques. They have a two-hour session to terminate this group, but are aware that there is exploration group members need to do to gain more insight personally and as future group leaders. They agreed in their group planning process that with a group of well-educated students they would attempt to reach consensus with any decision they put before the group members. This is how they decided to go forward at this point. Their understanding is that the group members are here to work, so how can the 2 hours be utilized most efficiently in terms of learning as much as possible, and most effectively as they terminate the training experience?

### Step 5:   Implement and evaluate how well the technique worked

SUSAN:        (*coleader*) I expect that you all are experiencing different reactions to this experience. We have only this one session left, however, so we need to make some decisions about what to do in closing.

SUZANNE:      No doubt we all should know something by now. I think it is hard to know what to do sometimes. Like figuring out what the group had done, and is doing now. I hate to admit it again, but I would be kind of embarrassed if you asked me what to do right now.

FELIPE:       Don't worry! We are not asking you all to be group leaders just yet. It is helpful if you pay attention to how you *do* feel right now and why.

SUSAN:          So, what might this mean? Because we are all trying to learn from this group, we would like to offer you two options. One thing we can do is ask you all a series of questions and process your experience in terms of your overall impressions and what you have learned at this point.

FELIPE:         The other thing we considered is breaking first into smaller groups, or subgroups, depending on how you relate to several variables we can identify.

LUCY:           I'm open to either one.

SUZANNE:        I've been listening and thinking that I want to talk a little more about leadership, and that maybe a subgroup who would want to talk about it would be cool. Then we can talk all together.

SUSAN:          Okay, then. If there is consensus on subgrouping first, then we will split into two groups. *(All members nod in agreement.)* Those who want to explore group leadership meet here with me, and those who want to explore more about group membership, meet over there with Felipe. Let's give this about 40 minutes, take a break, and then finish with the series of questions we prepared.

## If in a Class or Workshop, Then:

### Practice the choice

Pair up with another student and try out your choices. Give each other feedback. What might work? What might need to be changed? Compare your choices with those provided by the authors.

### Process the choice

What have you learned? What are you learning about this process for selecting group techniques? What are you learning about yourself as a group leader? What might you be able to use the next time?

---

PERFORMING (ENDING) CI 7.4

Group Type: *Counseling*
Best Practice Area: *Performing*
Group Development Stage: *Ending*

## Done

## HISTORY

Recent world events scattered young American soldiers from all military branches around the Middle East. As many of them returned to the United States, the general at the local army base identified that some of the returning soldiers were having a difficult time transitioning back into their normal lives. Charles Atkins, a professional counselor, has run a counseling group for male soldiers who returned en masse two months ago. They have met twice a week as a group, discussing many of their fears about the future of our country, the possibility (or lack of) world peace, and finally about their roles as husbands and fathers. All expressed great sadness about their friends and comrades who would not return and who had lost their lives in battle.

In the last meeting Charles reminded the group that it was originally set up to run for 12 weeks and they had only one week left, or the equivalent of two meetings. A lot of personal sharing has gone on in the group and they have formed a tight bond, despite the fact that some of the group members were officers and some were enlisted men, who would not normally work so closely.

## CRITICAL INCIDENT

CHARLES: I need to remind you once again that we have two meetings left in our group. It is very important that you all be thinking and talking about your future plans for self-care and about your military careers.

NED: All I know is there is too much left to talk about to quit now!

CHARLES: This is not about quitting. We had an agreement at the beginning of the group that there would be 24 sessions in 12 weeks. Tonight is session 22. I am only reminding you about what we agreed on from the start.

PATRICK: Can't we change that now? I would also like to continue this group. It is the only place where I can really have someone else understand what it's like when your best buddy gets blown up right in front of you. My wife would never understand that!

NED: My son was born while I was gone. I just can't get over the feeling that I should have been here!

CHARLES: These are important things to talk about, believe me! It is very satisfying to me personally to hear that you all have really appreciated this group. The fact remains, we are almost finished.

## WHAT TECHNIQUE DO YOU CHOOSE?

Individually or in small groups jot down or discuss several options for what technique you would use in this situation. What factors must be considered?

## STEPS TOWARD SELECTING A TECHNIQUE

Here is our thinking:

### Step 1:   Identify the group type and purpose, best practice area, and developmental stage

A group that enables significantly emotional issues to surface is probably the most difficult to end. What is apparent here is the intensity of emotion brought on by the group's purpose to deal with issues surrounding military personnel returning to their homes. Many, but not all, have difficult memories to carry with them. Though the group is set to end soon, the members are having difficulty letting go. The group leader is faced with high emotions and yet, has an obligation to his own practice to deal with this issue of termination.

### Step 2:   Analyze the presenting situation by applying ecological concepts

Context is an important ecological concept in this incident. Unusual circumstances often call for unusual decisions, such as the delicate one about what to report within the group between officers and enlisted personnel. The military has its own social system in many respects, so the member's comment that no one else would understand may be realistic. At the same time, expectations are clear and the length of time set for the group was established with all members in agreement at the outset.

As a counseling group the valuable resources are in its members, as well as the leader. Interconnections in this case are possibly complicated because of the various levels of rank of the group members and the military social system under which they have been trained and live. On the other hand, the group leader is a community counselor, who was called in to implement and lead this group at the request of the base's commander. Sustainability is perhaps the ecological concept that has been brought to the foreground in this case. Not to be confused with maintaining the formalized group, per se, but sustaining the relationships and growth professed by the group's members.

### Step 3:   Review possible group techniques, considering focus and level

***Performing Toolbox #33,*** You Are a Book. Tell members to pretend they are a book. Ask: "What is your title? Are you illustrated? What's your style, tone? Will people want to read you? What will entice them to read you? Which chapters were the hardest to write? After reading you cover to cover what will people think then?" At the end: "What changes would you make?"

*Focus:* Cognitive and affective.
*Level:* Individual.

These military men have a need for deep cognitive understanding about what they have experienced and what their futures hold. For some, it may be difficult to express openly their emotional needs, which are difficult to ignore after such an intense military engagement. This technique offers a thorough exploration of their self-concepts and can be modified in several ways to suit a particular incident or experience. Utilizing all of the questions provides for an adequate exploration of both cognitive and affective aspects of their lives, while allowing some room for interpretation.

***Performing Toolbox #74,*** Experiential Focusing. Clients are led through a six-step process to see their internal self working to provide answers to life's challenges, by helping to connect their physiological emotional responses with their psychological selves.

*Focus:* Cognitive and affective.
*Level:* Individual.

Experiential Focusing is a means to allow group members to see how their internal self is working for answers to life's challenges. Focusing can help group members become aware of how their internal self is affected by external situations and demands. Experiential Focusing is a technique that can become deeply moving and yet it offers an efficient way of making interconnections between mind and body.

### Step 4:   Select a best-fit technique

Both techniques heighten the stakes in engaging the group in communicating deeply personal perceptions of their reunification with families, friends, and coworkers. The book technique is unpredictable in its usefulness to connect these soldiers with how their families and friends perceive them upon arriving back in the United States. It is appropriate to "test the waters," though a deeper understanding may not be reached unless there is sufficient time to fully process what the group members share. The length of time needed to process each member's ideas may limit the depth to which he might like to go. This also may be important depending on military rank or security level. Although not particularly efficient in terms of use of time, there are two sessions left and it may just take all of both sessions to give members a chance to report. The side effects are potentially emotional and may not help the leader bring closure to the group.

Experiential Focusing is very therapeutic if the group members can apply themselves to the exercise. The technique may not be appropriate in all group settings, but in this case, it seems like a powerful way to touch on the most critical elements of the soldiers' transitioning back into the American community. It could be quite effective in its ability to help the soldiers visualize and imagine how their behaviors are affected by their emotions. At the end of a group, it would reinforce what this leader had tried to achieve in assisting the soldiers to be in touch with the here-and-now, physically and emotionally.

### Step 5:   Implement and evaluate how well the technique worked

CHARLES:   These are important things to talk about, believe me! It is very satisfying to me personally to hear that you all have really appreciated this group. The fact remains, we are almost finished.

NED:   I want to understand how I am supposed to act like everything is okay. It just isn't! I get all gnarled up inside just thinking about what could be happening over there right now.

CHARLES:   That is exactly what I am talking about, Ned. I want you all to do something very different tonight and it will require your undivided attention. It's called Experiential Focusing and that is what I need you to do right now—focus. Ready to begin?

## If in a Class or Workshop, Then:

### *Practice the choice*

Pair up with another student and try out your choices. Give each other feedback. What might work? What might need to be changed? Compare your choices with those provided by the authors.

### *Process the choice*

What have you learned? What are you learning about this process for selecting group techniques? What are you learning about yourself as a group leader? What might you be able to use the next time?

# In Sum

Putting things together, bidding adieu, taking care of unfinished business, making plans to apply what has been learned, and evaluating one's experience in the group represent some of the many functions served in the ending of a group. For many, getting some sort of closure and parting from others for a final time can be traumatic. For most, termination of relationships is a challenge. And, as we have pointed out, in our fast-paced society that is frequently filled with temporary relationships, being able to leave appropriately is a necessary life skill to develop.

Group leaders need to find ways to help members take stock, make sense of their experience, and wrap things up. Leaders also need to feel a level of personal comfort in this area.

A group can provide an excellent arena for learning how to consolidate and forecast. Moreover, if these goals are met, group members will find it possible to draw meaning from their group experience, and to move forward to sustain their learning outside the group in their ongoing lives.

# References

Bennis, W., & Slater, P. (1968). *The temporary society*. New York: Harper & Row.

Corey, M.S., & Corey, G. (2006). *Groups: Process and practice* (7th ed.). Belmont, CA: Brooks/Cole.

Gladding, S. (2003). *Group Work: A Counseling Specialty* (4th ed.). Upper Saddle River, N.J: Merrill Prentice Hall.

Lieberman, M., Yalom, I., & Miles, M. (1973). *Encountergroups: First Facts*. New York: Basic Books.

Trotzer, J. (2006). *The counselor and the group: Integrating theory, training and practice* (4th ed.). Philadelphia, PA: Accelerated Development.

# Techniques in Processing Counseling and Psychoeducation Groups

Processing is the third Best Practice area in group leading. Referred to informally as the "third P" (following planning and performing), processing is used by group leaders to help members make sense and draw meaning from the events and experiences that are occurring within and between group sessions or meetings.

Attention to the importance of processing began with the research findings of Lieberman, Yalom, and Miles (1973), who found that one key to successful group experiences was helping members understand their experience. Therefore, it is very important that group leaders learn how to use techniques that are geared to helping members focus on their experience and learn from it. Otherwise, the best experience is unlikely to translate into tangible application in other settings.

Much less attention has been given to the importance of processing between sessions. Sometimes this activity is thought of as supervision or, in other cases, as consultation, depending on the circumstances. Between-session processing also can occur when a solo leader reflects intentionally on his or her previous group session, and when coleaders meet subsequent to group sessions or meetings to review and reflect on their work together in the group. The Deep Processing Model (Conyne, 1999) was developed as one method to assist group leaders in between-session processing and it has direct application to the proper use of group techniques.

In Chapter 8 we focus on processing group events and experiences that occur within sessions or meetings—termed "within-group processing." In Chapter 9 we focus on processing that a leader or coleaders can engage in between sessions to help them put into perspective and better understand what has been occurring and how to best adapt for coming sessions or meetings. We term this form of processing "between-session processing." Both forms of processing are important for group leaders to practice.

# 8

# Processing Techniques to Use Within Group Sessions or Meetings

**ADVANCE ORGANIZER**

This chapter contains the following material:

**The "Self-Reflective Loop"**

**Within-Session Processing**

**Critical Incident Training Within-Session Processing**

**In Sum**

Group leaders need to be "reflective practitioners" (Conyne, Wilson, & Ward, 1997). There is so much to observe, to do, and to understand in groups that processing is necessary just to try to keep up. Besides, processing yields huge benefits that can greatly improve practice and generate new knowledge—about self, others, and group work, in general.

Processing can be defined simply as reflecting on events and experiences to produce meaning. See Ward and Litchy (2004) for an extended discussion of how processing can be used effectively by group leaders, including a rich discussion of several intragroup processing models.

## The "Self-Reflective Loop"

Yalom (1970) is chiefly responsible for giving impetus to the importance of processing, when he described the "self-reflective loop" in group therapy. He emphasized that the "power cell" of group activity is found in its process focus, the attention to the here-and-now relationship between interpersonal transactions. Yet, he also pointed out that process illumination is critically important, and without it, strong affect that occurs can lead potentially to negative consequences. Process illumination occurs through reflecting on here-and-now behavior, affect, events, and experiences that have just occurred. Another term for engaging in self-reflective loop behavior is within-session processing.

Little attention was paid to Yalom's contention initially. Later, Lieberman and colleagues (1973) verified the self-reflective loop concept through findings of their seminal research study on encounter groups. Data showed that the leader function of *meaning attribution*, along with the appropriate use of other important functions (caring, executive functioning, emotional stimulation), was necessary for productive and safe groups. When group leaders perform meaning attribution they provide concepts for how to understand, explain, clarify, and interpret behavior and experience.

What a surprise this empirical discovery was! Here-and-now experience and emoting were not enough for positive growth and change, contrary to a main practice of groups in the 1970s. These experiences needed to be converted to cognitive understanding—that is, to help members to attribute meaning to events. This empirically tested insight is essential to good group leader practice; whereas here-and-now process is fundamentally central to group work it must be accompanied by reflection, and processing is the vehicle for that to occur.

## Within-Session Processing

Processing can occur both within and between sessions and meetings. In this chapter, we will focus on within-session processing. What techniques can group leaders employ to conduct session processing and to heighten its effectiveness?

Within-session processing can help leaders and members understand and clarify behavior and thoughts and gain perspective on how the group itself is functioning. As DeLucia-Waack (1997) observed, "The processing of critical events and issues is critical to all forms of group work. Even if events are unplanned, they often must be processed to clarify group interactions and assure interpersonal learning" (p. 82).

---

**Best Practices in Processing**

*Group leaders develop and maintain a Processing schedule*

- Processing occurs within sessions
- Processing occurs between sessions

*Group leaders engage in reflective practice*

- Leaders synthesize theory and practice, dynamics, and interrelationships
- Leaders attend to their own values, cognition, and affect

*Group leaders evaluate process and outcomes*

- Results used for planning, improvement, and revisions
- Leaders appropriately and ethically disseminate results

---

**Figure 8.1**
Processing Best Practice Guidelines

Various training approaches have been developed to assist in teaching within-session processing (e.g., Cox, Banez, Hawley, & Mostade, 2003; Glass & Benshoff, 1999; Kees & Jacobs, 1990). Moreover, a variety of methods for conducting within-session processing is available. These methods illustrate a broad scope, attending to: (a) observing and giving feedback (Hanson, 1972); (b) organizing feedback by using a content-process grid (Conyne, 1977) and a three-by-three process matrix (Glass & Benshoff, 1999); (c) using journal letters (Cummings, 2001) and interactive process notes (Hall & Hawley, 2004); and (d) taking advantage of a cognitive, step-wise map (Stockton, Morran & Nitza, 2000).

Consistent with previous sections of this book containing Best Practice Guidelines in Planning and Performing, Figure 8.1 displays Processing Best Practice Guidelines. These Guidelines have been recommended by the Association for Specialists in Group Work (1998).

We will turn next to a presentation of critical incidents. In this case, the critical incidents will be directed at group leader techniques for within-session processing in psychoeducation and counseling groups.

## Critical Incident Training in Within-Session Processing

### CRITICAL INCIDENTS

#### PROCESSING (WITHIN) CI 8.1

Group Type: *Counseling*
Best Practice Area: *Within-Session Processing*
Group Developmental Stage: *Beginning*

### Academic Center Dilemma

## HISTORY

Dr. Jessica Cummings is in her first year as the director of the Academic Center at a small liberal arts college in the Midwest. As the first full-time director of the center, Dr. Cummings has spent a great deal of time working among various student groups to gain an understanding about the issues that cause students to falter academically. In her role as an academic counselor Dr. Cummings discovered that many students have come to college underprepared, though some students just seem to have a difficult time transitioning into a residential college setting.

At the end of the fall semester, Dr. Cummings invited seven struggling students to create a counseling group to deal with the discouragement they have experienced. The new semester began and in this third week of class, the group has met only twice for an hour and a half each time. In this third session one of the students, Amber, began to talk about her distaste for her math professor's informal clothing style. Another student, Paula, excitedly stopped her by changing the subject to the all-campus convocation scheduled for the next day. The other group members made a few comments before Amber talked again for about 10 minutes, this time focusing on how discouraged she had become because she just could not bring herself to even try to like her math professor. One of the other students, Rachel, said that she thought it sounded like a bad attitude all the way around. Then there was silence. Dr. Cummings had been watching the group members awkwardly fumble around when it seemed like everyone was suddenly aware that it was very quiet.

## CRITICAL INCIDENT

DR. CUMMINGS: I just lost you all there. I had the sense that Amber was trying to talk about something meaningful to her, but I wonder what happened with the rest of you.

RACHEL: You don't have to like your professor to learn something.

AMBER: Oh, and I suppose you like all of your professors!

RACHEL: I didn't say that. Just—you don't have to like them.

PAULA: I like *my* professors, just not the grades I got last semester! I even like the convocations that are coming up. Plus, the Activities Board is hosting a card party!

DR. CUMMINGS: Let's stop right here and take a minute to sit quietly. I think many of you are on different pages and it would be helpful here if we could all get on the same page for this hour and a half.

## WHAT TECHNIQUE DO YOU CHOOSE?

Individually or in small groups jot down or discuss several options for what technique you would use in this situation. What factors must be considered?

## STEPS TOWARD SELECTING A TECHNIQUE

Here is our thinking:

### Step 1: Identify the group type and purpose, best practice area, and developmental stage

This is a counseling group for students to work together in identifying issues in their lives on a residential college campus that have negatively affected their academics. Because it is only the third meeting, the group is considered in its beginning stage of development. The best practice area of processing within sessions will allow the group leader to focus on the group's lack of movement and poor cross communication between members.

### Step 2: Analyze the presenting situation by applying ecological concepts

Dr. Cummings is aware of the difficulty these students are having coming to a group that exists because of their poor academic performance. In her initial interviews with the students they had expressed embarrassment because they all had professed to be very good students in high school. Dr. Cummings knows how important her leader function is especially with regard to meaning attribution, or helping the students make meaning of the experience to promote future academic success. As the leader she knows there is value in the collaboration of the students to discover and discuss the issues of transitioning into a residential college.

Though early in the group's formation, Dr. Cummings intends to help the students process what they say in a way that is not only meaningful, but also assists the interconnection among the group members. A particularly important skill to gain from the group interaction is clear and appropriate communication in member-to-member exchanges. This skill is one that is sustainable in all of their college experiences. Remembering what influences are external as well as within the group, Dr. Cummings wants to do what she can to enhance the context in which the students and leader are working together.

### Step 3: Review possible group techniques, considering focus and level

There could be many reasons for a group to get "stuck." Although Dr. Cummings wants to allow plenty of free time for members to discuss their issues, this incident appears to have some members stuck. At this point, however, Dr. Cummings is not clear on what is happening. She wonders if the group members are feeling stuck, or if it is only her perception. Maybe they are working in their own way.

***Processing Within Toolbox #4,*** My Group Experience. Allow members to express their feelings about being in a group (or being forced into a group).

*Focus:* Cognitive and affective.

*Level:* Individual and group.

This technique illustrates collaborating with members by engaging them in discussing their experience in the group, emphasizing the naming of their feelings about it.

***Processing Within Toolbox #13,*** My Expectations. Using a modified version of the technique (which focuses only on silent members), have each member face the group and say, "When I look at you all I think you expect me to . . ." This technique is for exploring members' expectations of others.

*Focus:* Cognitive, affective, and behavioral.

*Level:* Individual, interpersonal, and group.

Perhaps there is a need for a slightly different approach in engaging these students in group processing. Dr. Cummings thinks the group is stuck, but she has yet to check that out with the group members.

### Step 4:   Select a best-fit technique

Both techniques seem appropriate in having all of the group members begin a discussion about their group experience so far. The first technique, #4, simply asks the students to discuss their feelings about the group. It would be an effective technique to get the students focused on what is happening within the group context, and putting themselves into it through exploring the members' emotional impact on one another. The second technique, #13, offers a different way of discussing what meaning the group has for the students. It encourages deeper reflection by asking members to clearly state how they understand the group is to work together. Out of this dialogue might come an improved understanding.

### Step 5:   Implement and evaluate how well the technique worked

DR. CUMMINGS:    Let's stop right here and take a minute to sit quietly. I think many of you are on different pages and it would be helpful here if we could all get on the same page for this hour and a half.

PAULA:    I'm sorry. I know I went off track there, but I feel so restless today.

DR. CUMMINGS:    I am going to start by telling you how I am experiencing this group right now. What I want you to do is pay attention to your feelings right now and about this group so far. I'll go first and you can see what I mean. Right now I am feeling concern and some anxiety. This group has been very exciting for me, but right now I think we might be stuck.

RACHEL:    (*eagerly*) I don't feel stuck. I feel really tired, but I'm always tired. I know that I am not in a good mood tonight. I do like coming to this group, though I still feel pretty embarrassed.

## If in a Class or Workshop, Then:

### *Practice the choice*

Pair up with another student and try out your choices. Give each other feedback. What might work? What might need to be changed? Compare your choices with those provided by the authors.

### Process the choice

What have you learned? What are you learning about this process for selecting group techniques? What are you learning about yourself as a group leader? What might you be able to use the next time?

---

## PROCESSING (WITHIN) CI 8.2

Group Type: *Counseling*
Best Practice Area: *Within-Session Processing*
Group Developmental Stage: *Ending*

## *Looking Back, What Has Happened Here?*

### HISTORY

This counseling group is in its 15th and final 2-hour session. The group's purpose is to help its eight members (five females, three males) become more comfortable and effective in their interpersonal communication and to help them feel less socially isolated in their lives. Led by two staff counselors of the university counseling center, this group has been characterized by ups and downs, with long silences and ragged interactions, but also it has been marked by improving comfort levels among members and some gains in communication skills overall. In short, a lot has happened over the previous 14 sessions and the leaders, Fred and Jennifer, are looking forward to helping the members process these events and their experiences.

In their planning for this last session, Jennifer and Fred were uncertain about how to open the final session. Was the group developed enough that a fairly simple, group-oriented, open-ended question might generate processing interaction? Or, would a planned structured technique be more facilitative? They decided to proceed with an open-ended invitation, having assessed the group and its members to be ready for that kind of unstructured technique.

At the start of the last session, after some preliminary small talk, Jennifer begins, drawing from the relatively open-ended within-session technique #17, My Learning.

### CRITICAL INCIDENT

JENNIFER:  We've come a long way together since our first session. Fred and I are wondering if we might take some time now to look back. What have we learned?

(*There is a long, uncomfortable silence.*)

JENNIFER:  Hmmm . . . I am wondering what to make of this long silence. What's going on? Anyone willing to share?

(*Shorter silence*)

BILL:  (*a group member, with anger in his voice*) This just isn't working for me! I've got some stuff to say to some of you here, and I'd like to get to it!

## WHAT TECHNIQUE DO YOU CHOOSE?

Individually or in small groups jot down or discuss several options for what technique you would use in this situation. What factors must be considered?

## STEPS TOWARD SELECTING A TECHNIQUE

Here is our thinking:

### Step 1:  Identify the group type and purpose, best practice area, and developmental stage

To review, this is a counseling group of eight university students in its final session and with a focus on helping members become more socially comfortable and skilled.

### Step 2:  Analyze the presenting situation by applying ecological concepts

As we have seen, all ecological concepts are always relevant and important. Moreover, they interact with each other and do not stand as independent factors. In this case, the final session raises meaning making and sustainability as the most significant. At this time, leaders need to be especially concerned with helping members learn from their group experience and develop plans for implementing strategies in their ongoing life experience. This is not the time to bring up new material, but to review and consolidate what has come before, with an eye to sustained application outside the group.

### Step 3:  Review possible group techniques, considering focus and level

A number of relatively unstructured techniques may be considered in relation to this incident (see within-session techniques #8 and #34 as examples). Let us examine one of those techniques.

***Processing Within Toolbox #8,*** Diversion Tactics. Divert attention from one member by addressing group behavior and reactions.

*Focus:* Affective and cognitive.
*Level:* Individual and group.

Here, the leaders might choose to encourage a shift from Bill's affect to the thoughts and feelings of others in the group. This unstructured technique might be used as a way to resist the surge to bring up new emotional material at the "final hour" of the group through enlisting input from others that might be more centered on integration rather than on stimulating new affect.

***Processing Within Toolbox #34,*** Rearview Mirror. This technique is semistructured. It asks members to imagine they are in a car that is being driven (by them or someone else) away from the group immediately following the last session;

all the other members are visible through the rearview mirror. What would you like to say to members about what you have learned from them or from the group itself? There is still time to say it now in the group.

*Focus:* Cognitive.
*Level:* Individual.

### Step 4:   Select a best-fit technique

As is often the case, either of these techniques (or others) are appropriate and might work. The first has the advantage of being simple, and it seeks to pull others into the discussion. It could be modified to invite contributions that are restricted to looking back, not to generate new ones. The semistructured option of the Rearview Mirror is a bit more complex, using visualization to reframe the initial question, and it affords the chance to refocus consideration around what already has been gained rather than developing new material. In both cases, it would be necessary to acknowledge Bill's contribution and feelings but not to get misdirected in the final moments of the group to consider previously uncharted territory. Misdirection would lower a technique's usefulness and lead to a number of negative side effects, including not having enough time to work through newly presented emotional content.

### Step 5:   Implement and evaluate how well the technique worked

BILL:   (*a group member, with anger in his voice*) This just isn't working for me! I've got some stuff to say to some of you here, and I'd like to get to it!

FRED:   You've got some important and, it sounds like, *new* things to say, Bill . . . but, we just are out of time for new things—we couldn't do justice to them. So, can you stay with us here as we look to what we have learned so far from each other and the group, what we might be able to use outside as this group closes down?

BILL:   Maybe I should learn to speak up sooner, don't know. Anyway, what do you have in mind?

FRED:   Okay, good. Let's try it this way. Can each of you close your eyes and imagine for about 5 minutes that you are in a car, driving away from this last session and you see in the rearview mirror all other members of the group standing on the sidewalk outside as you pull away. What have you learned from everyone, from the group? What can you take from here and use with friends, family, on campus? Can you note those things, and we will come back for a discussion during the last few minutes of our time together.

(*Allow 5 minutes for visualization.*)

FRED:   Okay, now open your eyes and come back to our discussion. Good . . . Bill, I wonder if we might start back with you now. What are you taking from us?

## If in a Class or Workshop, Then:

### *Practice the choice*

Pair up with another student and try out your choices. Give each other feedback. What might work? What might need to be changed? Compare your choices with those provided by the authors.

### Process the choice

What have you learned? What are you learning about this process for selecting group techniques? What are you learning about yourself as a group leader? What might you be able to use the next time?

---

PROCESSING (WITHIN) CI 8.3

Group Type: *Psychoeducation*
Best Practice Area: *Within-Session Processing*
Group Developmental Stage: *Beginning*

## *Feelings About Diversity*

### HISTORY

Over the last decade, Torville has grown from a largely rural, homogeneous community into an ethnically diverse city suburb. Contributing to a major population increase in the past four years and to the shift in the cultural demographic are two factors: a significant influx of immigrants from Mexico and Puerto Rico, and the relocation of over 100 families from Japan due to the recent opening of a Japanese-owned manufacturing plant.

Concerned about the impact of the rapid ethnic shift on the students and faculty of Torville's public schools, the district superintendent consults with Dalmar and Vana, school counselors from a neighboring district who have led pscyhoeducation groups focusing on this issue. Subsequently, the school board have invited Dalmar and Vana to lead a series of day-long groups devoted to helping faculty and staff consider the implications around ethnic diversity and its impact on group processes in the classroom.

Because it is summer break, faculty and staff are given free continuing education hours for their required participation in one of these psychoeducation groups, which is limited to 24 people. A day-long session begins with Dalmar and Vana giving a 1-hour interactive lecture, after which participants are divided into two subgroups, each facilitated by one of the counselors. The next two hours are spent processing the lecture content and the implications for the classroom. The afternoon component follows a similar format.

Following one morning's mini-lecture titled "Myths Concerning Culturally Diverse Groups," Dalmar facilitates a subgroup of five male and six female teachers. All the males have been teaching for at least 15 years; one is a retired history teacher who is filling in for a teacher on health leave. The female teachers, all hired within the last six years, include two Latina Americans and one Asian Americans, all hired in part for their bilingual skills.

### CRITICAL INCIDENT

Though Dalmar has a curriculum developed to guide the discussion, he begins with an open-ended question to assess the group's readiness to work on the material just presented.

DALMAR: All right, to begin our discussion, I'd really be interested in your responses to what you've just heard. Anyone have anything they'd like to say about the opening presentation? Any thoughts that came to mind on the myths we identified? Perhaps something that occupied your thinking?

FRANK: (*math teacher*) I get what you're saying. It's just that—well, I don't really see what this stuff has to do with helping students learn that parallel lines never intersect or that multiplying two negative numbers gives you a positive. Sure, language can be a barrier to learning the necessary facts. But other than that, I just don't see how having this discussion about cultural differences will make any difference on exam day. (*Raising a hand apologetically*) Nothing against you, you gave a great talk. But to be perfectly honest, I question why we have to sit through a whole day of this crap.

(*Without a pause, another teacher builds on Frank's statement.*)

JERRY: (*starting to talk almost before Frank has finished his sentence*) I'll second that. I'd like to know where they come up with money for something like this, and they can't find money for new lab equipment. I've been doing group projects with my students for the last 12 years, and I don't think that cultural diversity really has any effect on how the teams work together. In fact, from my experience I'd say that's the natural order of things—for the cultural groups to work together, I mean. Ya know, the Japanese students helping each other, the Spanish-speaking students teaming up, and so on.

(*As Jerry speaks, Dalmar scans the group and notices that all the female teachers are either looking at the floor or watching him. On the opposite side of the circle, Aaron, the retired history teacher, shifts uncomfortably in his chair.*)

SUSANA: (*Spanish-speaking art teacher, speaking confidently and with obvious spirit*) Why do we have to sit through this crap? The natural order of things? What the hell kind of comments are those? (*looking directly at Jerry*) Yeah, and you think things are going fine in your classes when all you're doing is encouraging unhealthy cliques. How does that help students learn to live in a multicultural world, I'd like to know? (*turning toward Dalmar*) I'd say this is going to be an interesting next couple of hours.

## WHAT TECHNIQUE DO YOU CHOOSE?

Individually or in small groups jot down or discuss several options for what technique you would use in this situation. What factors must be considered?

## STEPS TOWARD SELECTING A TECHNIQUE

Here is our thinking:

### Step 1:  Identify the group type and purpose, best practice area, and developmental stage

Dalmar and Vana are conducting a psychoeducation group to help faculty and staff of a public school system explore the implications of diversity and its effect on group processes in the classroom. To allow an opportunity for all group members to participate, the two counselor-facilitators have opted to split the initial group of 24 into two smaller groups for the postlecture processing time. Though previous working relationships likely exist among many of the members, with respect to this group and the current objectives, members are developmentally in the beginning stage of performing.

### Step 2:  Analyze the presenting situation by applying ecological concepts

As we have often stated throughout this text, context is everything. Torville, a long-established and relatively stable community, is experiencing rapid growth and a significant shift in the ethnic and cultural makeup of the exploding population. To address concerns about the healthy adjustment of faculty, staff, and students to this shift, the school system has asked Dalmar and Vana to lead psychoeducation groups for the faculty and staff. A one-day group is perhaps limiting, but that constraint is typical of the less-than-ideal contexts and circumstances in which group facilitators must often do their work.

Even an experienced group leader can feel overwhelmed and uncertain in the face of a powerful reaction, such as the comments prompted by Dalmar's opening question in the critical incident just described. Faced with a group that could potentially implode before it begins, Dalmar might well be thinking, "Uh-oh, that didn't go at all like I'd expected. Where in the world do I go from here?" However, we suggest that Dalmar and the group have learned how meaning is being attributed to the group experience and to the topic of diversity by at least three of the participants. And although we cannot be sure what meaning other group members may be drawing from the experience, including the verbal comments already voiced, their body language does provide Dalmar with evidence that suggests other participants besides Susana may disagree with the views Frank and Jerry have expressed. Although in terms of time together the group is still in the earliest stages of development, the topic of cultural diversity has already elicited strong feelings and opinions from several participants. By considering options that would harness the energy of the members who have been bold enough to speak candidly, Dalmar would likely gain perspective on how to proceed, while at the same time bringing others into the process. All members need to connect to the topic and one another for the group to benefit fully from the individual strengths each member has to offer. Can Dalmar lead the group in a way that will create a unique social order, resulting in a community, in which varying opinions can be heard, not just those few that have been rather forcefully expressed so far?

In her response, Susana has directly challenged Frank's and Jerry's opinions. Although conflict is not undesirable, given the strength of the comments and the early stage the group is at in its development, Dalmar has a challenge ahead of him: giving value to the assertiveness of the members who have spoken, while at the same time guiding all the members to verbalize their opinions and feelings in a way that promotes the group's work during the remainder of its life (i.e., the rest of the day).

**Step 3:    Review possible group techniques, considering focus and level**

***Processing Within Toolbox #2,*** Process Points.

*Focus:* Cognitive.
*Level:* Group.

Using this technique, Dalmar takes control of the situation very quickly, realizing that the group has not had any time to establish ground rules and so on. At the same time as he acknowledges that several group members have shared some valuable information that would make for a great discussion, Dalmar suggests it would be helpful for each person to contribute a rule that might guide comments and conversation as the group continues to process the topic of cultural diversity. Members then have several minutes to come up with and then share a rule with the others. Consensus is required for a rule to be adopted. With these agreed-upon guidelines in place, Dalmar asks that the initial conversation be repeated, but within the boundaries of the group rules.

***Processing Within Toolbox #5,*** Say It Another Way.

*Focus:* Cognitive.
*Level:* Group.

In a slightly different application of this technique, Dalmar takes a less direct leader role. After first giving value to the comments of the three members by acknowledging their honesty, he then asks the group to collectively consider the advantages of stating thoughts and feelings in a manner that allows for feedback from other group members. For example, Dalmar points out that Jerry could state his position in a way that concludes with a statement inviting feedback, such as "I'm wondering if any of you want to respond to what I've just said."

**Step 4:    Select a best-fit technique**

Dalmar elects to use the Process Points technique. The group is at a critical point. Whereas Dalmar believes that the energy of the few members who have shared their reactions verbally can benefit the group, he also realizes the need to establish some guidelines quickly, before further discussion. He believes that bringing all the members into the process will promote the group's development and sustainability throughout the remainder of the day. This technique is simply executed and allows the group to quickly put important rules in place. Although an unintended side effect of this technique might be the loss of here-and-now energy, providing a structure for the group through the process of consensus building offers the greater benefit of promoting group collaboration. Another side effect might be extended discussions about proposed rules. Dalmar will need to take a proactive role in moving the group quickly through this process, acknowledging members' contributions while heading off extended discussions of proposed roles.

### Step 5.   Implement and evaluate how well the technique worked

DALMAR:   (*holding up a hand*) I need to interrupt and put this discussion on hold for a few minutes. (*looks around the group*) Will you let me do that?

(*Group members who were looking down or looking away from the group now turn toward Dalmar.*)

DALMAR:   Thanks. Okay, now—Frank, Jerry, Susana—first, let me say that I really appreciate your honest responses and the energy you've invested in our discussion already by stating your beliefs so strongly. Believe me, every group needs that. But it can take awhile for everyone in a new group to get to that gut level of honesty. So if you can just hold on to that energy, I think we have the potential for a great day together. But I think we need to back up a bit—I'm sensing that as a group we may not all agree on the best way to transact our group business today. (*makes eye contact with Frank, Jerry, and Susana*) As you three were talking, I was trying to listen carefully to what you were saying, but also to what other group members might be saying—maybe not in so many words, but in their body language. What I saw—well, I noticed some people's body language saying that they were uncomfortable; maybe so uncomfortable that they were at the point of mentally walking away from the group. Whenever that happens—no question, the group always loses out. The rest of us can keep talking, but we're really missing out, losing really important contributions those members could make to our discussion. Am I making sense here? Everyone with me?

(*Some group members nod strongly or slightly; others appear attentive.*)

DALMAR: Okay—thanks for sticking with me. So, here's what I'd like to suggest, with everyone's permission. I'd like us to take a few minutes while each of you comes up with one rule that you think would be helpful for us to follow as a group. For example, we've already been doing a good job of respecting the person who is speaking. No one has talked over anyone else.

JACKIE:   (*science teacher*) Yes—exactly what I was thinking. It would really be helpful to have some ground rules in place, or well, you know what can happen in these "hot topic" discussions. We all spout off our opinions, but we never get past that to any kind of resolution or even finding a bit of common ground. Look, I'll be honest, too. I could really use some help. I've got more students per class than I've ever had before. If I can't help students learn to get along with each other and respect each other—I guess what I'm saying here is that I could use some effective tools for my classroom, to help me teach better and help the kids learn better.

AARON:   (*hesitantly*) Ummm—I'm not exactly sure what my position is here. I'd like to add something but, well, I'm just a substitute for the year and . . .

FRANK: Geez, Aaron, you've been around here longer than any of us. (*looking around the group with a half smile*) To tell the truth, you were teaching students in this district before some of us were born.

AARON: (*looking toward Dalmar*) Maybe we're getting a little ahead of ourselves again. Should we try to agree on some basic rules first? (*turning toward Frank*) And once we're settled on that, well—then I'll tell you what I've been thinking.

(*With Dalmar leading the discussion, the group develops a set of rules that include respecting opinions that are different, avoiding derogatory language, and stopping every 30 minutes to see who has not had a chance to participate.*)

FRANK: Okay, Aaron, it's been bugging me. What did you want to tell us earlier?

AARON: (*slowly rolling up his left sleeve, a serious, thoughtful look on his face*) Frank, Jerry, remember back when people would ask me every spring why I kept wearing long-sleeved shirts even after the weather got warm—especially back when the AC in the schools didn't work well—or didn't work at all? And I would make that joke about the sun giving me freckles? (*Jerry and Frank nod.*) It was a lie. I started saying that because I didn't want people to think of me as different—exclude me— and I kept telling the same lie even after I knew better. (*holding out his arm to show the tattoo*) I'm an Auschwitz survivor. That's what I was thinking about earlier—back when Dalmar and Vana were first talking— thinking that we can either welcome people who are different from us or maybe end up hating them. I know I'm "old school" about some things in education, but this diversity stuff—it's important. If we can't help these kids learn to live together and work together in the classroom, well, I don't think we're doing our job.

DALMAR: (*speaking quietly*) Thanks . . . thank you, Aaron. I think you've given us a very good place to reenter the conversation we were having earlier about why this topic might be important.

## If in a Class or Workshop, Then:

### Practice the choice

Pair up with another student and try out your choices. Give each other feedback. What might work? What might need to be changed? Compare your choices with those provided by the authors.

### Process the choice

What have you learned? What are you learning about this process for selecting group techniques? What are you learning about yourself as a group leader? What might you be able to use the next time?

PROCESSING (WITHIN) CI 8.4

Group Type: *Psychoeducation*

Best Practice Area: *Within-Session Processing*

Group Developmental Stage: *Ending*

## *Hasn't This Group Made a Difference?*

### HISTORY

In an effort to improve student retention, Winslow State College established the Office of Student Retention (OSR). As a result of creative planning by OSR leadership, several academic advisors with backgrounds in counseling and group skills were hired to work with first-year students identified as at risk for not being retained beyond the first year. Typically, such students appear unmotivated and unsure about career aspirations, may be lacking in social skills, and often have not had the opportunity to develop the study habits necessary for success in college.

After considering successful retention programs, the OSR chose to implement the psychoeducation group format in working with at-risk first-year students. During the first semester, each group meets once a week for 90 minutes. With 8 to 10 students per group, the leaders use a curriculum that addresses an array of topics and themes such as study skills, test-taking strategies, time management, loneliness, and accessing campus resources.

The advisors leading the various groups spend time together each week engaged in peer supervision. As the end of the first semester approaches they are unanimous that the groups have provided a kind of assistance to students not achievable in more traditional one-on-one sessions. Students seem connected to each other, using the groups as a source of both social support and study partners. At the same time, common themes that have emerged during recent group meetings suggest that the students are experiencing growing anxieties about their academic performance and their ability to fit into the campus community.

### CRITICAL INCIDENT

Midway through one group meeting focused on preparing for finals week, the following conversation occurred, its themes representative of similar conversations in many of the other groups.

BRAD:       I don't know where the rest of you are at, but I'm really feeling like I don't have my act together for finals. I mean, like, I have a ton of reading to do, plus I'm pretty sure I'm gonna need at least a C on my biology final to even pass the class, and—I don't even want to think about what else.

SHANDRA:   Same here. Like last night, Adrian and I were up way late working on a project and I was *so-o* not wanting to be here today—I mean, I could use an hour of sleep 'cause I've got a lo-o-ong one comin' up tonight, too.

LLOYD:       (*the advisor and group leader*) I'm hearing a definite theme from several of you. I'm guessing that this is going to be a group consensus, but I'd like to make sure. Can we have a show of hands? Everyone agree with the comments we've had so far?

(*All students raise their hands except for Kendra.*)

LLOYD:       So Kendra, pretty gutsy of you to buck the general trend. Want to give us your take?

KENDRA:     Hey, don't get me wrong—I mean, sure, I've had my share of days when I've thought about skipping a group meeting. But then last week when we had another group project in psych and I was stuck with that dude again—you know, the one I told you about who was in one of these groups and bailed after midterms? Man, that guy doesn't know if he's coming or going! And I got to thinking about how I'd probably be right there with him if it wasn't for this group. (*scanning the others*) So what's with everybody? You all planning to check out *now*? I can't believe this!

(*Several seconds of silence follow.*)

LLOYD:       Seems like we're at an interesting point in the life of our group.

DENZEL:      Yeah—like the game's over—quitting time.

ADRIAN:      I'm there, too! Sorry, Kendra—it's been great and all, but . . .

KENDRA:     Come on—reality check! You all just said it: final projects, papers, exams breathing down our necks. So shouldn't we be talking about hanging together to get us all through the next 2 weeks—not talking about breaking up? Hasn't this group made a difference?

(*Again, silence follows.*)

## WHAT TECHNIQUE DO YOU CHOOSE?

Individually or in small groups jot down or discuss several options for what technique you would use in this situation. What factors must be considered?

## STEPS TOWARD SELECTING A TECHNIQUE

Here is our thinking:

### Step 1:   Identify the group type and purpose, best practice area, and developmental stage

Lloyd is an academic advisor leading a psychoeducation group. The purpose of the group is to help first-year college students who have been identified as being at risk for not being retained. The best practice area for this group is performing, as they are likely in the late stage of group development.

### Step 2:   Analyze the presenting situation by applying ecological concepts

Regardless of the type of group, points of conflict or difficulty are likely to surface, even during the later stages. This group is at just such a critical juncture, with all members but one indicating that other contextual or situational factors (e.g., the need to complete assignments and study for exams) are more pressing than maintaining the group. Lloyd is impressed by the implications of the preceding conversation. First, it reflects the emergence of a unique social system that is allowing members to freely discuss and express thoughts and opinions. Second, Lloyd is hearing members attach a sense of importance to studying and learning, an indication that sustainability may well be occurring, as members begin to take the group's work beyond the confines of the weekly discussions. As well, the study partnership between Adrian and Shandra suggests successful interconnection among group members. Last, Lloyd is fascinated to see how group members are attributing meaning to their experiences. On one hand, most group members appear to be saying, "We got what we came for. Now, can we move on and do this on our own?" However, at least one member is saying, "Yes, that's true. But we've got a critical time coming up and maybe we have our most important work as a group still ahead of us."

### Step 3:   Review possible group techniques, considering focus and level

Faced with this situation, Lloyd appreciates more than ever the peer supervision he has been receiving; he will certainly want to process this session with his colleagues. But for now, as the leader of the group, he needs to think quickly and help translate today's group energy into a positive growth opportunity. The members are discussing important aspects of their experiences both as part of this group and in the larger context of being college students. Thus, he is considering a technique with a focus in helping the group members connect cognitive processes with the decisions that they face. After all, it is their thought processes that appear to be concluding that the group should be canceled. As far as level is concerned, a technique that would target the individual, interpersonal, and group aspects would be helpful so that members could explore the implications of their current situation at each of these levels.

***Processing Within Toolbox #38,*** Grid for Experiences and Events in Group Work.

*Focus:* Cognitive and affective.
*Level:* Individual, interpersonal, and group.

In choosing this technique, Lloyd believes that the grid on which it is built will help group members identify and clarify not only what is happening, but also how it is taking place. He is also thinking that this technique begins to help the members not merely make sense of what is currently occurring, but becomes a much needed process as they begin the important task of termination: reviewing, analyzing, discussing, and drawing meaning from key experiences and events that have occurred in the group.

Tersely, the group members are asked to complete a grid in which horizontal labels ask for "What" and "How" information. For example, the group's discussing anxiety around taking tests would be the "What" and talking one at a time might be an example of "How." Vertical labels of "I," "You," "We," and "Us" require the members to ask at what level the "What" and "How" occurred. After members have completed their respective grids, they share them with the other members. Among other factors, what often emerges is clarification in how members are making meaning of events and experiences.

Lloyd believes that this group technique could focus the current incident to help the members understand processes and events and lead them to more informed decisions concerning the life of the group.

***Processing Within Toolbox #39,*** Systems-Centered Subgrouping.

*Focus:* Cognitive and affective.
*Level:* Interpersonal and group.

In the techniques toolbox, we also placed this technique within the performing category. As with many techniques, this one has multiple uses, just as a carpenter's tool can be used in different ways, depending on the particular task at hand. In this group context, Systems-Centered Subgrouping requires group members to process other members' comments. Additionally, the group leader hopes this technique will help members grapple with ecological concepts in a mutually supportive way.

Particularly, Systems-Centered Subgrouping is founded on the assumption that the basic units of a group are its functional subgroups—in themselves a type of interconnection. Once a subgroup appears—such as that represented by Brad, Shandra, and Denzel in their common desire not to be in the group—a group leader can see that subgroup as a fulcrum for change, which in this case might be utilized for growth, thus avoiding a fight–flight response from that group's members. Systems subgrouping calls for a communication style that a leader can readily encourage. For example, as Lloyd identifies the subgroup of Brad, Shandra, and Denzel, he might want to help the group recognize these three members as a valid subgroup and then invite other group members to join the subgroup as a way of identifying with those members and the stance they share. Such a strategy allows the entire group to process the situation because all members must discriminate among, communicate, and integrate perceptions of differences. Likewise, Lloyd could encourage any member who is connecting with Kendra, even slightly, to enter into a discussion with her about the points on which they agree.

### Step 4:  Select a best-fit technique

In addition to focusing the discussion, the Grid for Experiences and Events in Group Work helps the members of the group make meaning in a contextual manner. As a technique, it is also particularly suitable for allowing members to reflect on what is happening in the current moment, as well as facilitating a transition into appropriate termination processes in a way that promotes sustainability. In addition to satisfactorily addressing what group members are expressing, the grid facilitates reflection on the depth of the relationships built as a result of the group. The technique is efficient, requiring little in the way of additional resources; however, Lloyd will need to spend some time explaining it to the group. One possible side effect, then, is that the time utilized to outline the technique could allow the current energy of the group to dissipate.

### Step 5:   Implement and evaluate how well the technique worked

Based on these considerations, here is what we might try:

KENDRA:   Come on—reality check! You all just said it: final projects, papers, exams breathing down our necks. So shouldn't we be talking about hanging together to get us all through the next two weeks—not talking about breaking up? Hasn't this group made a difference?

(*Again, silence follows.*)

LLOYD:   Okay, group, we have a couple of possibilities as to where we go from here. One choice we have is to simply go along with the majority and dismiss the group for today—or even for the rest of the semester. But all of us have invested a lot of time and energy in this group over the last few months, and I think we'd be doing ourselves a disfavor by going our separate ways without reflecting on what's happened in this group since we've been together. So I'd like to suggest we try an approach that can help us get beyond the content of our conversation so far today, and help us understand how we're doing as a group—even help us see how the choices that have been put on the table might impact us individually, interpersonally, and as a whole group. If we're all prepared to do what I have in mind, then I think it will also give us a good way to begin to wrap things up for the group, because we have only two sessions left. Will you go with me on this?

DENZEL:   (*groaning dramatically*) Arrrggghh! I *knew* you were going to come up with something like this. I guess we've been together long enough to have *you* figured out. (*Denzel rolls his eyes, and several other members of the group look at each other, grinning.*)

LLOYD:   (*smiling*) So, can I take that as a yes?

DENZEL:   Yeah—sure, why not? I mean, hey, we're here, and maybe that says something about us, too—so maybe it wouldn't be such a bad thing to talk about, ya know, "us"—the group—where we've been at and all. Maybe Kendra has a point about it being important for us to stick together right now—make sure no one totally loses it in the middle of all this end-of-semester hell.

ADRIAN:   Yeah, like maybe we could talk about what happens next semester—when we don't have this group any more? So we've learned something about how to study. But, well, say I get this professor and I'm having a tough time understanding him because of his foreign accent—how am I gonna deal with that when I don't have somewhere like this to vent?

KENDRA:   I've already said my piece—I'm for anything that keeps us working together. You've always had our back.

LLOYD:   Denzel? The rest of you? What are you thinking about all this?

DENZEL:   No skin off your nose, Lloyd, but I'm still thinkin' I'd rather be doing something else. And here I am anyway—this is what I've gotta do to get ahead, so I'm doin' it. Lay it on, man—let's get going.

LLOYD:    (*looking around the room and seeing no objection*) You know, what's happened here tonight—that didn't occur magically. Just the fact that people felt like they could be pretty honest and blunt about what they thought—that's a big thing. And it happened because of the work we've been doing this semester—individually, interpersonally, as a whole group—all of it. There's a grid we can use that will help us chart the work we're doing tonight, along with what we've done in the past. I think if we work through this together, it'll give us a sense of where we are, how we got here, and to start to answer your really great question, Adrian, what this all means for you as you head into these next 2 weeks and start to think about next semester.

DENZEL:    This is starting to sound like math! Do I need a graphing calculator? No, seriously, keep going. I can handle it.

LLOYD:    Hey, thanks for that vote of confidence! Okay, to give it to you in short form—here is what the grid contains: across the top, the focus dimensions refer to *what* we talk about (for example, we just discussed being here versus not being here) and the *how* dimension refers to *how* we talked (like we talked one at a time, or some of us were pretty intense, but others weren't taking the topic very seriously). That kind of thing. We each talked one at a time or some of us were very serious while others were lighthearted and not serious about the topic. Down the side of the grid, the *level* dimension identifies what part of the group was involved. (I, you, us, we, as in more than one of us) and us (as in the whole group). All right, now, let's try this out. Last week we talked about strategies you could use in preparing for comprehensive examinations. As I'm sure you all remember, it was a pretty hot topic, and after my presentation we had a unique discussion. Here . . . each of you grab a piece of paper, make a grid like this, and going by what you remember, jot down what seemed important to you. Try and complete the eight cells. Then we'll share what we have.

## If in a Class or Workshop, Then:

### Practice the choice

Pair up with another student and try out your choices. Give each other feedback. What might work? What might need to be changed? Compare your choices with those provided by the authors.

### Process the choice

What have you learned? What are you learning about this process for selecting group techniques? What are you learning about yourself as a group leader? What might you be able to use the next time?

## In Sum

Events and experiences occur during group sessions sometimes at near-warp speed, sometimes at what seems to be a snail's pace—and at all points in between. Rest assured that group members nearly always can benefit from some way to stop the action and examine the meaning of within-session activity.

Why? Because learning and change are as much a result of reflecting as about doing. A different way to state this point is that learning and change result from continual cycles of reflecting-on-doing. Group leaders need to develop effective and appropriate ways to produce reflective action within group sessions, while empowering members to become adept at this process themselves. Within-session processing techniques can provide helpful direction to assist members in gaining these necessary reflective skills.

## References

Association for Specialists in Group Work. (1998). *Asso-ciation for Specialists in Group Work best practice guidelines*. Retrieved from http://www.asgw.org

Conyne, R. (1997). Developing framework for processing experiences and events in group work. *Journal for Specialists in Group Work, 22*, 167–174.

Conyne, R. (1999). *Failures in group work: How we can learn from our mistakes*. Thousand Oaks, CA: Sage.

Conyne, R., Wilson, F. R., & Ward, D. (1997). *Comprehensive group work: What it means and how to teach it*. Alexandria, VA: American Counseling Association.

Cox, J., Banez, L., Hawley, L., & Mostade, J. (2003). Use of reflecting team process in the training of group workers. *Journal for Specialists in Group Work, 28*, 89–105.

Cummings, A. (2001). Teaching group process to counseling students through the exchange of journal letters. *Journal for Specialists in Group Work, 26*, 7–16.

DeLucia-Waack, J. (1997). The importance of processing activities, exercises, and events to group work practitioners. *Journal for Specialists in Group Work, 22*, 82–84.

Glass J., & Benshoff, J. (1999). PARS: A processing model for beginning group leaders. *Journal for Specialists in Group Work, 24*, 15–26.

Hall, J., & Hawley, L. (2004). Interactive process notes: An innovative tool in counseling groups. *Journal for Specialists in Group Work, 29*, 193–205.

Hanson, P. (1972). What to look for in groups. In J. Pfeiffer & J. Jones (Eds.), *1972 annual handbook for group facilitators* (pp. 21–24). La Jolla, CA: University Associates.

Kees, N., & Jacobs, E. (1990). Conducting more effective groups: How to select and process group exercises. *Journal for Specialists in Group Work, 15*, 21–29.

Lieberman, M., Yalom, I., & Miles, M. (1973). *Encounter groups: First facts*. New York: Basic Books.

Stockton, R., Morran, K., & Nitza, A. (2000). Processing group events: A conceptual map for leaders. *Journal for Specialists in Group Work, 25*, 343–355.

Ward, D., & Litchy, M. (2004). The effective use of processing in groups. In J. DeLucia-Waack, D. Gerrity, C. Kalodner, & M. Riva (Eds.), *Handbook of group counseling and psychotherapy* (pp. 104–119). Thousand Oaks, CA: Sage.

Yalom, I. (1975). *The theory and practice of group psychotherapy*. New York: Basic Books.

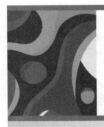

# 9

# Processing Techniques to Use Between Group Sessions or Meetings

**ADVANCE ORGANIZER**

This chapter contains the following material:

**Value of Between-Session Processing**

**History of Neglect**

**Implementing Between-Session Processing**

**Deep Processing as One Method**

**Critical Incident Training in Between-Session Processing**

CRITICAL INCIDENTS

CI 9.1: "Supervisor-Supervisee Conflict"
   Group type: *Psychoeducation*
   Best Practice Area: *Between-Session Processing*
   Group Developmetal Stage: *Middle*

CI 9.2: "Listening to Group Members"
   Group Type: *Counseling*
   Best Practice Area: *Betweem-Session Processing*
   Group Developmental Stage: *Beginning*

CI 9.3: "Reminiscence Group"
   Group Type: *Counseling*
   Best Practice Area: *Between-Session Processing*
   Group Developmental Stage: *Ending*

CI 9.4: "The Hour is Late"
   Group Type: *Counseling*
   Best Practice Area: *Between-Session Processing*
   Group Developmental Stage: *Ending*

**In Sum**

## Value of Between-Session Processing

Chapter 8 discussed techniques that group leaders can use within group sessions or meetings to help members process events and experiences, thereby accelerating and deepening learning. Within-session processing is very important. It also has received considerably more attention than the focus of this chapter—*between-session* processing.

Leaders need to engage in between-session processing because it provides a means for them to review and reflect on how their group is going and how they are performing in it. When a coleadership model is being used (which we usually recommend), between-session processing provides an invaluable opportunity for generating leader feedback and for reflecting together on group events.

For instance, we cannot easily count the number of times we have been perplexed about a group session, asking ourselves, "What in the world happened there?" Meeting with our coleader or supervisor to focus on the session prior to the next one often has helped sort out the session's events in a helpful way and identify how to proceed in a positive direction.

## History of Neglect

In truth, however, general group practice has tended not to systematically include between-session processing, to the detriment of effective group leading. Why has between-session processing not been a common practice for group leaders? First, its value was not routinely taught during training and it was not included in most textbooks. The focus of most group leadership training and of the professional literature was on performing group work, not on its planning or processing, as we have observed before. Second, between-session processing takes time, and time is something that is sorely lacking for most mental health and school counseling practitioners, who have so many other duties and responsibilities to deliver. Finally, and related to the dimension of time, practitioners and their schools and agencies function in an environment that demands production. For example, in mental health agencies client contact hours and revenue generation are frequent expectations, and in schools counselors' schedules are usually crammed with meetings and multiple other ongoing responsibilities. This emphasis on productivity too often restricts, or eliminates, sanctioned time available for important functions that may be viewed by administrators as being "nonproductive," such as between-session processing.

## Implementing Between-Session Processing

The advent of best practice guidelines, however, has led to the valuing of both planning and between-session processing. It is now understood, at least theoretically, that effective performance of group leadership also must incorporate planning and between-session processing. Therefore, training and the professional literature have been adapted to include these areas. So, as graduates move into the practice arena, they will allow increasing time for planning and between-session processing to occur.

Of course, leaders must set aside time for between-session processing, and then stick to the schedule. We recommend that a leader, or coleaders, plan to meet following each group meeting or session to review and reflect on group progress and on how leadership is proceeding. We have found from experience that roughly one hour of processing to two hours of group leading (1:2 ratio) seems to be both beneficial and feasible to accomplish within busy schedules. Of course, if more processing time can be made available, all the better!

This meeting might take place in various ways. A leader can process independently between sessions, making use of logs, letters, journals, or following some other form of guidance, such as the cognitive map suggested by Stockton et al. (2000). Weekly supervision is a familiar practice for counselors and, of course, it can be used to focus on group work. Coleaders can meet to engage in between-session processing, as we have stated, and this strategy is one that we have found to be particularly helpful.

## Deep Processing as One Method

However between-session processing is implemented, it is wise to follow a general strategy or model for guidance. We will summarize a model with which we are familiar, called deep processing (Conyne, 1999), that was developed specifically for between-session processing.

The deep processing model involves five steps, with each one becoming progressively deeper: (a) *transpose*, or accurately describe what happened in a previous group session or meeting, without any interpretation; (b) *reflect*, or add leader awareness of one's own thoughts, feelings, and sensations in relation to what occurred during the period being considered; (c) *discover*, or seek to integrate conceptual knowledge (i.e., relevant concepts, theory, and research) with observations and reflections; (d) *apply*, or try to link information produced through the first three steps of the model with what might be done in upcoming sessions; and (e) *evolve*, or intentionally identify group leader principles that would seem to be generalizable across group situations and would be usable in the future.

## Critical Incident Training in Between-Session Processing

What do group leaders need to know and be able to do between sessions or meetings in order to make sense of what is occurring in their groups? Following are critical incidents of between-session processing with counseling and psychoeducation groups. As with the critical incidents that have been presented earlier, they are intended to provide concrete experience with applying the PGTM in the selection and use of group techniques.

**CRITICAL INCIDENTS**

PROCESSING (BETWEEN) CI 9.1

Group Type: *Psychoeducation*
Best Practice Area: *Between-Session Processing*
Group Developmental Stage: *Middle*

## *Supervisor–Supervisee Conflict*

### HISTORY

This psychoeducation group was established to help college students manage and prevent stress more effectively. It has met for 8 of its planned 20 sessions.

The group is led by Ashley Terlesky, a licensed counselor who just began her position as staff counselor with the Harris State College Counseling Center this year. She is enthusiastic about counseling in general, but she feels somewhat less confident about her group-leading skills. Group was not emphasized in her counseling training.

Dick Fredericks is an experienced staff person who is respected for his competency in providing and in supervising individual counseling. He also has supervised groups for several years. Dick has felt for some time, though, that he was somewhat out of touch with developments in group work and in group supervision.

Ashley and Dick had been meeting in their weekly supervision sessions for six weeks now. Although the group seemed to be progressing satisfactorily, there has been some attrition and Ashley seemed to be uncertain how to focus on both stress management content and skills and how to balance that with attention to the process of the group. Dick was growing more impatient with what he saw as his own "blundering around," not being able to use a more coherent form of supervision with Ashley. He thought that "an old dog can always learn new tricks," and he wanted to find a more organized way to try out in his own supervision.

A few weeks ago Dick had registered for a continuing education two-day training workshop on group leadership supervision. He had told Ashley he was going to this training, and that he might bring back some of it to try out.

The method Dick learned is called Deep Processing (Conyne, 1999). It includes five interdependent steps that were described earlier.

Dick had found this deep processing approach interesting and promising. He liked how it helped organize a direction to proceed that did not demand learning new theory or techniques or require giving up one's own tried and true approaches to group work. He and Ashley had been using the deep processing approach for a couple of weeks now and were beginning to feel quite comfortable with it.

### CRITICAL INCIDENT

Dick welcomed Ashley to the ninth supervision session. They began their review of the last session using the deep processing model, by starting at Step 1, Transposing:

DICK:     So, Ashley, let's begin as we have been by you describing what happened during that session, okay?

ASHLEY:  Well, if it's all right, I'd much rather jump to a big issue that I'm not sure what to do about . . .

DICK:     Sure, we'll get to that, but let's go our usual way, starting with the events as they occurred.

ASHLEY:  You know, Dick, I like this model, but sometimes—like now—it feels too restrictive.

## WHAT TECHNIQUE DO YOU CHOOSE?

Individually or in small groups jot down or discuss several options for what technique you would use in this situation. What factors must be considered?

## STEPS TOWARD SELECTING A TECHNIQUE

Here is our thinking:

### Step 1:  Identify the group type and purpose, best practice area, and developmental stage

This solo-led psychoeducation group is at the middle stage of its development, where issues of connecting and producing generally are appropriate. Because we are focusing here on the best practice area of between-session processing, how the leader engages with her supervisor with group events and experiences from one session to another is the concern.

### Step 2:  Analyze the presenting situation by applying ecological concepts

Supervisor and supervisee are facing a conflict. How should they proceed? This conflict can be viewed as a positive event. As Ashley, the group leader, challenges Dick's application of the deep processing approach, it provides the opportunity to examine how they are doing, how application of the new model is going, what might be the best way to proceed, and how to make such decisions. If handled well, this challenge can strengthen the degree of interconnection they experience, can bolster their working collaboration, and can promote a clearer understanding of their social system. If handled poorly, fragmentation and frustration can occur.

Ashley exercised a choice to raise for consideration a different way of proceeding. This takes some courage, but it reflects a basic trust in the relationship that she perceives exists with her supervisor. Dick now has a choice: Does he exercise his authority as a supervisor to move ahead with his plan, thus reinforcing the social system being charted through the deep processing model, or does he choose to work with Ashley to adapt it? This choice may well influence the quality of their interconnection.

### Step 3:   Review possible group techniques, considering focus and level

***Processing Between Toolbox #9,*** Deep Processing Model.

*Focus:* Behavioral, affective, and cognitive.
*Level:* Group.

The deep processing model is found in Between–Session Processing Toolbox technique #9. Its five steps of transpose, reflect, discover, apply, and evolve are what Dick and Ashley are following. It provides an organized set of guidelines for reviewing and making choices about group-leader interventions. Yet, its sequential application is being questioned by Ashley at this point. She may need an adaptation.

***Processing Between Toolbox #11,*** Group Assessments. This technique addresses the importance of assessment and evaluation as these processes relate to accountability and self-discovery.

*Focus:* Structural, because the use of this technique calls for suspending the normal steps of the deep processing model to question what may be the most useful course of action at this point.
*Level:* Group.

### Step 4:   Select a best-fit technique

This may be a good time to review what is the best way to move ahead right now in supervision. Should the supervision process proceed as the model suggests? Or should the process be adjusted to fit the supervisee's current need? How this review takes place and what is decided will impact the present and future course of supervision, and of Ashley's group leadership itself.

What is the right way to proceed? There is a tension between maintaining fidelity with a model or theory and its adaptive application. There also may be a tension surrounding the perceived authority of a supervisor when a supervisee desires to behave discordantly. Values held by both the supervisor and the supervisee become important in helping resolve these actual and potential tensions.

Which approach being considered offers a more sufficient solution? Which one is more "on target," helping Ashley resolve her immediate questions while also providing a valid opportunity to review the previous group session?

What direction for supervision will provide the best possible outcome, both for supervision itself and even more important, for application by Ashley in the group she is leading? What choice will lead most directly to effective group leadership?

How do time and energy influence the decision to be made? Arriving at adaptations can take more of both elements, at least initially, than would moving straight ahead with the plan that had been constructed. Yet, in the longer range, perhaps a responsibly created adjustment might prove to be even less costly in terms of effort and time.

Proceeding with the first step of the model might reinforce a coherent method of working and maintain the regulated social system Dick and Ashley have established. Altering it to fit the situation, however, might allow for a kind of freedom that is needed, and allow both Dick and Ashley to feel more empowered to adapt the model as they see fit. Spending relatively more time focused on how to conduct supervision, as opposed to what the group may need, could negatively affect group leadership and member progress.

**Step 5:  Implement and evaluate how well the technique worked**

DICK:   Hmmm . . . Ashley, maybe we should just step back and talk a bit about what is best right now—I'm certainly open to that.

ASHLEY: Whew, I'm glad! Okay, that's good. Can I say that I really like this deep processing approach, but sometimes maybe we might just tweak it some, when that seems really necessary?

DICK:   Maybe like now? To start with what is really pressing for you, then to catch up with what's called for in the other steps? That sounds like a good way to go to me!

ASHLEY: Yes, that's it . . . great. So, here's what got me about the last session. I am tied up in knots about how to get at the stress prevention part of all this and to get people to learn from one another.

## If in a Class or Workshop, Then:

### Practice the choice

Pair up with another student and try out your choices. Give each other feedback. What might work? What might need to be changed? Compare your choices with those provided by the authors.

### Process the choice

What have you learned? What are you learning about this process for selecting Group techniques? What are you learning about yourself as a group leader? What might you be able to use the next time?

---

## PROCESSING (BETWEEN) CI 9.2

Group Type: *Counseling*
Best Practice Area: *Between-Session Processing*
Group Developmental Stage: *Beginning*

## *Listening to Group Members*

### HISTORY

Nurse Joiner, who started a psychoeducation group for her patients with adult onset diabetes, has a new problem. Although she had trouble getting the patients to attend regularly in the beginning, there is now a core group of seven who have asked for more counseling and less education in the group. The other two nurses suggested that Nurse Joiner find a coleader who could provide counseling, while she would be providing stability with her presence, and trust with her patients.

Initially, Nurse Joiner's reaction was disappointment because she had considered her educational programming to be quite sound. She included everything from diet information to basic anatomy and biology lessons. In her opinion, the patients had been very engaged and almost hungry for the information. The request for counseling now makes her nervous, because it would change the group purpose and she knows she is not qualified on her own. Her fellow nurses' suggestion to bring in a coleader is a good one, so Nurse Joiner feels somewhat resigned to the idea. She can't help but be concerned, though, about the best practices of changing the purpose of an existing group.

## CRITICAL INCIDENT

The three nurses have been meeting together for peer supervision each week. Their discussions are a very important part of Nurse Joiner's group experience so far, but her concerns may be outside this comfortable realm of experience the three women share.

NURSE JOINER:  It is time I made a decision about my diabetes group. Just think— I used to be so frustrated to even get the patients to come, and now they want more!

NURSE BLAIN:  (*one of the other parish nurses*) Your group really has made a difference!

NURSE JOINER:  Yes, I think so too, but I just don't know if I can simply change the goals and expectations without some other, perhaps more important, changes.

## WHAT TECHNIQUE DO YOU CHOOSE?

Individually or in small groups jot down or discuss several options for what technique you would use in this situations. What factors must be considered?

## STEPS TOWARD SELECTING A TECHNIQUE

Here is our thinking:

### Step 1:  Identify the group type and purpose, best practice area, and developmental stage

Nurse Joiner originally identified a need in her community, which has been effectively addressed in a group format. In fact, the group has been so effective that her group members want to pursue a deeper level of interaction, from a psychoeducation group to a counseling group. Processing with the two other nurses between sessions has been an important best practice supporting her role as a group leader, and emphasizing the value of supervision. Bringing in a coleader is the next important step, but Nurse Joiner is still concerned that she has more to do. The group is not in its beginning stage, except that as a counseling group it would change purpose and would have an additional leader, meaning that dynamics would change perhaps more than the members realize. Nurse Joiner is planning as though it will be a new group, beginning stage.

### Step 2:    Analyze the presenting situation by applying ecological concepts

The ecological concept of interconnection seems particularly relevant in thinking about a group of patients who have come together with similar health issues, but gained a strong bond of community, which they don't want to sever. Nurse Joiner created a social system in the group that has included collaboration with the members. They feel empowered to make a request to take the processing in the group to a deeper and more meaningful level.

The peer supervision with the other two parish nurses has been helpful to Nurse Joiner in emphasizing the clients' social context. As a relatively new group leader Nurse Joiner has developed several of her leadership skills, including attending to process in the group sessions. In terms of experience with counseling, she is aware of her ethical responsibility to discover an appropriate coleader. Her collaboration thus far with the other parish nurses and health care professionals in her community provide her with a sense of confidence in her ability to work with a coleader. Networking within the community has been an integral part of working with patients in a culture of low socioeconomic status, such as the one in which her clients live, so Nurse Joiner is aware of professionals with whom she can trust to continue to develop and sustain a positive experience for her clients.

### Step 3:    Review possible group techniques, considering focus and level

Facilitating a counseling group is a different role for a group leader than facilitating a psychoeducation group. Nurse Joiner is struggling with sharing her responsibility with a coleader and changing the group's purpose from a psychoeducation group to a counseling group. Leader dynamics, as well as overall group dynamics, will change.

***Processing Between Toolbox #8,*** Leader ABCDEthical. Use ABCDE worksheets to enhance ethical decision making (assessment, benefit, consequences and consultation, duty, education).

*Focus:* Cognitive.
*Level:* Individual and group.

This is an appealing technique for several reasons, but primarily because it aids in the discovery of ethical concerns. Nurse Joiner feels as if she needs help making a decision, too.

***Processing Between Toolbox #11,*** Group Assessments. Add group assessment and/or self-evaluation for accountability and self-discovery at the end of each session.

*Focus:* Cognitive, affective, and behavioral.
*Level:* Individual.

The assessment of her group to date may be helpful in analyzing in-depth the dynamics that have worked well, what has been so positive for her patients, and what she wants for her own role as a leader or as a coleader.

### Step 4:    Select a best-fit technique

Either technique is an organized way of reviewing and making choices about group leader interventions. With important decisions to make about the group's future, Nurse Joiner thinks the sequential application of the ABCDE technique would be especially helpful at this time. Supervision is a great place to discuss the components of the ABCDE technique, and it does not require familiarity so that all three parish nurses could brainstorm together through the decision-making components.

The other technique to do a group assessment also seems very appropriate in light of Nurse Joiner's indecision about changing the group type and leadership style. Having a coleader will be a new experience for Nurse Joiner, but it, too, is appealing, particularly as she is enjoying her growing group skills. Her reliance on supervision with the other two parish nurses has supported and sustained her until now. If the group changes, so will the supervision. What choice will lead most directly to effective group leadership and planning for the future?

Nurse Joiner is in the position to explore her own perspectives about the group's meaning for her community work. The ABCDE technique is a well-formatted evaluation that will allow Nurse Joiner to consider all of the important variables that she has identified in her decision about the group's future. Beginning with an analysis like this, Nurse Joiner may actually be empowered to increase her own commitment level to the group. The technique is focused carefully on aspects that include ethics in the decision-making process, which is the technique's highlight and would address all of the concerns that she has shared with her peers.

### Step 5:  Implement and evaluate how well the technique worked

NURSE JOINER:   I have had trouble making important decisions like this before, but I have an idea that will help. It would be great if you two could work through this with me, because I really value your input and you know me so well!

NURSE HILL:   Okay. What do you need right now to help you make these decisions?

NURSE JOINER:   I have a technique that you all might like anyway. It was developed to help in any decision-making process, but it is just what I need right now because it includes an ethical exploration.

NURSE BLAIN:   Sounds great! It seems like we run up on ethical choices several times a day. I, for one, would like to see this technique.

NURSE JOINER:   If we do it well, we may just learn something about ourselves along the way!

## If in a Class or Workshop, Then:

### *Practice the choice*

Pair up with another student and try out your choices. Give each other feedback. What might work? What might need to be changed? Compare your choices with those provided by the authors.

### *Process the choice*

What have you learned? What are you learning about this process for selecting group techniques? What are you learning about yourself as a group leader? What might you be able to use the next time?

> Group Type: *Counseling*
> Best Practice Area: *Between-Session Processing*
> Group Development Stage: *Ending*

## *Reminiscence Group*

### HISTORY

In North America the population of older adults is increasing as the elderly are living longer and baby boomers are aging. Consequently, there is a corresponding increase in the need for mental health services targeted to this important segment of society. Sasha and Lindy, two counselors at Sunshine Haven, a large retirement community, have responded by developing and implementing a 10-session reminiscence group. As the two have discovered, reminiscence groups can provide a context to help group members connect with each other, often leading to reduced social isolation and stress and an increase in well-being.

Sasha and Lindy are currently coleading a reminiscence group that shares many similarities with past reminiscence groups they have led together. Group members have enjoyed each two-hour group session and seem to have formed significant interpersonal relationships with each other. During the second half of session nine the theme "The Best Years of Our Lives" was introduced by the co-leaders as a way to focus group members' interactions. Although most members were lively and engaged in the topic, toward the end of the session Sasha and Lindy became aware of an emerging idea expressed by a few members. However, with only one session remaining, both coleaders are reticent to probe the group for possible meaning, particularly because the last session is for looking back over the work that has occurred during the first nine sessions—not for initiating new topics.

### CRITICAL INCIDENT

PAUL:    (*visibly happy*) Oh, how I remember the day I bought a color television! It was Christmas Eve, 1968. It took us almost a year to save the money. Marybeth and I had saved for almost a year. And I can still see my kids' faces as David—that's my oldest boy—helped me carry it in from the car and hook it up. And then, can you believe it? No sooner did we have it working, than *Rudolph, the Red-Nosed Reindeer* comes on. You should have seen us all sitting around there in the living room—eyes glued to that screen . . . (*wiping a tear from his left eye*) You'da thought we were the luckiest people in the world. Those were—yessiree—those were good days!

JESSE:    (*from across the room, in a negative tone*) Yeah, those were the good-ole days—not like now, nope, not at all. (*shaking his head*). . .

PAUL:    (*after several seconds of silence*) Well, like I was saying—those were good times, good times. But I'm sure you all have some memories, too—like mine?

LINDY:     Paul, thanks for sharing this meaningful event for you and I'm sure your family, too. We have time for one more. Anyone else?

LEA:       (*speaking slowly and softly*) Well . . . you all know by now that I'm the quiet one in this group. But Paul—when you were talking about your children's faces when you came home with that color TV, I was, I couldn't help but think of my parents' faces—that look of sheer joy—when I graduated from high school. It was way back in 1943, but just now it seemed like yesterday. None of you probably remember, but Congress had just repealed the Chinese Exclusion Act. I can't really imagine what they must have been feeling—I mean, I hadn't been through all that in the same way. But, but I knew—I just knew—that they were so proud of me getting my diploma and having a life ahead of me as an American citizen.

GLENDA:    (*echoing Jesse's earlier remarks in a dull tone*) Those *were* the days.

SASHA:     (*after a few seconds of silence, realizing that the allotted time for the group is up*) Well, group, time has gone quickly—like usual! And as you all know, next week will be our last session. So that means we'll likely spend most of our time trying to wrap up and make sense out of what has happened over the last several weeks—and talk some about what happens when this formal group ends.

(*As is their routine, Sasha and Lindy meet later that day to process the group session, using this time to plan for the next session—in this case, the last session.*)

LINDY:     Wow! What a group session!

SASHA:     You said it! So, where do we go from here? Any ideas how we can use the last session to process some of those things so that the take-away will be positive for the group?

LINDY:     I'm not sure what you are getting at. I mean, well, here's what I've been thinking about the last few sessions—what Jesse and Lea have been saying. I'm wondering if those feelings maybe really represent what the group as a whole was saying and we just didn't pick up on it and address what they were trying to express.

SASHA:     Yeah, I'd have to agree with you—but that still leaves us with the question of how we use the time we've got left now to plan for next week, the final session. Should we forge ahead with our typical agenda for the last group meeting? Or do you think we should spend our time today deciding if we should take things in another direction, you know? At least consider if a different approach might be helpful to the group, given today's dynamics.

## WHAT TECHNIQUE DO YOU CHOOSE?

Individually or in small groups jot down or discuss several options for what technique you would use in this situations. What factors must be considered?

## STEPS TOWARD SELECTING A TECHNIQUE

Here is our thinking:

### Step 1:   Identify the group type and purpose, best practice area, and developmental stage

Sasha and Lindy have been coleading a counseling group that seeks to improve the quality of life for elderly men and women in a retirement community. The coleaders are engaged in between-session processing regarding the last session of the group, even though circumstances in the just-concluded session would suggest that several group members may be ruminating about serious concerns.

### Step 2:   Analyze the presenting situation by applying ecological concepts

As the coleaders ponder a way to process what is happening in the group, they will likely benefit from recalling that the success of reminiscence groups rests in helping members forge interconnections. This has been accomplished, in part, as group members have built relationships with each other, often based on shared recollections and past experiences. In that process, group members also are afforded the opportunity to recast or attribute new meaning to the past and consider what this suggests for the present and the future. Jesse and Glenda are two group members who might be finding it difficult to do this kind of work, but have the energy to say so, even though the group's formal existence is near an end. Now, as a result of the ninth session, Sasha and Lindy also share a growing belief that what Jesse and Glenda are expressing is common among the other group members.

The context of a retirement community is also a key factor and may be related to how members are experiencing this group. Perhaps some see the retirement community as a great vacation, whereas others view the setting as a dreary conclusion to life. These two views about the retirement community perhaps represent two ends of a continuum, with other group members somewhere in between.

In this case, sustainability emerges as a central ecological concept. Group members' perspectives on life and death matters are critical, and must be incorporated into the considerations of working with this group. In fact, it is likely that the response to the imminent end of the reminiscence group itself represents how members might be viewing end-of-life concerns.

### Step 3:   Review possible group techniques, considering focus and level

***Processing Between Toolbox #1,*** Session Review.

*Focus:* Cognitive.
*Level:* Group.

A possible between-session processing technique that might be beneficial for the coleaders is to spend time reviewing what happened in the previous sessions to bring about the specific set of circumstances they now find occurring within the group. Additionally, the coleaders have other past experiences with reminiscence groups that may be applied productively to the current situation.

***Processing Between Toolbox #7,*** Goal Review.

*Focus:* Cognitive.
*Level:* Group and individual.

Over the life of a group the original goals can easily be forgotten. It might be helpful for Sasha and Lindy to review the objectives they established, either prior to the group beginning or early into this particular group. As well, the coleaders might want to incorporate individual members' goals into this review process. Such a technique evaluates "How have we done?" and contributes to planning by asking "What now?" With one group session remaining, this might be an important technique to utilize.

### Step 4:   Select a best-fit technique

It is our experience that too often groups come to an end without proper time set aside to revisit the goals that were originally established by the leaders and/or members. We applaud Sasha and Lindy for thinking in this direction. However, using the time to review the past sessions allows a broader scope for discussion and can easily accommodate a review of goals, too. As well, attending to goals only may or not be sufficient for understanding what has occurred in the group. Reviewing past sessions is therefore a more fitting strategy, given the current conditions, and will likely be helpful in gaining a proper appreciation for the group and in planning a beneficial final session. The pitfall of a broad approach that requires a review of nine previous sessions is obviously one of efficiency; the coleaders will need to focus their appraisal in a manner that is practical.

### Step 5:   Implement and evaluate how well the technique worked

SASHA:   So I'm thinking we could use the next 30 minutes to review the past group sessions for themes that might connect to Jesse and Glenda's comments.

LINDY:   Do you think that will be enough time?

SASHA:   Maybe. Maybe not. But let's see where that takes us. If we use this time to review and then move on to planning for the last session, based on our review . . . Well, if we aren't seeing a clear path, then we can come back to the review process, or think about getting together some other time to finalize things before the final session.

LINDY:   Sounds good—okay, I'll keep track of time.

## If in a Class or Workshop, Then:

### *Practice the choice*

Pair up with another student and try out your choices. Give each other feedback. What might work? What might need to be changed? Compare your choices with those provided by the authors.

### Process the choice

What have you learned? What are you learning about this process for selecting group techniques? What are you learning about yourself as a group leader? What might you be able to use the next time?

---

PROCESSING (BETWEEN) CI 9.4

Group Type: *Counseling*
Best Practice Area: *Between-Session Processing*
Group Development Stage: *Ending*

## The Hour Is Late

### HISTORY

Although the ideal group would have uninterrupted time together, when group sessions are lengthy, group rules may allow for a short break or two. For example, a counseling group meeting for two-hour sessions might permit members to take 10 minutes to stretch, get a drink of water, use the restroom, and so on. Such breathers can interrupt the natural flow of discussion or activity and cause one or more members to disengage from the group's work, thus hindering both individual and group goals. However, breaks also afford group leaders a few minutes to process what has been happening in the session up to that point. Because this kind of processing takes place when group members are not actively working together, we think of it as between-session processing.

Between-session processing can play a critical role in the latter stages of a group's life. As the reminiscence group critical incident illustrated, important issues often emerge near the end of a session and/or as the group's final session together approaches. The challenge for group leaders is to find a way to deal with such issues, while at the same time helping members prepare for the coming termination of group.

For this group, as for the reminiscence group, the hour is late; it is session 11 of a 12-session counseling group. Following the usual break, the group leader has planned to introduce a pretermination activity that will provide a foundation for the final session. However, as the time for the break approaches, the following takes place.

### CRITICAL INCIDENT

LES:    (*visibly shaking*) I—uh—I have something, umm, something to say to y'all. I need to tell ya that, well, that I've sort of been lying, uh, right from day one. Remember way back at the beginning—ya know, when we all talked about why we joined this group? And I, well, I—I (*stuttering and looking at the floor*) said all that about how I wanted to be a better daddy to my boys, and that, what the heck, my health insurance was gonna cough up for it, anyway. Yeah—well, truth is I got court-ordered to come here after my ex, after she fed her

|            |                                                                                                                                                                                                                                                                                                                                                                                                                                                                                                              |
|------------|--------------------------------------------------------------------------------------------------------------------------------------------------------------------------------------------------------------------------------------------------------------------------------------------------------------------------------------------------------------------------------------------------------------------------------------------------------------------------------------------------------------|
|            | lawyer a bunch of stuff, stuff that wasn't really the way things were at all. I was, I guess I was just too embarrassed to . . . But now, umm . . . (*stops talking, but continues to look at the floor, head bent*)                                                                                                                                                                                                                                                                                            |
| JUDITH:    | But now?                                                                                                                                                                                                                                                                                                                                                                                                                                                                                                      |
| LES:       | But now (*lifting his head briefly to look around the room at the group before dropping his gaze to the floor again*), well, after all the time we've been together here, I pretty much trust you guys, so I've been sitting here the last two weeks wanting to say something—ya know, come clean—but I just couldn't. Maybe it's hard to believe, but I've been thinking a lot lately, feel like I'm finally figuring some things out, like how lousy I am at being a daddy. (*looking up*) Look, I could really use your help. If I don't make some changes, and fast, there's no way that judge is gonna give me back my visitation rights. |
| ADAM:      | (*glancing around the group*) It looks to me like some of you are feeling that you could really use a break. But Les, I want to say that I appreciate how honest you've been with us, and (*looking tentatively at the group leader*) I think that we should use the entire hour—the rest of our time—if that's what we need to take to help Les out.                                                                                                                                                             |
| KERRI:     | Well, I have to say that I'm just not there, sorry. I kinda hear ya, Les. Yeah, sure, it's a crappy place to be. But it sounds to me like you're only ready to get honest with us because time's almost up and you're getting desperate. It would really have been nice to hear all this a few weeks ago. Look, if we're going down this road after the break, I wanna have my say, too—about the B.S. I think I'm hearing.                                                                                        |
| DALA:      | Can we please take a break? Geez—I really need a smoke.                                                                                                                                                                                                                                                                                                                                                                                                                                                       |
| MILES:     | Yeah—me, too. It's way past 7:00 and I gotta use the restroom, too.                                                                                                                                                                                                                                                                                                                                                                                                                                           |
| GROUP LEADER: | (*looking around the room and noting that the body language of others is clearly signaling their agreement with Dala and Miles*) I hate to break right now, given that we're at a critical point here—but if we can't give our full attention to helping Les, it might be best if we take a quick breather. So, what do you all think? Break or no break? Les, how're you doing? What works for you?                                                                                                          |
| LES:       | (*glancing around the group, but repeatedly looking at Kerri*) I know how this looks and I—I promise I'll listen to you all, even if you wanna rag on me. (*turning to the group leader*) But I could use a cigarette, too—just a break, not like I'm trying to run off or anything. After we come back, I wanna hear what Kerri and the rest of you have to say.                                                                                                                                             |
| GROUP LEADER: | (*reading a general consensus for a break in the body language of the group*) Okay, then, let's take 10.                                                                                                                                                                                                                                                                                                                                                                                                    |

## WHAT TECHNIQUE DO YOU CHOOSE?

Individually or in small groups jot down or discuss several options for what technique you would use in this situations. What factors must be considered?

## STEPS TOWARD SELECTING A TECHNIQUE

Here is our thinking:

### Step 1:  Identify the group type and purpose, best practice area, and developmental stage

Although we do not know this group's exact purpose we do know it is a counseling group in the ending stage of group development. The group leader will make use of the break to engage in some between-session processing; she will consider how best to proceed with Les's belated disclosure, which is now competing with her plan to help the group begin the termination process.

### Step 2:  Analyze the presenting situation by applying ecological concepts

As the group leader retreats to a private space for the break, she thinks about the rich and rewarding work that many members in this group have accomplished. Ecologically, a spirit of collaboration is at work. Thus, rather than using her prerogative as leader to make a unilateral decision to continue the group session or to take a break, she asked for group input first, and then used their contributions as part of the decision-making process. Considering Les's current need in the context of sustainability, a hall-mark of any successful group, the group leader believes that he is likely at a pivotal point in making changes that could greatly impact his relationship with his children. However, considering the group as a whole, she knows that termination processes are key for helping all the members engage in making meaning of the group experiences, and for attempting to transfer this learning into sustainability for the entire group.

### Step 3:  Review possible group techniques, considering focus and level

*Processing Between Toolbox #7,* Goal Review.

*Focus:* Cognitive.
*Level:* Interpersonal.

Whereas termination is a group process, that process is guided by the leader. Thus, in reviewing the goals she outlined for this group, the group leader has deliberately built in time for termination to take place. She knows from experience that proper attention to termination promotes many of the ecological concepts we have previously outlined. At this point, the group leader must resolve an issue of time management in order to reach this objective of successful closure for the group. As she considers her goals in the context of the current situation, she processes two questions: (1) Can the group afford the time to help Les and still achieve successful termination? (2) Will curbing Les's plea in order to move into her termination activity promote the ecological concepts, such as collaboration, that the group leader values?

*Processing Between Toolbox #1,* Session Review.

*Focus:* Cognitive.
*Level:* Group.

Another approach would be to use these few minutes alone to quickly review the group's past sessions. Using this technique, the group leader might briefly jot down the significant events and themes of the group's history, especially over the more recent sessions. By engaging in this overview, the group leader can not only begin to gain a sense of the work accomplished during the life of the group, but also assess what needs to happen in order for the group to come to a successful termination. Through this process, the group leader may discover how much flexibility there is in her plan that will allow time for Les, with the group's help, to work on the current revelation. For example, the group may have at some level begun the work of termination, and/or Les may be trying, with his recent disclosure, to prevent the group from ending after the next session.

### Step 4:   Select a best-fit technique

Either technique would help the group leader engage in constructive between-session processing. Although both techniques could potentially be utilized to help the group leader make a decision about the direction in which to take the group after their break, with only 10 minutes available to her, we believe she should select only one technique for her between-session processing. Given that the leader already places high value on the goal of allowing adequate time to terminate, we suggest Session Review as an efficient and effective way to help gauge the degree of flexibility she has in her current group plans to address the current situation with Les, without cutting short the other important termination activities.

### Step 5:   Implement and evaluate how well the technique worked

The group leader spends the next few minutes reviewing the current session, as well as the last few sessions, jotting down notes about the major themes and processes, as well as each member's level of participation. In spite of the hurried nature of the process, she realizes that many members' comments in today's session have been couched in past-tense language, suggesting that the group is already naturally moving toward termination. Given the momentum already present, the group leader decides to give the group the option of spending some of the remaining time listening and providing feedback to Les. Although allowing this use of time will abbreviate the termination activity she has planned, the leader believes there will still be sufficient time to engage productively in that process.

GROUP LEADER:   (*after giving the group a few minutes to get settled again*) Les, how are you feeling now? Ready to pick up where we left off before the break?

LES:   Well, uh—not exactly looking forward to keepin' it goin', but, yeah, since I started this, I could use some help to figure out where to go from here. This group, it's been, well, I honestly don't think I'm the same guy that I was when the group started. But when it ends—ya know, when I don't have this group to remind me to try to do things different—I'm pretty sure I'm gonna just go back to doing things the old way, even though I don't want to.

KERRI:   I know I was pretty hard on you—not one to sugar coat, I guess—and, yeah, I'll probably say more things you're not gonna like. But, well, what you just said—I think you really meant it and I hear you. Keep going.

GROUP LEADER:   Real quick—I need to interject here. (*looking around the group*) We've got a pretty tight time schedule and a lot to do yet. (*looking at Les*) Les, we may not accomplish everything today, but I think we can make some good progress. Could we set a limit of 30 minutes to work with Les and then do a 5-minute summary of what we've done? I need the last 25 minutes to introduce a few themes that are going to be important for us as we think ahead to next week and our last session together.

MILES:   Got it covered. (*rolling up his sleeve to show the group his watch*) I'll let you know when we've got 10 minutes left, and then give the five-minute warning.

ADAM:   (*shaking his head at Miles with a grin*) Mr. Timekeeper—right on the job as usual. Next group we're in, could I maybe get a crack at the job?

GROUP LEADER:   Okay, okay—Kerri, would you say again what you said to Les just before the break and let's see if we can move on from there.

## If in a Class or Workshop, Then:

### Practice the choice

Pair up with another student and try out your choices. Give each other feedback. What might work? What might need to be changed? Compare your choices with those provided by the authors.

### Process the choice

What have you learned? What are you learning about this process for selecting group techniques? What are you learning about yourself as a group leader? What might you be able to use the next time?

## In Sum

Processing between sessions, an ASGW best practice area, allows leaders the opportunity to learn from their experience and to apply it in future sessions and groups. A solo leader can keep a journal of each session and meet with his or her supervisor for analysis and judgment. Coleaders can take advantage of a built-in system for mutual feedback about each other's in-session performance, a process that can be enhanced when they have developed a workable relationship inclusive of group leadership goals they have set. Of course, making consistent time available for between-session processing presents a real-world challenge for all group leaders for reasons we discussed earlier.

Committing to finding the time is a necessary step. Once implemented, application of between-session processing learning will benefit both the current group situation and, by extension, add rungs to the group leadership scaffold that is being constructed for future group leading.

## References

Conyne, R. (1999). *Failures in group work: How we can learn from our mistakes*. Thousand Oaks, CA: Sage.

Stockton. R., Morran, D. K., & Nitza, A. (2000). Processing group events: A conceptual map for leaders. *Journal for Specialists in Group Work, 25*, 343–355.

# PART V

# Techniques for Additional Types of Groups

Groups, of course, are ubiquitous in Western society. They are part and parcel of daily life for nearly everyone, unless one is living on the edge of civilization, out of the range of others.

Most people participate in groups in a bewildering number of settings: in schools, political functions, neighborhood activities, religious centers, recreational facilities, athletic teams, music ensembles, mental health centers, community centers, work, and in informal social gatherings of all kinds. Productivity is very much a joint, project-based activity in today's world. Social support tends to occur through dyadic and group connections. In fact, much of our personal identity is developed and formed through interpersonal and group involvement.

It is no wonder, then, that professional group work has become diversified. No longer is it constrained to the more traditional forms of helping—what we know of as group counseling and psychoeducation groups. The largest number of training programs in counseling, social work, and psychology prepares students in these two forms of group work. Reflecting that reality, this book is centered on those two group work applications. Additionally, though, group work increasingly finds itself expressed through group psychotherapy and task groups.

Always a strong foundational force in group work, group psychotherapy is an essential means of providing service to people who are suffering from deeper levels of mental, emotional, and psychological dysfunction. As well, much of what we have learned about interpersonal and group dynamics has emerged from group psychotherapy researchers and clinicians. As our society continues to become more stressful and chaotic, coupled with an insufficiency of trained clinicians, group psychotherapy will continue not only to be important, but it also can be expected to expand its significance and scope in training and practice.

Dwarfing all other forms of group work, task groups easily are the most common in the United States and many other countries. Within organizations, for example, employees spend considerable parts of their work weeks in group meetings. At the same time, when asked about their least favored work activities, many employees are quick to offer up "meetings." There is so much to improve in how meetings are run, how classrooms are structured, how task forces function, and in all forms of task group work. Counselors, psychologists, social workers, and others who are skilled in group-work leadership and in group techniques can contribute much to enhance group functioning. "Give group techniques away" is a mantra that can serve well to guide efforts in this area.

Chapter 10 addresses group techniques in task and in psychotherapy groups. We hope it will help expand your thinking about how to use group techniques more broadly in both settings and populations.

# 10

## *Group Techniques in Task and Psychotherapy Groups*

**ADVANCE ORGANIZER**

This chapter contains the following material:

**Task Groups**
> *Task Group Performance Model*
> *Task Groups in Action*
> *Improved Task Group Leadership*

**Psychotherapy Groups**
> *Therapeutic Factors*
> *A Great Need for Group Psychotherapy*
> *Going Deeper*

**Critical Incident Training in Task and Psychotherapy Groups**

CRITICAL INCIDENTS

CI 10.1: "Making It Work: What to Do With a Large Group"
> Group Type: *Task*
> Best Practice Area: *Planning*
> Group Developmental Stage: *Prior to first session*

CI 10.2: "Getting Started"
> Group Type: *Task*
> Best Practice Area: *Performing*
> Group Developmental Stage: *Beginning*

CI 10.3: "The Importance of Planning"
> Group Type: *Psychotherapy*
> Best Practice Area: *Planning*
> Group Developmental Stage: *Prior to first session*

CI 10.4: "You're the Expert!"
> Group Type: *Psychotherapy*
> Best Practice Area: *Performing*
> Group Developmental Stage: *Beginning*

CI 10.5: "Meet!"
> Group Type: *Task*
> Best Practice Area: *Between-Session Processing*
> Group Development Stage: *Beginning*

**In Sum**

We have been focusing so far on the groups that counselors and other helpers work with most often—counseling and psychoeducation groups. However, group work encompasses additional group types beyond counseling and psychoeducation, and they are being used with increasing frequency.

The most obvious of these other types are task groups and psychotherapy groups. The Association for Specialists in Group Work (ASGW), in its *Professional Training Standards* (ASGW, 2000), identified and described these additional group-work types, as well as counseling and psychoeducation groups. In Chapter 2 we briefly defined task and psychotherapy groups. But that was many pages ago, so here are those definitions once again:

> *Task Groups:* These groups are used to resolve or to enhance performance and production goals within a work group, through attention to team building, collaborative problem solving, and system change strategies.

> *Psychotherapy Groups:* Through psychotherapy groups, members learn how to reduce psychological and/or emotional dysfunction by focusing on bringing past history to the present and incorporating diagnosis and assessment within an interpersonal orientation.

## Task Groups

Hulse-Killacky, Killacky, and Donigian (2001) said it well with regard to group work in the past century:

> One of the most interesting phenomena of the 20th century has been the growth, development, and presence of group work. From the earliest formal groups, such as Pratt's psychotherapy group for patients with tuberculosis in the early 1900's, to more recent self-help and cooperative learning groups, we have witnessed the emergence of a massive array of groups, from therapy settings to board rooms. (p. 6)

In the 21st century, the scope and speed of development of group work can only be expected to increase.

In the previous quotation, the reference to "board rooms" provides one example of a task group setting, in which corporate board meetings occur. There are many examples of task groups and where they can occur: committees, task forces, discussion groups, study circles, problem-based learning groups, neighborhood councils, strategic planning sessions, bible studies, and many others. Task groups, in fact, are ubiquitous in our culture. They are an important part of our everyday lives.

Their obvious presence, though, does not mean that task groups are either effective or satisfying. As has been observed (e.g., Conyne, 1989; Conyne, Rapin, & Rand, 1997, 2006; Conyne, Wilson, & Ward, 1997), although task groups share much in common with other forms of group work, their emphasis on concrete goal accomplishment makes them unique from other group types and also particularly challenging to lead.

Too often task groups, in fact, are not led well. We do not need to refer to any professional literature to verify this claim. Instead, all we need to do is to turn to our own experience with them. How many find planning groups enjoyable? Are you eager to attend your weekly staff meeting? How productive are the task forces you may have been part of? In our collective experience, it is the rare person who looks forward to task group meetings because they tend to be fraught with boredom and other problems.

There is a significant disconnect, then, between the high frequency of task group meetings that are held on a daily basis and the degree to which their members would like to avoid attending them. The resulting lack of productivity, coupled with high dissatisfaction, is wasteful.

Thus, there exists a very large need for counselors and others who are skilled in group work to address. Counselors can improve the level of task group work in communities and workplaces by making their group services available as leaders, trainers, consultants, and as enlightened members.

The methodology exists to guide task group leadership by counselors and other helpers. We cite two examples.

## Task Group Performance Model

A precursor of the PGTM was described by Conyne and others (see Conyne, Wilson, et al., 1997; Conyne, Rapin, et al., 1997), called the task group performance model. This model applies a collaborative problem-solving approach to critical incidents and focuses on how groups can relate human processes to achieving clear-cut performance goals (see Wheelan, 2004). Moreover, whereas context is important in all groups, for task groups context assumes additional significance. For instance, a task force established by county administrators to produce a community prevention plan is always part of a larger system and must report to that larger system. Thus, in this example, the task force was created by county administrators to produce the community prevention plan, which then must be submitted to the administrators for approval and action. Another example showing the importance of context refers to an academic program department chair:

> Chairs must understand, however, that before the department meeting is held, it is important to consider the setting, the agenda, the nature of the business to be conducted, and the probable reactions of those in the meeting. Given a moderate-size faculty, an hour department meeting costs thousands of dollars of professional time. The chair must recognize just how important this time is to the faculty in the room, and to the institution, and to make the best use of the department meeting. (Chu, 2006, at tomorrows-professor@lists.Stanford.EDU)

## Task Groups in Action

Another useful model to assist counselors and other helpers to work with task groups was developed by Hulse-Killacky et al. (2001). It asks that group leaders seek to appropriately balance content (what group members discuss) and process (how group members discuss content) across the developmental phases of a task group. These phases were identified by the authors as "warm-up," "action," and "closure." The resulting schema provides a kind of "roadmap" that task group leaders can use to guide their leadership techniques.

## Improved Task Group Leadership

Counselors, psychologists, social workers, educators, and all human service professionals who have been trained in group-work leadership—usually related to counseling and psychoeducation groups—can apply their skills more broadly to improve the functioning of task groups. These group skills need to be "given away," so that the productivity of communities, businesses, classrooms, government, and other settings in which task groups routinely occur might be enhanced. Attention to process issues and helping bring a collaborative, problem-solving approach to group functioning represent viable ways to enhance task group performance. Who else is in a better position to inject such approaches within task groups than human service professionals?

## *Psychotherapy Groups*

It is a matter of emphasis, or a point of view, that is used to demarcate group psychotherapy from group counseling. Consequently, the lines between the two group types should be only lightly drawn, perhaps dotted, as the distinctions are fuzzy.

Following the *Professional Training Standards* of the Association for Specialists in Group Work (ASGW, 2000), however, we find it useful to note workable distinctions between counseling and psychotherapy groups, while recognizing their overlapping variance. Other experts (e.g., Barlow, Fuhriman, & Burlingame, 2004), recognizing the complexities involved, are comfortable embracing group counseling and psychotherapy within one umbrella, citing a general definition of group therapy that includes groups applied for guidance, prevention, counseling, and training (Dagley, Gazda, Eppinger, & Stewart, 1994). Barlow et al. (2004) use the terms "counseling" and "psychotherapy" interchangeably when discussing group methods.

We think of group therapy as generally being the deepest type of group work, used to help members reformulate personal constructs, personality characteristics, and worldview. Moreover, group psychotherapy is used with group members whose intrapersonal and interpersonal functioning is diagnosed or diagnosable and in need of significant repair. If counseling group members experience difficulty and upsetting "problems in living" that anyone in our society might face at any time (e.g., loneliness, anxiety, meaninglessness), they are generally able to conduct their life without major disruption, dissatisfaction, or ineffectiveness. Psychotherapy group members, by contrast, experience such intense, profound, and pervasive psychological and emotional cleavages that their lives are broadly and substantially disrupted.

Counselors, especially mental health counselors, may find providing group therapy to be a job requirement. All counselors working with groups of any type will find it occasionally necessary to work from a group therapy perspective. Knowledge and skills in promoting therapeutic factors are vitally important for counselors and other helpers working with therapy groups or in other groups taking on therapylike conditions.

## Therapeutic Factors

As Kivlighan and Holmes (2004, p. 23) observed, Yalom's (Yalom & Leszcz, 2005) delineation and description of 11 therapeutic factors as the "essential elements of group-promoted change" is his single most influential contribution to group therapy. It is impossible to read any group-work text today without encountering a discussion of these factors. The therapeutic factors can be defined briefly as:

- **Instilling hope:** Leaders helping members to feel optimistic about the group as a place for improvement.
- **Universality:** Aloneness is supplanted by a sense that others in the group experience similar difficulties.
- **Imparting information:** Group leader provides useful information and suggestions.
- **Altruism:** Helping others provides personal benefits to the helper, as well as to the helpee.
- **Corrective recapitulation of primary family group:** Group provides members with positive opportunity to correct negative family experience.
- **Developing socializing techniques:** Group provides opportunities for members to interact socially in a positive manner and to learn helpful approaches.
- **Interpersonal learning and input:** Members learn through self-disclosure of others.
- **Interpersonal learning and output:** Members can try out interpersonal learning and receive feedback.
- **Cohesiveness:** Group members feel connected to each other, to the group, and feel a "sense of belonging."
- **Catharsis:** Members express affect directly, allowing them to feel better.
- **Existential factors:** Members assume personal responsibility and find increased meaning in their lives.
- **Imitative behavior:** Members learn by observing others.

## A Great Need for Group Psychotherapy

With one in five American adults suffering from a diagnosable mental disorder in any given year (National Institute of Mental Health [NIMH], 1998), or roughly 57,650,000 individuals (Gullotta & Bloom, 2003), there is a pressing need for counselors and other helpers to deliver group therapy. This is the case for three reasons: (a) there are far too few trained helpers to meet the daunting demand for service, (b) group delivery of service is more efficient than individual delivery, and (c) group therapy works (Conyne, 2004).

## Going Deeper

The basic group-work leadership competencies learned by counselors and other human service practitioners provide the foundation for working with psychotherapy groups. However, additional training usually is required due to the depth and pervasiveness of problems experienced by many psychotherapy group members.

As contained in the ASGW *Professional Training Standards* (ASGW, 2000), group psychotherapy leaders need to be able to apply principles of normal and abnormal human development by using group-based strategies with group members who may be experiencing chronic and/or severe maladjustment. Appropriate preparation for group psychotherapy practice includes course work in abnormal human development, family pathology and family therapy, assessment and diagnosis of mental and emotional disorders, individual therapy, group therapy, and supervised training experiences in a therapy group.

The PGTM you have been studying throughout this book is very helpful not only for counseling and psychoeducation groups, which have been the focus of the book, but also for task and psychotherapy groups, which are being considered in this chapter. The PGTM steps of identify, analyze, review, select, and implement and evaluate guide leaders in choosing and using group techniques that fit situations occurring across all group types.

Let's now take a look at how the model can be applied in task and psychotherapy groups.

## Critical Incident Training in Task and Psychotherapy Groups

### CRITICAL INCIDENTS

#### TASK AND PSYCHOTHERAPY GROUPS CI 10.1

Group Type: *Task*
Best Practice Area: *Planning*
Group Developmental Stage: *Prior to first session*

### Making It Work: What to Do With a Large Group

#### HISTORY

Frequently individuals who are in positions of leadership are challenged when the number of participants for a function exceeds a manageable size. Defaulting to more traditional approaches, business leaders, educators, and even mental health professionals often wind up lecturing to groups for long stretches of time. Of course, lecturing to people in a group setting fails to harness the potential that groups lend to the task at hand, as group interactions and other dynamics are ignored.

The following critical incident has been slightly enhanced, but is nonetheless a real-world example of how two of this book's authors (Bob and Mark) used the PGTM model to implement task groups with a college class of 30 students that they coinstructed. In a planning meeting several weeks prior to the first class Bob and Mark discuss their concerns.

## CRITICAL INCIDENT

MARK:    So, how many are enrolled for the class this year?

BOB:    It looks like 30—about the same as past years.

MARK:    I'm always glad to see so many students interested in taking this class, but . . .

BOB:    But what?

MARK:    But it's just too many. We've talked about this before. The class doesn't seem to really pick up energy and life until the last four or five weeks when we have students divided into groups of four to work on their final assignment.

BOB:    Keep going.

MARK:    It's just that—well, I always cringe when I see the straight rows of desks and students all seated, one behind another. I wish we could use some sort of group format earlier in the course.

BOB:    Oh, I completely agree! It's the material. It's so dense and novel for most of the students that I usually feel they need those intensive lectures I give in the first part of the course. But if we could incorporate a group discussion format as a way to cover the material they've been studying that would engage students—sure, it would be a tremendous shift and away from a straight lecture mode.

MARK:    No argument from me. But how?

BOB:    Perhaps we could scan the toolbox for some help?

MARK:    Great idea.

## WHAT TECHNIQUE DO YOU CHOOSE?

Individually or in small groups jot down or discuss several options for what technique you would use in this situation. What factors must be considered?

## STEPS TOWARD SELECTING A TECHNIQUE

Here is our thinking:

### Step 1:  Identify the group type and purpose, best practice area, and developmental stage

Educational classes are typically considered to involve task groups of clearly stated objectives (e.g., students will gain a certain mastery of the subject being studied). Bob and Mark are in the planning stage and working to transition away from a lecture format toward group work as a way to achieve the course objectives.

### Step 2:  Analyze the presenting situation by applying ecological concepts

There are two levels of analysis important to consider. First, Bob and Mark are challenged by a set of past experiences that influence their current view of teaching a particular class (e.g., making meaning). Bob and Mark seem eager to use group work as a format for teaching. On the other hand, Bob sees the material as challenging to deliver in a group format and Mark is concerned by the large numbers of students. How does a leader run a group with 30 members? Nonetheless, they are working collaboratively to see if options exist. A second level of analysis is the future class itself. Though there is not a lot of information about the nature of the course, Mark mentions an important contextual factor, involving the traditional arrangement of the classroom and desks. Attending to this will likely be important to any successful venture in using group work within the classroom setting.

**Step 3:   Review possible group techniques, considering focus and level**

*Planning Toolbox #21,* Floating Facilitator.

*Focus:* Structural.
*Level:* Group.

It goes without saying that successful group work in a traditional classroom setting requires that seating be adjusted to accommodate students and instructors to maximize interaction and foster interconnection. With this as a foundational step that Bob and Mark will likely attend to, they are considering the possibility of placing students into five groups of six students, dispersed around the room. Each group would discuss the dense readings and novel material, perhaps guided by a set of questions provided by Bob and Mark. They would then take on the role of floating facilitators. As experts on the material being discussed by the students in each group, Bob and Mark would shuttle among the various groups to help facilitate the discussion of the material and answer questions that are naturally occurring within each group's exchange.

*Planning Toolbox #22,* Fishbowl (revised).

*Focus:* Structural.
*Level:* Group.

The Fishbowl technique typically involves arranging an inner circle of group members working on a task or problem and surrounding this group with a second group that silently observes the inner group at work. At defined points established by the leader(s) the inner group stops its work and receives nonjudgmental, observational feedback from the outside group. Usually this feedback is process focused, but not always. Then the inner group continues its work with this newly infused feedback.

Bob and Mark are considering how to creatively use this approach in the classroom setting with the 30 students currently enrolled. They are wondering if one instructor could lead a group of 15 students in a discussion about the material the students were to read and study, while the other instructor and the remaining 15 students form an outer circle and observe the discussion, not so much looking to make process observations, but looking for practical points that have not been discussed or ways to synthesize the group's work into meaningful application. Bob and Mark are thinking that after the inner group members are finished with their task, the outer group members would provide their feedback, allowing for cross-group communication. From one class session to the next the groups would switch roles; so, the inner group would become the observing group in the next class session.

### Step 4:   Select a best-fit technique

Both group techniques are suitable approaches in taking a large number of individuals and creating a context in which members are more likely to actively participate in a discussion about the academic material. The value of the floating facilitator model is that students are in smaller-sized groups than proposed in the Fishbowl technique. Difficulties that may emerge with multiple groups operating simultaneously is that two leaders cannot be fully engaged in all the groups, all the time. Additionally, this format in a single classroom would likely create a level of distractibility that in reality impedes group work. Finally, groups may not easily benefit from the group work occurring in other groups.

Conversely, the Fishbowl technique allows for all the students to be involved without the distractions of multiple cooccurring groups. As well, the flow of information is more effective in that all the students hear what the others are contributing. A clear limitation to the Fishbowl technique is that groups of 15 are still somewhat large and may discourage full participation from various students.

Bob and Mark believe that a best-fit technique in this critical incident centers on all students being able to benefit from the leaders' knowledge of the material, while having an opportunity to participate in a discussion format task group. The Floating Facilitator technique, though valuable in allowing for smaller groups, also places groups in a more vulnerable position of not having ongoing guidance and may be difficult in a single classroom. As such, they elect to implement the Fishbowl technique.

### Step 5:   Implement and evaluate how well the technique worked

BOB:      This is great! Still, 15 can be a large group. We'll need to be watching for students who perhaps tend to stay on the sidelines and not participate.

MARK:    *(taking copious notes, looks up from his legal pad)* Right. Perhaps we need to be also thinking about questions that could draw these individuals into the discussion.

*(At the first class Bob and Mark reviewed the Fishbowl approach to be used in subsequent class sessions. At the next class the technique was used with great success.)*

## If in a Class or Workshop, Then:

### *Practice the choice*

Pair up with another student and try out your choices. Give each other feedback. What might work? What might need to be changed? Compare your choices with those provided by the authors.

### *Process the choice*

What have you learned? What are you learning about this process for selecting group techniques? What are you learning about yourself as a group leader? What might you be able to use the next time?

TASK AND PSYCHOTHERAPY GROUPS CI 10.2

Group Type: *Task*

Best Practice Area: *Performing*

Group Developmental Stage: *Beginning*

# *Getting Started*

## HISTORY

Tyla Nole is a hospital administrator who has recently accepted the task of leading a group of hospital division directors as they implement new policies and procedures that seek to improve patient satisfaction. The charge from the hospital's executive board also includes an ongoing component in which the group will function in a quality control capacity, with responsibilities for reviewing and discussing ongoing concerns relative to patient care expressed by patients, family members, and hospital staff.

Excited by the fresh opportunities, Tyla is also keenly aware that this new responsibility is not completely without potential pitfalls. In an era in which patients typically have a number of health care settings from which to choose, hospitals that historically enjoyed being the "only game in town" must now compete. Complicating the situation further is that, in addition to the emphasis on patient satisfaction being a new consideration for many of the divisions throughout the hospital, one assessment technique, such as a patient satisfaction questionnaire, may not work equitably across settings. For example, a division comprised mainly of busy outpatient clinics may garner a lower patient satisfaction rating in response to a question about available appointment slots in comparison to a more specialized division easily able to accommodate a similar number of patients during the same time period.

## CRITICAL INCIDENT

Tyla went to considerable lengths to plan for the first meeting. Knowing the value of each group member's time she prepared important material and distributed it two weeks prior to the first meeting. She then called each director and shared her vision for the first meeting and beyond, attempting to build a relationship with each group member. Imagine her shock when at the first meeting the following occurred within the first few minutes.

TYLA:        So, we'll be working to find ways to recommend procedures that can serve all our respective divisions.

DR. FRED:    *(director of psychiatry, responding quickly in an impatient tone)* Frankly, I don't really know how we can expect to do that. We don't even know what goes on in other divisions or what procedures they have in place. And should we even be assuming that changes are necessary? As far as my division is concerned, we think our procedures are working quite effectively as they stand!

## WHAT TECHNIQUE DO YOU CHOOSE?

Individually or in small groups jot down or discuss several options for what technique you would use in this situation. What factors must be considered?

## STEPS TOWARD SELECTING A TECHNIQUE

Here is our thinking:

### Step 1:   Identify the group type and purpose, best practice area, and developmental stage

Tyla is leading a task group whose purpose is to evaluate and improve patient satisfaction throughout a hospital. As the group's first meeting, it is representative of the beginning stage of group development.

### Step 2:   Analyze the presenting situation by applying ecological concepts

Information provided about the hospital suggests that contextually or organizationally, it is segmented into divisions. Although there is a temptation to imagine that the group members, all division directors, would make for a homogeneous group, administrative demands likely vary significantly from division to division (e.g., an outpatient clinic vs. an inpatient unit). Hence, as Tyla considers the various group members, she might benefit from appreciating these contextual factors and how they promote or hinder collaboration. In fact, the differing backgrounds and training of the division directors may constitute diversity concerns. Dr. Fred, a psychiatrist by training, likely approaches his work much differently than the division director in charge of emergency medicine, or the director of social work. In attending to these differences in group members' training and experience, Tyla would be appreciating multicultural influences. In facing this current critical incident and selecting a technique to help the group, Tyla might benefit from thinking about these ecological concepts and the ways in which she can find commonalities, while at the same time appreciating the variabilities represented. Therefore, giving priority to forging interconnections and creating a collaborative atmosphere become key considerations in deciding on appropriate techniques. For example, Tyla might have assumed that her prior work in distributing material and placing a personal phone call to each group member was satisfactory, when in reality the task group members might have little buy-in to this newly formed social system.

### Step 3:   Review possible group techniques, considering focus and level

***Performing Toolbox #14,*** Resume for Membership.

*Focus:* Cognitive.
*Level:* Individual and group.

Appreciating Dr. Fred's comments, Tyla might suggest to him and the other group members that perhaps it would be an appropriate use of the group's time to understand not only the collective task, but also each member's potential contribution to the work of the group. Thus, Tyla asks members to use the next several minutes to individually write down the personal and professional characteristics that make them a valuable member of this group. Having completed this assignment, the group members are instructed to work as a team and produce a "group resume" that reflects their strengths as a team, specifically as they relate to the larger task of the group.

***Performing Toolbox #10,*** Self-Description.

*Focus:* Cognitive and structural.
*Level:* Individual, interpersonal, and group.

There are a variety of ways to use this technique at this early juncture in the life of the group. For example, Tyla might acknowledge Dr. Fred's concerns, along with those of other group members. To help move the group along in a beneficial direction, she would then ask each one to write on a piece of paper a single word describing a strength or positive attribute that she or he brings to the group. Having written their words, members are given a few minutes to mill around the room and read one another's words, after which they have been asked to match up with another individual whose word is dissimilar to the one they themselves chose. Each dyad then uses the next several minutes to discuss their words. As a final step to bring the members back together, the dyads report to the rest of the group; each member of a dyad introduces the other member, along with that person's word and the reasoning behind the choice of that particular word.

### Step 4:   Select a best-fit technique

We believe that either of the two preceding techniques has the potential to assist the group's overall development and, eventually, the central task of patient satisfaction. Both techniques are fitting for groups at the beginning of their development, although, as we have attempted to underscore, Tyla must not simply jump to either of these techniques without some acknowledgment of what Dr. Fred has said. As well, both techniques provide sufficient opportunity for members to begin to talk about themselves and the strengths they bring to the group. The strength of the Self-Description technique is that members have an opportunity to begin forming collaborative relationships through the dyadic exchange. As well, process actively engages all members of the group. The advantage of the Resume for Membership technique lies in the production of a final document that requires a high level of group collaboration to complete. However, unlike the Self-Description technique, this latter strategy allows for greater variability in the level of participation, with members potentially able to play a significantly more or less active role in the process. Therefore, to ensure full participation at this critical stage of group formation, we suggest that Tyla implement the Self-Description technique.

### Step 5:   Implement and evaluate how well the technique worked

TYLA:         *(making eye contact)* You know, Dr. Fred, you've made some valid points—and—well, I appreciate your willingness to raise those concerns. And I'm betting that others might be having similar kinds of thoughts.

DR. FRED:   I would think so—after all *(looking around)*, I'm sure we're all wondering where this leaves the work we've done in our division.

TYLA:        (*looking around the room at the other members and seeing a few heads nodding in agreement*) All right, then, it seems to me that maybe we need to set this agenda aside (points to a paper) for now and take some time to figure out a few things . . .

DR. GUPTA:   You have something particular in mind?

TYLA:        Actually—yes, I do. I know you've all interacted with each other at some level as professional colleagues, but I'm wondering if you would agree with me that we're facing a new task here? And—well—maybe it's a little fuzzy for all of us as to what professional perspectives and abilities we can bring to this particular table. Would you be willing to spend the next 30 to 45 minutes in an activity that I think will at least give us a handle on where we're all coming from and give us some direction—some sense of the most productive way to proceed from here? I think Dr. Fred has made a good beginning in pointing out that I might have been jumping into things too quickly.

DR. FRED:    (*nodding*) Yes—yes, this is exactly what I meant. We really need to agree on some basics before . . .

DR. GUPTA:   (*jumping in*) I completely agree. I mean, here I am with friends and colleagues—we're supposedly on the same team—and I'm looking around and thinking that I have no idea what most of you are facing when it comes to this whole "patient satisfaction" project.

TYLA:        Okay—excellent. Looks like we're agreed on where we need to begin. Now, if everyone would take a minute to write down on a piece of paper one word—a word that specifically relates to the issue of patient satisfaction as you see it.

## If in a Class or Workshop, Then:

### *Practice the choice*

Pair up with another student and try out your choices. Give each other feedback. What might work? What might need to be changed? Compare your choices with those provided by the authors.

### *Process the choice*

What have you learned? What are you learning about this process for selecting group techniques? What are you learning about yourself as a group leader? What might you be able to use the next time?

---

### TASK AND PSYCHOTHERAPY GROUPS CI 10.3

Group Type: *Psychotherapy*
Best Practice Area: *Planning*
Group Developmental Stage: *Prior to first session*

## *The Importance of Planning*

## HISTORY

Since last spring, when Jim completed his graduate training in mental health counseling, he has been working in a community mental health center, where the primary delivery method of services to clients is individual treatment. In his brief time at the center, he has been somewhat surprised to find that a considerable number of clients present with behaviors and characteristics that are often associated with chronic forms of depression. In fact, Jim's caseload has become saturated with such individuals. Interestingly, many of these clients, although certainly not all, have not been gainfully employed since the closing of two large factories.

During weekly supervision, Jim suggests the possible benefits in using psychotherapy groups as a way of providing effective treatment to the clients who appear to have similar treatment needs. Jim's supervisor supports the idea, especially on reviewing Jim's increasingly large client load. Further, psychotherapy groups would somewhat alleviate payment concerns, as group therapy is typically more affordable for clients. Both concur that launching two psychotherapy groups would be beneficial. Still, Jim's supervisor readily admits that this would represent a shift in how services are currently provided to clients.

## CRITICAL INCIDENT

SUPERVISOR:   Yeah, I take your point—well, it's just that group work has never been a focus of this practice. (*pausing briefly*) But it's not that I don't value group work—it's what I spent about half my time doing during my postdoc training, you know, facilitating counseling and psychotherapy groups—the same kind of thing you're suggesting for us here. I agree completely that getting people with similar concerns together can have a lot of value. Yeah, I think this could prove to be therapeutic.

JIM:          So, are you saying this is something I can do?

SUPERVISOR:   Sure—but . . .

JIM:          But what?

SUPERVISOR:   (*smiling slightly*) But there's some things we need to consider if we want this to get off the ground successfully. Planning, for one—we'll need to start there. So, tell me—what do you see as coming next, if we want to add groups to what we're already doing?

## WHAT TECHNIQUE DO YOU CHOOSE?

Individually or in small groups jot down or discuss several options for what technique you would use in this situation. What factoros must be considered?

## STEPS TOWARD SELECTING A TECHNIQUE

Here is our thinking:

### Step 1:  Identify the group type and purpose, best practice area, and developmental stage

The topics of group work and depressive behaviors are rather broad categories and may or may not be within Jim's scope of expertise. Assuming that he has suitable training and/or is receiving appropriate supervision, Jim will need to consider the type of group that is best suited for this population. In reality, most groups do not fit neatly into categories. For example, counseling or psychotherapy groups may have psycho-education aspects or vice versa; psychoeducation groups can include elements of counseling. Here, it is likely that the chronic concerns defining the clients with whom Jim is working would be best served through psychotherapy groups. Jim is therefore in the planning phase as he develops and implements a psychotherapy group approach.

### Step 2:  Analyze the presenting situation by applying ecological concepts

A variety of concepts are applicable when planning a group. Context is certainly essential as Jim considers how his efforts fit into the mission and vision of the community agency that employs him. Will this new service necessitate that the policies and procedures of the center be revised and/or clarifications added? What potential challenges might arise in finding or creating suitable space to accommodate such a group? What impact will groups have on center resources?

Another key concept for consideration is personal connection. In contrast to individual therapy, groups (in this case psychotherapy groups) rely on interconnections. What planning is required as Jim moves from an individual approach to a group approach? What factors are key in helping individuals with depression learn to work together, and how can those initial interconnections be successfully sustained?

One important consideration here is the work of bridging from the individual to the group. Depression is very personal, because individuals experiencing depression frequently feel isolated from others. Therefore, Jim may want to also value the importance of working from a collaborative stance. That is, the group members are without doubt the experts in their respective life stories. How will Jim plan to partner with the group members to create a shared process? Closely related to planning for inter-connections and collaborative stance is planning for social system. A psychotherapy group for depression is characterized by a distinctive set of expectations, rules, norms, and experiences. For example, what acceptable group member behaviors with respect to attendance and punctuality might emerge from this concept?

In sum, Jim is planning to launch psychotherapy groups in a setting that has not previously utilized this approach. Special attention needs to be given to the context; a successful beginning requires it. Secondarily, but in many ways no less important, Jim's success will hinge on his ability to implement a model that is vigilant in shifting from an individual level of analysis to an interpersonal focus, emphasizing the importance of attending to the creation of a unique social system (both in his workplace, as well as in the newly formed groups). In successfully accomplishing this commendable goal, Jim must be particularly mindful of "doing with, rather than to."

Clients do not need to be "experimented on." And though it is unlikely that Jim and his supervisor would do so, clients' perceptions are of critical importance.

## Step 3:   Review possible group techniques, considering focus and level

***Planning Toolbox #2,*** Assessment Visit.

*Focus:* Cognitive.
*Level:* Individual.

As he pondered this supervisor's question, Jim immediately recalled how the cofacilitator from his master's internship experience interviewed prospective group members. Jim believes this approach to forming a group is valuable and connects with identifying potential group members who will both benefit from a group psychotherapy experience and likely work with others in developing interconnections.

***Planning Toolbox #8,*** Attitude Assessment.

*Focus:* Cognitive and affective.
*Level:* Individual.

Though similar to the Assessment Visit technique, the Attitude Assessment is not limited to appraising only group members. In a broader sense, attitudinal information can include group members as well as others who have a stake in the development and implementation of the groups. In this case, the most obvious stakeholders would be Jim's fellow employees.

## Step 4:   Select a best-fit technique

At first, making the choice point the decision between (a) electing to visit with people who wish to join the group, and (b) administering an attitude assessment about groups, may seem unfair because the two options are not necessarily mutually exclusive in all contexts. However, in this critical incident no groups are yet "promised." Though both techniques seem similar, visiting with people who wish to join a group that has not yet been established may be somewhat problematic in that it can raise potentially unrealistic hopes in the soon-to-be members. On the other hand, conducting an attitude assessment emphasizes a feasibility or inquiry approach to the future possibilities of starting a group, and may be more appropriate to potential members already struggling with disappointed hopes.

Neither technique may be entirely satisfactory in the complete planning for a successful psychotherapy group. Still, gathering attitudinal information will provide a valuable foundation from which to build, especially when formulating a plan to move from an individual approach toward an interconnected and collaborative approach. The goal also could be accomplished from interviewing prospective group members, a valuable foundation from which to build.

It is difficult to imagine how planning for a successful psychotherapy group could occur without doing some basic survey work about the attitudes of key individuals in the work setting, as well as those of potential group members. Interviewing only prospective group members would be a valuable screening technique, but would provide no information about others who may be impacted by initiating psychotherapy groups.

Completing an attitude assessment about groups is a complex technique involving several individuals. Supervision as an initial step, however, is simple, involving Jim primarily working with one other person. All other factors being equal, when given a choice between simple and complex techniques, choose the most economical or straightforward approach.

As we have noted, whereas the two techniques look similar on the surface, they could have very different results, depending on the contextual factors. Interviewing potential members for a psychotherapy group at this stage of planning is premature and could have significant consequences on individuals with depression. For instance, if the groups do not materialize, or do not begin immediately, interviewed individuals could reinforce faulty thinking by perceiving that they were rejected from participating in a group. Alternatively, the kind of attitude assessment that seeks to test the waters regarding the likelihood of launching and maintaining psychotherapy groups has minimal negative side effects. Positive side effects from either technique could be stimulating others to think about the possibilities of initiating the groups and creating a social system that supports the process of instituting such groups.

### Step 5:   Implement and evaluate how well the technique worked

| | |
|---|---|
| SUPERVISOR: | *(after a long pause)* Still with me, Jim? |
| JIM: | Uh-huh—just thinking. |
| SUPERVISOR: | Thinking about . . . ? |
| JIM: | A lot—to be honest! For starters—well, what would you think about an attitude assessment of groups? |
| SUPERVISOR: | Sounds to me like a starting point worth considering. So, let's say you generate some questions around this, and the next time we meet, we'll talk about what you've come up with— try to create a draft plan to get us started. |

*(Jim meets with his supervisor and they develop several questions and methods to gather information regarding attitudes around groups. The Attitude Assessment gathers information from both employees with whom Jim works, as well as from clients who may be appropriate candidates for psychotherapy groups. After Jim has collected information and has results from his assessment he again meets with his supervisor.)*

| | |
|---|---|
| SUPERVISOR: | Okay, let's hear what you've got for us. |
| JIM: | Well—all sorts of things actually. *(shaking his head slightly)* For starters—Kara and Megan *(the secretaries)* are concerned about seating in the waiting room. Then Brad—he's in charge of billing—says the computers haven't been programmed for billing based on group sessions. |
| SUPERVISOR: | Anything from the client side of things? |
| JIM: | Yeah, that, too. A few potential group members sound interested, but seemed apprehensive about confidentiality issues. Oh, yeah, and one person wanted to know exactly what the difference in cost would be. |

## If in a Class or Workshop, Then:

### Practice the choice

Pair up with another student and try out your choices. Give each other feedback. What might work? What might need to be changed? Compare your choices with those provided by the authors.

### Process the choice

What have you learned? What are you learning about this process for selecting group techniques? What are you learning about yourself as a group leader? What might you be able to use the next time?

## TASK AND PSYCHOTHERAPY GROUPS CI 10.4

Group Type: *Psychotherapy*
Best Practice Area: *Performing*
Group Developmental Stage: *Beginning*

## You're the Expert!

## HISTORY

Do you remember Jim from the previous critical incident? He succeeded in planning psychotherapy groups for the mental health agency in which he is employed as a counselor. Two weeks ago he launched two psychotherapy groups (a morning session and an afternoon session). The clients screened and selected to participate are individuals who present with behaviors that are often associated with chronic depression. The groups are closed; they will continue for a total of 25 two-hour sessions, meeting once a week. As he leads the group, Jim will continue to meet weekly with his supervisor.

The initial sessions of both groups seemed to be successful. As the sole facilitator, Jim had both groups involved in several activities that required the members to talk about themselves, the first step of the process in getting to know each other and establishing interconnections. During the second session Jim observed a marked decrease in the level of participation from all the group members in one of the groups, and a similar, but milder decrease in the other group. He had hoped that the unresponsiveness was a temporary situation, perhaps due to the rainy overcast weather that day.

Today's morning group, meeting for their third session, started out routinely enough with a check-in, during which members take turns summarizing the past week and what they remember from the last group session. After this introduction, as in the previous session, group members quickly became silent, avoiding eye contact with each other, and especially with Jim, the group leader.

Following the session, but prior to the afternoon session, Jim reported to his supervisor and admitted dismissing the group after only an hour, feeling that the silence had become unbearable. During this unplanned and brief supervision session, Jim also expressed self-doubt regarding his role as an effective group leader. In addition, Jim admitted his growing belief that the same series of events would be replicated in the afternoon session as well. When Jim's supervisor explored with Jim these experiences, Jim was able to gain a perspective that allowed him to optimistically plan for the afternoon session. As Jim's supervisor took the initiative in exploring these experiences with Jim, he was able to reframe his perspective in a way that allowed him to plan with much more optimism the upcoming afternoon session. As he continued his preparation for the next group session, Jim spent some time digesting a few articles on group development that he had not yet had the opportunity to read.

As had happened in the morning group, the afternoon group session started out routinely enough, though only six of the nine group members were present. After a brief check-in period the following occurred.

## CRITICAL INCIDENT

JIM:       I'm wondering if anyone has anything to share with the group today?

(*Silence ensues, as all the members look alternately at the floor, their hands, and the corners of the room.*)

JIM:       (*after about a minute of complete silence*) Okay—so no takers? I'm not sure exactly what to make of the silence. I'm, I'm wondering if some of you have concerns that I'm not aware of?

(*Another notable period of silence follows*)

NAOMI:   (*in a quiet, but pleading voice*) You're—(*clearing her throat*)—you're the expert here, right? Can't you help us?

(*All group members' eyes fix on Jim, as several heads move up and down, silently seconding Naomi's appeal.*)

## WHAT TECHNIQUE DO YOU CHOOSE?

Individually or in small groups jot down or discuss several options for what technique you would use in this situation. What factors must be considered?

## STEPS TOWARD SELECTING A TECHNIQUE

Here is our thinking:

### Step 1:  Identify the group type and purpose, best practice area, and developmental stage

This is a psychotherapy group in which the group and the group leader are stuck. Although very little seems to be happening, the silence and minimal group member input suggest that there is, in reality, a great deal going on. Given the way in which the group is performing right now, they are no doubt developmentally in the beginning stage. This, in part substantiated by Naomi's risky call for help, with its underlying assumption that the leader is the sole source of guidance and answers, suggesting that the group's roles and goals may be ill-defined or unclear to its members. Certainly, Jim did not intend for the group members to confer this status on him.

### Step 2:   Analyze the presenting situation by applying ecological concepts

Developmentally speaking, we know that in the beginning stages of a group, leaders and coleaders often must assume many of the leader functions. Therefore, there is some justification for the members looking to Jim for help. Accepting the current situation as understandable, Jim might consider reviewing how the ecological concepts can help him make more sense of this critical point in the group's development. For example, what contextual factors have allowed group members to make inferences about his position as leader and expert of the group? Does the setting itself (e.g., the organization, the building, the arrangement of the furniture, etc.) confer on him, in the group's view, a certain level of expertise? Jim will also benefit from evaluating his efforts thus far in helping the group form a unique social identity: an identity that prizes collaboration among all group members and that creates a sense of strength and trust through the value placed on mutual support.

### Step 3:   Review possible group techniques, considering focus and level

***Performing Toolbox #31,*** Sentence Completions.

*Focus:* Affective and/or cognitive.
*Level:* Individual and group.

In this technique, Jim gives the group, or at least Naomi, what is expected. As a way of acknowledging her statement and taking charge, Jim asks the group members to complete several questions, which provide a means to begin exploring what is happening in the group. Individual members write down their response to the questions, which Jim must create on the spot. Afterward, members are encouraged to discuss as a group the responses they have just recorded individually. This activity has the advantage of both allowing Jim to take charge and lead the group, while at the same time inviting the members to engage in an activity that will shift some of the meaning making to them. Jim's well-crafted sentences should bring to light members' thoughts and feelings regarding the group members' current state and their expectations for the remaining sessions.

***Performing Toolbox #4,*** Collective Knowledge.

*Focus:* Cognitive.
*Level:* Interpersonal and group.

As with the previous technique, Jim acknowledges Naomi's comments and the nonverbal communication of the members. Building on this, he works from a collaborative stance and asks members to divide into pairs. In their pairs, members are asked to develop a list of group rules, goals, and expectations. After an appropriate amount of time, Jim has each pair report to the entire group. Using the information reported to evaluate what is occurring, Jim continues to help the group process and make meaning out of the experiences.

### Step 4:   Select a best-fit technique

The group is at a transitional point in its development. Jim elects to use sentence completion statements to explore feelings, thoughts, and ideas. Jim's approach in selecting a technique that helps connect affect with behaviors, and perhaps cognitive processes, is crucial to furthering group development. Also, he has elected to do so at an individual level because only one member has taken the risk to express honest levels of frustration with Jim. Whereas establishing and clarifying rules and goals is without question an important ingredient, Jim has a unique opportunity to connect the processes in the group with the selected Sentence Completions technique. The effort to divide into pairs (using Collective Knowledge) might result in an unintended side effect of losing the here-and-now energy that Naomi has risked initiating with her plea for help. On the other hand, a technique such as Sentence Completions, one that can build on the openness of a group member's statement/response, can prove to be a very effective group strategy. As an additional advantage, the Sentence Completions technique has a low level of complexity, and can easily be accomplished.

Giving consideration both to the silence over the last several sessions and to the concept of meaning making, we might easily propose a variety of alternative explanations for the minimal member participation, beyond the meaning suggested by the one group member's comments.

The choice point in electing to elicit an affective response is to help the individual group member connect a previously made cognitive statement to affect. Making this connection enables the group member to explore further the processes supporting the recent behaviors. Thus, using sentence completion statements to explore feelings has been selected as the most appropriate technique.

### Step 5:   Implement and evaluate how well the technique worked

JIM:       Thank you, Naomi. It's very helpful for the rest of us to hear how you're feeling—and I'm guessing that others may be having similar feelings. Would it be okay if I helped us start to explore this by starting several sentences, and then asking others here if they would finish the thought I start?

NAOMI:    Well—I'm not sure—I don't really have any idea what others are thinking right now. But, okay, yes—I think I would like to try that, and I think maybe other people would too. Would it be all right if you give us an example first—just so we kinda know?

JIM:       Sure—good idea. Here's an example: I say, "I'm thinking that your silence is because, as the group leader, I'm supposed to have the answers, but I haven't been doing a very good job of giving you the answers you need. Then you would finish the next sentence I give you. Like this: "When Jim doesn't lead me in this group, I feel . . . " Then you would add what you feel—in your head or perhaps even better, on a piece of paper that I can provide.

*(Group members unanimously agree to give this technique a try. After several questions, Jim asks members if they would feel comfortable sharing any of their responses to the sentence completion exercise.)*

MAGGIE:   All right, I'll go. When I agreed to come to this group I expected to have Jim teach us how to live with depression. And, um, okay, here goes—The way I feel right now about this group is that I've been cheated.

JIM:       Maggie, thank you—thanks for sharing your sentences. That's really important for us all! Anyone else? Did any of you write something similar to what

Maggie wrote? If you did—well, it's important that you share it with us. I can't speak for how anyone else feels, but I know I'd really like to hear from you.

LUIS:    Yeah—okay—I guess I can. I'm feeling sorta like Maggie, so I said something pretty much the same: When I agreed to come . . .

The technique is in itself oriented toward continual processing. The group has experienced conflict and is now processing the impact of unclear group members' expectations. From this, Jim will continue to create his own unique context in which he can continue to learn and develop as well as effectively assist group members. This Sentence Completions technique is, in itself, oriented toward continual processing. The group has experienced conflict, and they are now processing the consequences of the unclear expectations group members have been carrying. From this point, Jim will continue to create his own unique context in which he can continue to learn and develop, as well as effectively assist group members to do the same.

## If in a Class or Workshop, Then:

### *Practice the choice*

Pair up with another student and try out your choices. Give each other feedback. What might work? What might need to be changed? Compare your choices with those provided by the authors.

### *Process the choice*

What have you learned? What are you learning about this process for selecting group techniques? What are you learning about yourself as a group leader? What might you be able to use the next time?

### TASK AND PSYCHOTHERAPY GROUPS CI 10.5

Group Type: *Task*
Best Practice Area: *Between-Session Processing*
Group Development Stage: *Beginning*

## *Meet!*

## HISTORY

A planning committee has been established to recognize the 25th year of the counseling center at Rogers University by holding honoring activities within a Celebration Year theme. The cochairs of this committee include the counseling center director (Susan) and the coordinator of group services (Tony), both professional staff with considerable experience in group leadership. In addition, an intern (Doris) is helping with logistics. Planning committee members include three previous staff still in the area, an assistant dean of student services (Jean), the president of the student government at Rogers University (George), and a staff member (Betty) from the Career

Development Center. The committee has met twice so far, for 1 hour each time, in getting ready for the Celebration Year, which is 10 months away.

The first meeting, held October 1, went well in terms of getting people oriented generally to the task and to each other. The second meeting, held on November 15, was quite "ragged," with lots of ideas but no consolidation of them. Two members, on leaving, said that "maybe they could use some more direction." Susan, Tony, and Doris have been very busy and have not been meeting to discuss how the committee has been functioning.

## CRITICAL INCIDENT

In this third committee meeting, held on December 12, the following occurred about halfway into it:

JEAN:   *(assistant dean:)* Not to be difficult here, but it seems we are spinning our wheels quite a bit, don't you think? *(She looks around the table.)*

BETTY:   *(from Career Development)* I'd have to agree, Jean. *(addressing the cochairs and intern)* I wonder if you might have some plans or ideas you've been working on that we haven't yet heard of?

*(Before Tony or Susan could speak, the student on the committee suggests somewhat authoritatively:)*

GEORGE: Hey, here's a thought. I always meet with my cabinet in between meetings to figure out what's going on and what we should do next and I couldn't get along without that. *(addressing Susan and Tony)* Say, if you're not doing that, it might be a good idea!

## WHAT TECHNIQUE DO YOU CHOOSE?

Individually or in small groups jot down or discuss several options for what technique you would use in this situation. What factors must be considered?

## STEPS TOWARD SELECTING A TECHNIQUE

Here is our thinking:

### Step 1:  Identify the group type and purpose, best practice area, and developmental stage

This task group is in its beginning stage of performance and the coleaders are meeting to process in between sessions.

### Step 2:  Analyze the presenting situation by applying ecological concepts

Members are looking for direction. To assist with providing more direction, the cochairs might think about the kind of social system that is being established and the level of meaning making they are providing. That is, the existing social system does not include the cochairs and intern meeting to process what is occurring in the committee and what might be reasonable next steps. It may not be worked out yet, either, how the cochairs and intern are to work together in terms of respective roles and responsibilities. As well, it might be that the committee leaders, as well as the members, are not able yet to make sense of events and experiences that have occurred, which inhibits their capacity to move forward with any clarity.

Therefore, Susan, Tony, and Doris might meet to clarify their mutual roles and responsibilities and establish an ongoing schedule for between-meeting processing so they can review what has happened and strategize appropriate next steps to bring into the committee meeting. They also might plan how they could introduce this suggestion into the next committee meeting in an effort to collaborate with the members and to enlist their support.

**Step 3:   Review possible group techniques, considering focus and level**

***Processing Between Toolbox #5,*** Coleader Checks. Establishing a meeting among coleaders is necessary for any subsequent between-meeting processing results to be shared.

*Focus:* Structural; establishing a coleader between-session meeting requires disruption of the typical daily pattern, finding a time that fits all schedules, and holding to it.
*Level:* Group; the coleaders meet outside of group meetings to review all levels of intragroup activity.

In this critical incident, no meetings among the leaders have occurred to date. Therefore, there is no other viable technique to take the place of this one: Meet!

In order for between-meeting processing to occur, it first must be made a priority, be scheduled regularly, and then not be missed. Including within one's busy schedule time for regular between-meeting processing involves evoking a structural focus. The technique itself is aimed at several levels, but chief among them is the group and member interaction within it, as well as how events are proceeding in relation to what is working or might need changing. This type of processing also provides the leaders with the opportunity to examine how each is doing independently and in connection with each other. Sometimes between-meeting processing can become quite intense, especially when discussing difficult group issues or when coleaders provide each other with honest feedback and suggestions. In other cases, intensity may be low, as when identifying how many members were present and when describing events that occurred in the meeting. Its overall effectiveness is largely dependent on the nature of the working relationship between coleaders, including their mutual openness and trust.

**Step 4:   Select a best-fit technique**

How Susan, Tony, and Doris respond to George and the other committee members is the task at hand, after realizing that it would be a good idea for them to be processing regularly between meetings. As we have pointed out, attention needs to be given to the AAEES criteria of adequacy, appropriateness, effectiveness, efficiency, and side effects (AAEES) to assist with this choice.

Will between-meeting processing fit with the committee's functioning? With the activities of the counseling center? How can this approach be introduced to the committee members so as not to offend them or to clash with their values? Is asking the members for their reaction to between-group meetings an acceptable way to seek their support?

Is establishing a schedule for between-meeting processing sufficient for ensuring improved direction? Is it a noticeable positive step? Would anything else be needed in addition? Will the approach for introducing this technique be enough to enlist their support?

Will spending time reviewing and reflecting committee functioning help with keeping members on task and with moving the committee forward? Will it assist with helping members feel clearer about directions and, thus, contribute to improved productivity? Will asking members for their reaction produce a positive discussion and stand a reasonable chance of getting their support?

Scheduling an additional meeting each week obviously takes more time from already busy schedules. Does it seem more likely than not that this extra time will promote improved practice, help with monitoring progress, and assist with lowering misguided efforts? Is a more nuanced or complex way needed to seek members support, or is this straightforward enough?

Will this schedule of between-meeting processing positively or negatively affect other responsibilities? How can the negative ones be avoided?

**Step 5:   Implement and evaluate how well the technique worked**

One of the cochairs, let's say, Susan says: "Hmmm, you have me thinking now about what might be helpful. Your idea, George, seems a good one . . . Tony and Doris, what if we plan from here on out to meet after each committee meeting to debrief and to take a look at some next steps?"

Note that the suggestion takes George's idea into account, does not address any possible "haughtiness" that was part of his remark, and openly suggests a new tack, one that might help keep the committee stay more on track. Assuming Tony and Doris positively respond, then the following statement might be in order:

TONY:    (*addressing the committee members*) How does this sound to you; does it
         seem on target, appropriate, or not?

Here, the cochair tries to enlist the members to comment on this idea, to work from a collaborative stance, and to seek their support.

## If in a Class or Workshop, Then:

### Practice the choice

Pair up with another student and try out your choices. Give each other feedback. What might work? What might need to be changed? Compare your choices with those provided by the authors.

### Process the choice

What have you learned? What are you learning about this process for selecting group techniques? What are you learning about yourself as a group leader? What might you be able to use the next time?

## In Sum

Group work is a robust method, suitable for providing personal and interpersonal help (i.e., counseling, psychoeducation, and psychotherapy groups) and for improving productivity (i.e., task groups). In this book, because counselors, psychologists, and social workers use groups most frequently within counseling and psychoeducation contexts, we focused on those particular applications.

In this chapter, however, we examined psychotherapy and task groups. In psychotherapy groups, the work delves more deeply within the psychoemotional realm and group leaders need to use techniques that probe more deeply into the members' lives and are sensitive to greater risk. In task groups, leaders need to help members join together to forge ideas into feasible strategies for accomplishing established goals. As well, group specialists can consult with and train leaders and members of task groups—such as classrooms, neighborhood councils, and religious communities—to assist them in becoming more adept at using group processes in their work.

The up side to group work is huge. Group techniques, skillfully and creatively used, can help the existing opportunity become a reality.

## References

Association for Specialists in Group Work. (2000). *Professional standards for the training of group workers*. Retrieved from http://www.asgw.org

Barlow, S., Fuhriman, A., & Burlingame, G. (2004). The history of group counseling and psychotherapy. In J. DeLucia-Waack, D. Gerrity, C. Kalodner, & M. Riva (Eds.), *Handbook of group counseling and psychotherapy* (pp. 3–22). Thousand Oaks, CA: Sage.

Conyne, R. (1989). *How personal growth and task groups work*. Newberry Park, CA: Sage.

Conyne, R. (2004). *Preventive counseling: Helping people to become empowered in systems and settings*. New York: Brunner-Routledge.

Conyne, R., Rapin, L., & Rand, J. (1997). A model for leading task groups. In H. Forester-Miller & J. Kottler (Eds.), *Issues and challenges for group practitioners* (pp. 117–132). Denver, CO: Love.

Conyne, R., Rapin, L., & Rand, J. (2006). A model for leading task groups. *Counseling and Human Development, 38* [Whole issue].

Conyne, R., Wilson, F. R., & Ward, D. (1997). *Comprehensive group work: What it means & how to teach it*. Alexandria, VA: American Counseling Association.

Dagley, J., Gazda, G., Eppinger, S., & Stewart, E. (1994). Group psychotherapy research with children, preadolescents, and adolescents. In A. Fuhriman & G. Burlingame (Eds.), *Handbook of group psychotherapy* (pp. 340–369). New York: John Wiley.

Gullotta, T., & Bloom, M. (Eds.). (2003). *Encyclopedia of primary prevention and health promotion*. New York: Kluwer.

Hulse-Killacky, D., Killacky, J., & Donigian, J. (2001). *Making task groups work in your world*. Upper Saddle River, NJ: Merrill/Prentice Hall.

Kivlighan, D., & Holmes, S. (2004). The importance of therapeutic factors: A typology of therapeutic factors studies. In J. DeLucia-Waack, D. Gerrity, C. Kalodner, & M. Riva (Eds.), *Handbook of group counseling and psychotherapy* (pp. 23–36). Thousand Oaks, CA: Sage.

National Institute of Mental Health. (1998). *Mental health matters*. Washington, DC.: Author.

Wheelan, S. (2004). Groups in the workplace. In J. DeLucia-Waack, D. Gerrity, C. Kalodner, & M. Riva (Eds.), *Handbook of group counseling and psychotherapy* (pp. 401–413). Thousand Oaks, CA: Sage.

Yalom, I., & Leszcz, M. (2005). *The theory and practice of group psychotherapy* (5th ed.). New York: Basic Books.

# PART VI

# Closure

With Chapter 11 we close this book on how to use group techniques with increased purpose. Reviewing and processing what has occurred can add appreciably, and often immeasurably, in life and—as we have tried to show—in group work. Meaning attribution and reflection are critical functions for leaders and members of all kinds of groups, and engaging in these functions can augment and deepen learning and the potential for sustaining change.

In preparation for the final chapter, we ask you to consider the following three questions. Take some time and jot a few notes in the spaces provided (or use supplemental sheets, if needed):

What have you learned about using group techniques?

What have you learned about yourself in the process?

How will you apply your learning?

Now, on to the final chapter.

# 11

## *Summarizing Group Techniques*

**ADVANCE ORGANIZER**

This chapter contains the following material:

**Ecological Concepts in Group-Work Leadership**

**Group Techniques**

**The Toolbox Metaphor**

**PGTM Steps**

**The Three P's of Group Leadership**

**Group Types**

**Developmental Stages**

**Critical Incident Scenario Format**

**What Have You Learned About Yourself?**

**Self-Assessment in Using the Purposeful Group Techniques Model**

**In Sum**

In this final chapter, we want to engage you in reflecting and processing your learning of using group techniques by applying tenets of the purposeful group techniques model (PGTM). This step is similar to what you might do as a group leader in the final group sessions, where you are helping members focus on what they have learned, how they will apply their learning, and where they are headed—among other considerations.

As we mentioned in the preface, for some readers starting with this chapter may be helpful, as it provides a summary overview of the entire book. If you are beginning here, welcome! For the rest of you who are reading the book more traditionally, just carry on.

To get started, we ask that you respond to the questions contained in the four "Reflection Points" boxes that follow. Then, if possible, discuss each of your responses with a partner. We follow each box with a summary of our own.

Let's get started by considering the questions raised in the first Reflection Points.

## Ecological Concepts in Group-Work Leadership

### Reflection Points
#### (for individual analysis or group discussion)

1. Ecological concepts supply the foundation for selecting and using group techniques in the purposeful group techniques model (PGTM). Identify and describe these concepts. What makes an ecological perspective suitable for group leadership?

2. What is meant by the term "group techniques"? What is included?

3. A group techniques toolbox is presented as a resource. Yet, we cautioned about its use. What is the concern? Discuss this with a partner.

Groups themselves are comprised of individuals who interact and participate together for some purpose. To attain positive results, including a satisfying experience, these individuals need to do many things, including finding and agreeing on ways to connect with each other, combining their resources collectively, and sensing that their involvement contributes something positively. In short, effective and satisfying group work is dependent on the members forming an ecology that works for them and yields successful outcomes that are lasting.

The PGTM is premised on a set of six ecological concepts, as you have read: context, interconnection, collaboration, social system maintenance, meaning making, and sustainability. As leaders of any group, keep these concepts in mind as guiding principles. One of the fundamental functions of the group leader is to help individual members form connections through which they can accomplish their goals and feel a sense of personal satisfaction.

## Group Techniques

Simply put, we think of group techniques as the "actions group leaders take to move the group and its members forward." More precisely, the definition of group techniques we use is:

*Techniques are intervention applications ("tools of the trade") that are used by group leaders—and sometimes by group members—to focus group processes, try out behavior, accentuate thoughts and feelings, and provide opportunities for learning.*

There are literally hundreds of group techniques that have been developed. That is both a blessing and a curse. Although it is wonderful to have an array of possibilities available for use, it is essential that any technique be chosen and used carefully or, in our words, *purposefully.* That is not to suggest that techniques cannot be used spontaneously, growing out of the moment in a group session. What purposeful use means is that any technique fits the group context, is used to foster interconnection, is consistent with the rules and norms governing the group, develops or takes advantage of collaboration, allows for members to develop personal meaning in their experience, and promotes the sustainability of progress. In a nutshell, then, the purposeful use of group techniques results when they are selected and used in ways that are consistent with guiding principles—in the case of the PGTM, with ecological principles.

In Chapter 2 you were introduced to Table 2.1, which showed relationships among ecological concepts, strategies, and exemplary group techniques (see the following). Review the table and then try to identify three other group techniques for each concept. Discuss your work with a partner.

| Ecological Concepts to Support Group Techniques | → | Strategies Associated with Ecological Concepts | → | Exemplary Group Techniques |
|---|---|---|---|---|
| Context | → | "Conceptualize that context is everything." | → | Seating (Toolbox #26, Performance) |
| Interconnection | → | "Forge interconnections among members." | → | String Activity (Toolbox #84, Performance) |
| Collaboration | → | "Do with, rather than do to." | → | Sharing Group Trepidations (Toolbox #1, Performance) |
| Social System | → | "Create and maintain a functioning social system." | → | Physiogram (Toolbox #54, Performance) |
| Meaning Making | → | "Connect experience with knowing." | → | My Learning (Toolbox #17, Processing—Within-Session) |
| Sustainability | → | "Attend to changes lasting over time." | → | Six Month Reminders (Toolbox #30, Processing—Within-Session) |

Identify three other techniques that address context:

a. _____

b. _____

c. _____

Identify three other techniques that address interconnection:

a. _____

b. _____

c. _____

Identify three other techniques that address collaboration:

a. _____

b. _____

c. _____

Identify three other techniques that address social system maintenance:

a. _____

b. _____

c. _____

Identify three other techniques that address meaning making:

a. _____

b. _____

c. _____

Identify three other techniques that address sustainability:

a. _____

b. _____

c. _____

## The Toolbox Metaphor

Of course, this book is intended to address the issue of group-leading competence by focusing on group techniques. Along with Trotzer (2004), we think that group leaders need a kind of basic toolbox at their disposal to feel ready and able to do their work with zest and effectiveness. Similar to how a carpenter, a decorator, a plumber, a Web site designer, or an artist enters a job site carrying a box of tools for the trade, so it is that a group leader needs to enter the group-leading context with a set of tools for that trade—that is, the group techniques that are available for use.

For beginning group leaders there is nothing better than ready information from which to choose salient techniques, such as a toolbox, to move a group forward. Many of us did not have such a toolbox, but have learned by trial and error and "trusting our gut." Drawing from the work of leaders in the field has been an ongoing and arduous task, creating a plethora of choices for use in this book and in our own work. It takes time, however, to build a toolbox mentally or physically.

The value of planning comes very early in a group leader's experience, much like the substitute teacher's old adage, "Always have something in your back pocket, just in case the teacher did not leave enough to keep the students busy." Similarly, the notion of practice, practice, practice is true when group leaders are beginning to develop their expertise. Coleadership is an excellent way to develop skills while receiving immediate feedback with each session. Performing as a group leader with this kind of supervision is especially helpful while counselors are in training.

All that consideration aside, learning to trust one's gut is more than an affective response to group behavior. Assimilating a full understanding of the ecological concepts and how they assist the group leader's perspective at any given time is perhaps the most exciting set of tools available to counselors, experienced or not. As you grapple with how to integrate this new information into your understanding of group work, you may also realize how important these ecological concepts are to seeing a holistic picture of counseling in general.

Following is an example of how we organized group techniques in the Toolbox of Techniques (see the appendix). We have striven to make these techniques accessible and easy to use. Techniques are organized by best practice area (planning, performing, processing), and then within it by group-work type (counseling, psychoeducation, task, psychotherapy), developmental stage (beginning, middle, ending), ecological concepts (context, interconnection, collaboration, social system maintenance, meaning making, sustainability), focus (cognitive, behavioral, affective, structural), and level (individual, interpersonal, group). An example planning technique from the toolbox follows.

### Planning Technique Prototype

| Group Types | Best Practice PLANNING | Stage(s) | Ecological Concept(s) | Focus(i) | Level(s) |
|---|---|---|---|---|---|
| Psyed Couns | Hold a preliminary group session to orient potential members. | Begin | Context Collaboration Social system | Cognitive | Interpersonal Group |

## *PGTM Steps*

> ### Reflection Points
> #### *(for individual analysis or group discussion)*
>
> To guide the selection and use of group techniques, we developed the purposeful group techniques model (PGTM). As you know, this model contains the five major steps:
>
> 1. Identify
> 2. Analyze
> 3. Review
> 4. Select
> 5. Implement and evaluate
>
> Describe each of these steps and discuss how this model is intended to be helpful in using group techniques with purpose. Then discuss them with a partner.

Being an effective group leader requires many resources, not the least of which is to be an effective reflective practitioner. Being able to sense the context of a group, to observe what is occurring, to assess what is needed or missing, to have at one's disposal a range of techniques to choose from, to engage in a problem-solving process to select a best-fit technique, and then to use it and evaluate its use—all these steps are involved with being an effective reflective practitioner.

We designed the purposeful group techniques model (PGTM) to help group leaders become competent reflective practitioners. Mastery of its five steps, we have found, enhances the capacity of group leaders to be effective and helpful. Why? Because the PGTM breaks down a series of complicated steps into larger, more manageable ones that group leaders can learn and apply quite easily.

To review, the PGTM steps are:

### Step 1:  Identify the group type and purpose, best practice area, and developmental stage.

What is the context of the group? Its type (counseling, psychoeducational, task, psychotherapy, a mixture)? What area of best practice is relevant (planning, performing, within or between processing)? If in the performance area, what group developmental stage (beginning, middle, ending) best describes the group's present status?

### Step 2:  Analyze the presenting situation by applying ecological concepts.

What ecological concepts (context, interconnection, collaboration, system maintenance, meaning making, sustainability) are present? Which ones are missing?

**Step 3:   Review possible group techniques, considering focus and level**

What group techniques might be feasible for use? Which ones are you aware of and have used? Might the toolbox be helpful to you in generating possibilities?

**Step 4:   Select a best-fit technique keep in mind these criteria:**

- **Appropriateness:** For example, which technique would best fit the culture of the group and its members?
- **Adequacy:** For example, which technique would be strong enough, but not too strong, to have the desired effect?
- **Effectiveness:** For example, which technique could most fully achieve the goal?
- **Efficiency:** For example, what technique would require the fewest resources?
- **Side effects:** For example, which technique would minimize negative side effects while maximizing positive side effects?

**Step 5:   Implement and evaluate how well the technique worked**

Engage in within- and between-session processing. How did the technique work? Was it useful? Was it helpful for the members and the group? What would you change, if anything, for future use of this technique?

## *The Three P's of Group Leadership*

### Reflection Points
#### *(for individual analysis or group discussion)*

1. Group leadership spans across the focal areas of planning, performing, and processing, group leadership's three P's. Review and describe what is included in each "P."

2. Counselors lead different types of groups. Because the most frequently led are counseling and psychoeducation groups, we concentrated on them in this book. In addition, we devoted one chapter to task and psychotherapy groups because these also are important for counselors. What are the differences among these four group types? Which group type or types do you feel most attracted to, and why?

3. Performing occurs across developmental stages. We identified these stages as beginning, middle, and ending. Techniques are used to assist members and the group itself to progress positively through these stages. Discuss with a partner the major issues involved in each of these three stages.

You will recognize the planning-performing-processing illustration from Chapter 2.

Group leadership involves attention to the three P's of planning, performing, and processing (both within- and between-session). Group techniques are used within each of these areas to help move a group forward. As you have learned, if a group is

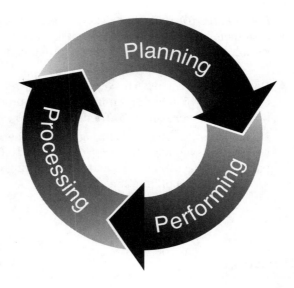

not planned well overall, or by individual sessions, the possibilities for success are compromised. Moreover, if leaders do not reflect on the group and its progress and do not help members do the same, the overall success of the group is lessened.

The *Best Practice Guidelines* of the Association for Specialists in Group Work (Association for Specialists in Group Work [ASGW], 1998) detail standards applicable to planning, performing, and processing, and we encourage you to refer to them. The toolbox contained in this book's appendix organizes 145 group techniques for use in the best practice areas of planning (21 techniques), performing (87 techniques), and processing (37 techniques).

## Group Types

Groups come in many varieties. We have focused primarily on two types of group work, counseling and psychoeducation. In addition, we devoted a chapter to two other important types: task and psychotherapy. Group work leadership can be applied to all of these types.

It is important to conceptually understand and distinguish between these group-work types. In reality, however, mixtures of group-work types occur. For example, a group might be intended primarily as a counseling group but it also might contain some psychoeducational exercises. There is nothing wrong with that and, in some cases, this kind of group-work blend might be preferred (Ward, 2006).

In any case, four major types of group work (ASGW, 2000) are available to counselors and others:

*Task Groups:* These groups are used to resolve or to enhance performance and production goals within a work group, through attention to team building, collaborative problem solving, and system change strategies.

*Psychoeducation Groups:* The purpose of psychoeducation groups is to educate members and develop their skills. Often they are geared to prevention of future problems. Leaders impart information and train in skills, within an interpersonal milieu.

*Counseling Groups:* These groups are used to help members improve their coping skills by focusing on interpersonal problem solving, feedback, and support within a here-and-now framework.

*Psychotherapy Groups:* Through psychotherapy groups, members learn how to reduce psychological and/or emotional dysfunction by focusing on bringing past history to the present and incorporating diagnosis and assessment within an interpersonal orientation.

## Developmental Stages

Each of the group-work types develops or evolves over time. This development has been charted and described by a large number of group developmental stage theories. Assessing the approximate developmental stage of a group is always a "guesstimate" due to the complex issues involved. However, being aware of the general stage of development can assist leaders in understanding events and experiences that are occurring. This understanding can promote the selection and use of group techniques that are most appropriate.

We have tried to keep our description of developmental stages relatively simple: beginning, middle, and ending.

### Performance Techniques at the Beginning Stage of Group Development: Getting Established and Transitioning

Techniques selected at the beginning stage need to be grounded in helping members begin to develop a social system and become oriented and begin the process of becoming interconnected.

### Performance Techniques at the Middle Stage of Group Development: Connecting and Producing

Techniques selected at the middle stage need to be building on previous conditions, enhancing the level of interconnection, adding collaboration among members to move forward, and helping members make sense and draw meaning from their experience.

### Performance Techniques at the Ending Stage of Group Development: Consolidating and Forecasting

Techniques selected at the ending stage of group development need to emphasize meaning and the sustainability of learning and change. What has been learned and what will carry forward to the future are essential questions at this point of any group.

## Critical Incident Scenario Format

### Reflection Points
#### (for individual analysis or group discussion)

1. Critical incidents were presented to assist you in learning how to choose and implement group techniques. What have you learned about using group techniques by considering this approach?

2. Group techniques can be thought of as having a focus (cognitive, affective, behavioral, or structural) and a level (individual, interpersonal, or group). Go to the appendix, which contains the toolbox, and select from the performance area one example of a technique that you particularly like for each focus and for each level. What is attractive to you about these seven techniques?

3. What have you learned about yourself as a group leader through studying the PGTM? How has your study stimulated you? What personal and interpersonal strengths have you noticed again, or for the first time? How has your knowledge of group leadership been affected? How will you put any of this learning into practice? Discuss these questions with a partner.

In the previous chapters, you learned about techniques and their use through working with critical incidents that were adapted from actual group sessions. We presented a situation for you to consider by following a consistent set of steps, leaving you at a choice point regarding what technique(s) you might select. You were then asked to review techniques contained in the toolbox, as appropriate, and to follow the PGTM steps to arrive at your choice. If you were involved with an educational or training session, you also had the opportunity to try out your choice and obtain feedback from others. Our intent was to help you learn techniques within a decision-making structure that will permit you to function effectively and appropriately as a group leader, while developing your expertise in exercising professional judgment as a group leader.

Adapted from Cohen and Smith (1976), techniques were categorized by their relative focus on thinking (cognitive focus), feeling (affective focus), doing (behavioral focus), and/or on shifting the focus (structural focus). Techniques also were categorized by their level of attention on one member (individual level), two or more members (interpersonal level), and the group as a whole (group level). These organized ways of thinking about group techniques aid leaders in group leading.

## What Have You Learned About Yourself?

Group leadership is a personal pursuit. All the theory, techniques, and supervised experience in the world—although very important and necessary—cannot replace or take priority over your personal and interpersonal impact on others. In a very real sense, you are your most important resource! What are you learning about yourself as you move through this book? What kinds of techniques seem most amenable to your own style? How has your ability to become a reflective practitioner changed, if at all? How are you putting all this information together with your own existing strengths?

To assist in your self-assessment, take a good look at the checklist that follows. Where are you presently strong? Where might you need additional work?

## Self-Assessment in Using the Purposeful Group Techniques Model

### INSTRUCTIONS:

Circle the relevant response for each question in each section. Write any self-assessment comments after the last section.

|  | Okay Now | Needs Growth |
|---|:---:|:---:|
| **A. ASGW *Best Practice Guidelines*** | | |
| Understand: | | |
| 1.  Planning | X | X |
| 2.  Performing | | X |
| 3.  Processing | | |
|    ✔ Within-session | X | X |
|    ✔ Between-session | X | X |
| **B. Ecological Concepts** | | |
| Understand: | | |
| 1.  Context | X | X |
| 2.  Interconnection | X | X |
| 3.  Collaboration | X | X |
| 4.  Social system maintenance | X | X |
| 5.  Meaning making | X | X |
| 6.  Sustainability | X | X |
| **C. Ecological Strategies** | | |
| Ability to: | | |
| 1.  Conceptualize that context is everything | X | X |
| 2.  Forge interconnections among members | X | X |
| 3.  Do with, rather than to | X | X |

| | Okay Now | Needs Growth |
|---|---|---|
| 4.  Create and maintain a functioning social system | X | X |
| 5.  Connect experience with knowing | X | X |
| 6.  Attend to changes lasting over time | X | X |
| **D.  Purposeful Group Techniques Model (PGTM) Skills** | | |
| Ability to: | | |
| 1.  Identify | | |
| ✔ Group type and purpose | X | X |
| ✔ Best practice area | X | X |
| ✔ Developmental stage | X | X |
| 2.  Analyze present situation | | |
| ✔ Ecological concepts present | X | X |
| ✔ Ecological concepts missing | X | X |
| 3.  Review group techniques | | |
| ✔ Focus | X | X |
| ✔ Level | X | X |
| 4.  Select best-fit techniques | | |
| ✔ Appropriateness | X | X |
| ✔ Adequacy | X | X |
| ✔ Effectiveness | X | X |
| ✔ Efficiency | X | X |
| ✔ Side effects | X | X |
| 5.  Implement and evaluate | | |
| ✔ Within-session processing | X | X |
| ✔ Between-session processing | X | X |

**E.  Self-Assessment Comments**

1.  In completing this self-assessment what have you learned about yourself?

2.  How might you integrate the results from this self-assessment into your growth and development as a group leader?

## In Sum

Of course, assessing your capacity in each of the elements in the self-assessment can be very helpful and provide some useful guidance. Yet, group leadership involves integrating these separate elements and then applying them within ongoing situations that arise.

Group leadership is a critically important function for counselors and other helpers. Being able to *do* group leadership, as opposed only to knowing *about* it, is a pressing need.

Group techniques provide group leaders with action possibilities. These techniques need to be used carefully, being guided by a cohesive framework. The purposeful group techniques model (PGTM) supplies one resource that group leaders can use to help shape what they do in the planning, performing, and processing of group leadership, with any type of group. PGTM steps (identify, analyze, review, select, and implement and evaluate) allow group leaders to consider and choose from a range of technique possibilities that suggest the best possibility for success. We hope you have found this model beneficial and that, as you draw from it, your group leadership effectiveness is enhanced.

Finally, we want to reiterate the importance of fitting this model, or whatever conceptual framework you choose to employ, with your own personal and interpersonal disposition, strengths, and resources. As we have emphasized, whereas the value of conceptual and technical competence cannot be denied, it is the integration of it with your personal and interpersonal qualities that will make all the difference.

# References

Association for Specialists in Group Work. (1998). *Association for Specialists in Group Work best practice guidelines.* Retrieved from http://www.asgw.org

Association for Specialists in Group Work. (2000). *Professional standards for the training of group workers.* Retrieved from http://www.asgw.org

Cohen, A., & Smith, R. D. (1976). *The critical incident in growth groups: Theory and technique.* La Jolla, CA: University Associates.

Trotzer, J. (2004). Conducting a group: Guidelines for choosing and using activities. In J. Delucia-Waack, D. Gerrity, C. Kalodner, and M. Riva (Eds.), *Handbook of group counseling and psychotherapy* (pp. 76–90). Thousand Oaks, CA: Sage.

Ward, D. (2006). Classification of groups. *Journal for Specialists in Group Work, 31,* 93–97.

# *Appendix*

**TOOLBOX OF TECHNIQUES**

| Group Types | Best Practice Area: PLANNING Techniques | Ecological Concept(s) | Focus(i) | Level(s) |
|---|---|---|---|---|
| Psyed<br>Couns<br>Psyther<br>Task | 1. *Ecological Profile:* Do an ecological profile (audit), considering context, interconnection, collaboration, social system, and meaning making. | Context<br>Interconnection<br>Collaboration<br>Social system<br>Meaning making | Cognitive | Group |
| Psyed<br>Couns<br>Psyther | 2. *Assessment Visit:* Visit with people who wish to join the group to assess goodness of fit. | Context<br>Collaboration<br>Social system | Cognitive<br>Behavioral | Individual |
| Psyed<br>Couns<br>Psyther | 3. *Preliminary Session:* Hold a preliminary group session to orient potential members. | Context<br>Social system<br>Meaning making | Cognitive<br>Behavioral | Individual<br>Group |
| Psyed<br>Couns | 4. *Interviews:* Key informant interviews. | Context | Cognitive | Group |
| Psyed<br>Couns | 5. *Group Plan:* Leader develops a group plan (see Chapter 4). | Context | Cognitive | Group |
| Psyed<br>Couns | 6. *Group Leader Goals:* The leader sets goals for the group. | Context | Cognitive | Individual |
| Psyed<br>Couns | 7. *Representative Group:* The leader gathers a group of people representative of those expected to participate in the group. | Collaboration | Structural | Group |
| Psyed<br>Couns<br>Psyther | 8. *Attitude Assessment:* Do an attitude assessment about groups, perhaps by mail, to review prior to the first session. | Interconnection<br>Meaning making | Cognitive<br>Affective | Individual |
| Psyed<br>Couns<br>Psyther<br>Task | 9. *Procedures Discussion:* Leader introduces essential procedures and discusses them with members. | Context<br>Collaboration<br>Social system | Cognitive | Group |
| Psyed<br>Couns<br>Psyther<br>Task | 10. *Leader Selection:* Select group leaders, and decide if there is to be a coleader. | Context<br>Interconnection<br>Social system | Structural | Group |
| Psyed<br>Couns<br>Psyther | 11. *Contracting:* Leader has members sign two copies of a contract, keeping one and returning one to the leader, specifying behaviors or attitudes to *(Continued)* | Context<br>Interconnection<br>Collaboration<br>Social system | Cognitive<br>Behavioral | Individual |

*Notes:* Planning techniques occur prior to the first group meeting; therefore, a developmental stage is not relevant. Group types include psychoeducation (psyed), counseling, (couns), psychotherapy (psyther), and task.

| Group Types | Best Practice Area: PERFORMING Techniques | Ecological Concept(s) | Focus(i) | Level(s) |
|---|---|---|---|---|
| | *(Continued from p. 219)* change and what they are willing to do to make changes. | | | |
| Psyed Couns Psyther Task | 12. *Boundary Planning:* Plan boundaries: logical, financial, authority, time, money, other (e.g., Never group on Sunday nights). | Context Interconnection Collaboration Social system | Cognitive Structural | Interpersonal Group |
| Psyed Couns Psyther Task | 13. *Planning Supervision:* Seek supervision. | Collaboration Social system Meaning making | Cognitive | Group |
| Psyed Couns Psyther Task | 14. *Seating:* Arrange seating to accommodate the most communication among group members. | Context Interconnection Social system | Structural | Interpersonal Group |
| Psyed Couns Psyther Task | 15. *Questionnaires:* Have members complete a questionnaire on how well they are coping with an area of concern. | Context Meaning making | Cognitive Affective Behavioral | Individual |
| Psyed Couns Psyther Task | 16. *Planning Consultation:* Seek consultation. | Context | Cognitive | Individual |
| Psyed Couns Psyther Task | 17. *Group Work Training:* Seek training. | Context | Behavioral | Individual |
| Psyed Couns Psyther Task | 18. *Group Work Education:* Seek education. | Context | Cognitive | Individual |
| Psyed Couns Psyther Task | 19. *Leader Self-Goals:* The leader sets goals for himself or herself. | Meaning making | Cognitive | Individual |
| Psyed Couns Psyther Task | 20. Ask Planning Members to discuss feelings of anxiety, mistrust, and insecurity. | Meaning making | Affective | Individual Group |
| Psyed Task | 21. *Floating Facilitator:* Leaders shuttle among small groups to help facilitate discussion of material and answer questions naturally occurring within each group's exchange. | | Structural | Group |
| Psyed Couns Psyther Task | 22. *Fishbowl (revised):* Leader arranges an inner group with members working on a task surrounded by a second group silently observing the inner group at work. At defined points the inner group stops and receives nonjudgmental, observational feedback from the outside group. | | Structural | Group |

| Group Types | Best Practice Area: PERFORMING Techniques | Stage(s) | Ecological Concept(s) | Focus(i) | Level(s) |
|---|---|---|---|---|---|
| Psyed Couns Psyther Task | 1. *Address Apprehensions:* Members divide into subgroups to discuss apprehensions about group participation, to prepare a group discussion about their major concerns. | Beg | Context Meaning making | Affective | Interpersonal Group |
| Psyed Couns Psyther Task | 2. *Topic Inventory:* Have group members create a list of statements about the group's topic or purpose. Statements may be true or questionable, but the group process must include consensus among each subgroup. Compile the statements and discuss as a group, with leader prepared to provide correct information or to assist group members to arrive at correct statements. | Beg | Interconnection Social system Collaboration | Cognitive | Interpersonal |
| Psyed Couns Psyther Task | 3. *M & M Icebreaker:* Select several colors of M & M candies to distribute among group members. Choose colors to represent specific activities for members to perform, such as red means shake other members' hands while saying your name, or yellow means ask another group member to tell his reason for coming to the group. | Beg | Interconnection Social system Meaning making | Affective Behavioral | Individual |
| Psyed Couns Psyther Task | 4. *Collective Knowledge:* In subgroups have members introduce themselves, then as a group name five ground rules for the larger group. Have subgroups report, sharing only what they have that is different from the previous group reports. Reach consensus as a large group regarding the adoption of the ground rules. | Beg | Interconnection Collaboration Social system Meaning making | Cognitive | Interpersonal Group |
| Psyed Couns Psyther Task | 5. *Motto Mosaic:* Each group member creates a short statement that will become his or her motto, and assists each member in identifying something special or unique about himself or herself. | Beg | Meaning making | Cognitive | Individual |
| Psyed Couns Psyther Task | 6. *Two Truths and a Lie:* Group members write down three short statements about themselves, two of which are true and one of which is not. Pair group members and have them share their statements. (*Continued*) | Beg | Interpersonal | Cognitive | Individual Group |

| Group Types | Best Practice Area: PERFORMING Techniques | Stage(s) | Ecological Concept(s) | Focus(i) | Level(s) |
|---|---|---|---|---|---|
| | *(Continued from p. 221)* Gather as a group and let each partner introduce the other member and group tries to determine which is true and which is not. | | | | |
| Psyed Couns Psyther Task | 7. *Trust Fall:* Member 1 closes his or her eyes and Member 2 stands behind. Member 1 falls back and Member 2 catches; object is to trust that someone will be there. | Beg | Interconnection | Behavioral Structural | Interpersonal |
| Psyed Couns Psyther Task | 8. *Using "I" Terms:* Leader instructs the members to use "I" terms. (Often needed when people make generalizations.) | Beg | Social system | Behavioral | Individual |
| Psyed Couns Psyther Task | 9. *Letter to Self:* Write a letter to self that will be opened at the last meeting (goals, expectations, etc.). | Beg | Meaning making | Cognitive | Individual |
| Psyed Couns Psyther Task | 10. *Self-Description:* Members offer a one-word description of themselves. Then they pair up by identification with others who used similar/ dissimilar words; finally, combine with another pair. | Beg | Interconnection Collaboration Social system Meaning making | Cognitive Behavioral Structural | Individual Interpersonal Group |
| Psyed Couns Psyther Task | 11. *Match Hunt:* Each member is given a list of human experiences, attributes, and hobbies to match with others in the group (e.g., plays music, likes to watch TV, or has a pet). | Beg | Interconnection Collaboration | Cognitive Behavioral | Interpersonal Group |
| Psyed Couns Psyther Task | 12. *Self-Disclosure:* Members do introductions by stating their name and saying anything about themselves that they want the group to know. | Beg | Context Interconnection Social system | Cognitive | Individual Interpersonal |
| Psyed Couns Task | 13. *Delphi Technique:* A decision-making process that uses opinions of members with the guidance of a facilitator to reach consensus by rank-order process. | Beg Mid | Collaboration | Cognitive | Individual Group |
| Psyed Couns Psyther Task | 14. *Resume for Membership:* Post these elements of a resume: Education, Experiences, Unique talents suitable to a job, Past successes. Members spend 5 minutes writing a resume as if applying for a job as a "member of the group." Then share and discuss as a group. | Beg Mid | Interconnection Social system Meaning making | Cognitive | Individual Group |

| Group Types | Best Practice Area: PERFORMING Techniques | Stage(s) | Ecological Concept(s) | Focus(i) | Level(s) |
|---|---|---|---|---|---|
| Psyed Couns Task | 15. *Blind Trust Walk:* Members take turns being blindfolded and led around by another. After, discuss the trust or lack of trust members experienced. | Beg Mid | Interconnection Collaboration Meaning making | Cognitive Affective Behavioral | Individual Interpersonal |
| Psyed Couns Psyther Task | 16. *Subgrouping:* Members create subgroups and then are assigned a number. The leader can call a number from each group to have that member respond for his or her group (to ensure equal participation). | Beg Mid | Interconnection Collaboration Meaning making | Cognitive Behavioral Structural | Individual Group |
| Psyed Couns Psyther Task | 17. *Question/No Question:* Using a random pattern of shapes, have two group members work together to re-create the pattern. Members sit back to back, with one member as artist while the other has the drawing. No questions are allowed by the artist, while the member with the drawing describes the pattern. Once completed, have them share. Repeat the exercise, but use a different pattern and allow the artist to ask questions for clarification. Share again. Demonstrates one-way versus two-way communication. | Beg Mid | Collaboration Social system Meaning making | Cognitive Behavioral | Individual |
| Psyed Couns Psyther Task | 18. *Goal Setting:* Have the group set goals for one session. | Beg Mid | Context Interconnection Collaboration Social system | Cognitive Structural | Group |
| Psyed Couns Psyther | 19. *Sociograms:* Have members do individual sociograms to indicate relationships in their lives. Share. | Beg Mid | Interconnection | Cognitive | Individual |
| Psyed Couns Psyther Task | 20. *Say It for Real:* Leaders can have resistant members verbalize attitudes or behaviors such as "I won't say anything," and asking "How are you going to do this? How will you keep things to yourself?" | Beg Mid | Interconnection Social system | Cognitive Affective | Individual Interpersonal |
| Psyed Couns Psyther Task | 21. *Time Tokens:* Pass out the same number of "time tokens" to all members. Each time they want to speak they must use a time token (to ensure wider participation). | Beg Mid | Social system Meaning making | Cognitive Behavioral | Individual Interpersonal Group |
| Psyed Couns Psyther | 22. *Self-Check:* Leader asks, "Can you take more responsibility?" | Beg Mid | Social system | Behavioral | Individual Group |

| Group Types | Best Practice Area: PERFORMING Techniques | Stage(s) | Ecological Concept(s) | Focus(i) | Level(s) |
|---|---|---|---|---|---|
| Psyed Couns Psyther | 23. *Permission:* Leader asks, "Would that be okay?" | Beg Mid End | Collaboration | Cognitive | Individual Interpersonal |
| Psyed Couns Psyther Task | 24. *Go-Arounds:* Have each member check in with a "go-around" at some point in the session. | Beg Mid End | Context Interconnection Social system | Cognitive Affective Behavioral | Individual |
| Psyed Couns Psyther Task | 25. *Assigned Readings:* Assign readings between group sessions, inviting reflection and learning. | Beg Mid End | Context Meaning making | Cognitive Behavioral | Individual Group |
| Psyed Couns Psyther Task | 26. *Seating:* Arrange seating to accommodate the most communica-tion among group members. | Beg Mid End | Interconnection Social system | Structural | Interpersonal Group |
| Psyed Couns | 27. *Therapeutic Activity:* Engage members in an activity with thera-peutic benefits, such as jogging or walking. | Beg Mid End | Interconnection Collaboration | Cognitive Affective Behavioral | Individual Interpersonal Group |
| Psyed Couns Psyther Task | 28. *Nominal Group Technique (NGT):* Up to six steps to initiate ideas, but unlike brainstorming, NGT does not require members' open exposure. | Beg Mid End | Interconnection Collaboration Meaning making | Cognitive | Group |
| Psyed Couns Psyther | 29. *Outer Circle:* When a forced client doesn't want to participate, have him or her create an outer circle where participation is not required. | Beg Mid End | Interconnection Social system Meaning making | Cognitive Affective Structural | Individual Interpersonal Group |
| Psyed Couns Psyther Task | 30. *Direct Feedback:* Leader offers feedback about a troublesome behavior (e.g., always answering with questions) in order to model respectful feedback. | Beg Mid End | Collaboration Social system | Cognitive Affective | Individual Interpersonal Group |
| Psyed Couns Psyther Task | 31. *Sentence Completions:* Use sentence completion statements to explore feelings, thoughts, and ideas. Elicit sharing of the experience. | Beg Mid End | Interconnection Meaning making | Cognitive Affective | Individual Interpersonal Group |
| Psyed Couns Psyther Task | 32. *Life Line:* Members draw a timeline of their life, including points of interest and critical turning points. Elicit sharing. | Beg Mid End | Meaning making | Cognitive Affective Behavioral | Individual |

| Group Types | Best Practice Area: PERFORMING Techniques | Stage(s) | Ecological Concept(s) | Focus(i) | Level(s) |
|---|---|---|---|---|---|
| Psyed Couns Psyther Task | 33. *You Are a Book:* Tell members to pretend they are a book: "What is your title? Are you illustrated? What's your style, tone? Will people want to read you? What will entice them to read you? Which chapters were the hardest to write? After reading you cover to cover, what will people think then?" At the end: "What changes would you make to the book?" | Beg Mid End | Meaning making | Cognitive Affective | Individual |
| Psyed Couns Psyther Task | 34. *Objective Listening:* Using any object, have the member who is speaking hold the object while others are silent.She or he gives it to the next speaker who must address the very last thing said (careful listening skills). | Beg Mid End | Social system | Cognitive Behavioral Structural | Individual Interpersonal Group |
| Psyed Couns Psyther Task | 35. *Fishbowl:* Construct a fishbowl arrangement where a subgroup sits in a circle outside an inner circle. Have members observe process. Then switch. | Beg Mid End | Interconnection Collaboration Meaning making | Cognitive Affective Behavioral Structural | Interpersonal Group |
| Psyed Couns Task | 36. *Brainstorm:* Members generate ideas in a nonjudgmental manner. | Beg Mid End | Interconnection | Cognitive Affective Behavioral | Group |
| Psyed Couns Psyther Task | 37. *Toys in Concert:* Give each member Tinker Toys or Legos and ask them to build a representation of what group cohesion looks like (could be done in pairs or triads). | Beg Mid End | Interconnection Meaning making | Cognitive Behavioral | Individual Interpersonal |
| Psyed Couns Psyther Task | 38. *Summaries:* Have the next speaker in the group summarize what the previous speaker just said (increase understanding and listening skills). | Beg Mid End | Interconnection Social system | Cognitive | Individual Group |
| Psyed Couns Psyther Task | 39. *Out with the Trash:* Have all members sit in a tight circle around the wastebasket. Have them all talk to the can at once about what is most on their minds. Leader calls "Stop" at some point. Often helps people (e.g., lively youngsters) calm down. | Beg Mid End | Collaboration Social system | Cognitive Behavioral | Group |
| Psyed Couns Psyther Task | 40. *Ethical Choice Chart:* Pass out worksheets with sections labeled Assessment, Benefits, Consequences, Duty and Education, leaving *(Continued)* | Beg Mid End | Interconnection Collaboration Social system Meaning making | Cognitive | Individual Group |

| Group Types | Best Practice Area: PERFORMING Techniques | Stage(s) | Ecological Concept(s) | Focus(i) | Level(s) |
|---|---|---|---|---|---|
| | *(Continued from p. 225)* room for group members to write. Useful for issues that arise which need attention to ethical decision making. | | | | |
| Psyed Couns Psyther Task | 41. *Sizing Up:* Ask members to size up everyone in the room, but not to share. (You are asking them to attend to group process and their own reactions.) | Beg Mid End | Meaning making | Cognitive Affective | Individual |
| Psyed Couns Psyther | 42. *Self-Puppets:* Using lunch-sized brown paper bags, glue pictures and words on them that represent the self, then use the bags as puppets to talk. | Beg Mid End | Interconnection Meaning making | Cognitive Affective Behavioral | Individual |
| Psyed Couns Psyther Task | 43. *Opposite Circles:* Have members form two circles, one inside the other, and to walk in reverse directions so that they face each other. Greet others without words. Stop at intervals and give various instructions, such as "find someone you think you have something in common with" or "someone you don't know," etc. | Beg Mid End | Interconnection Collaboration Social system | Behavioral Structural | Interpersonal Group |
| Psyed Couns Psyther | 44. *Genograms:* Have members draw genograms to understand family dynamics. | Beg Mid End | Interconnection Social system Meaning making | Cognitive Affective Behavioral | Individual |
| Psyed Couns Psyther Task | 45. *Person, paper, and pen:* Have each member decide on something they would like to change about their life. Ask for a brief description to discuss with the group with options for change. Take note of recommendations from the group. Try one idea and report back to the group. | Beg Mid End | Collaboration Meaning making | Cognitive Behavioral | Interpersonal Group |
| Psyed Couns Psyther Task | 46. *Caterpillar Activity:* Provide a paper with eight circles connected: draw an expressive face into segment #1, describe self in #2, hobbies in #3, present feelings in #4, birthplace in #5, where I would like to be in #6, activity I would like to do in #7, and unique special quality in #8. Elicit sharing. | Beg Mid End | Interconnection Collaboration Social system Meaning making | Cognitive Affective Behavioral | Individual Group |
| Psyed Couns Psyther | 47. *Family Sculpting:* Members use the other members to "sculpt" their own family by positioning others with body positions to represent their feelings and understanding about the family and family roles. | Beg Mid End | Interconnection | Cognitive Affective Behavioral Structural | Individual Group |

| Group Types | Best Practice Area: PERFORMING Techniques | Stage(s) | Ecological Concept(s) | Focus(i) | Level(s) |
|---|---|---|---|---|---|
| Psyed Couns Psyther Task | 48. *Sensing the Unseen:* Leader says: "None of us has ever seen the wind, but we know it is there. We are blessed with five senses, or if one is lost we compensate with others. Think of ways in which we know the wind is there, and together we will write a poem out loud." Examples: "I see the wind in . . ." (members add images), "I hear the wind in . . . ," "I smell the wind in . . . ," "I taste the wind in . . . ," "I touch the wind in. . . ." Substitute other words for wind, like *God* or *love.* | Beg Mid End | Interconnection | Cognitive Affective | Group |
| Psyed Couns Psyther Task | 49. *Silent Puzzles:* Distribute puzzle pieces cut into various formations of three to five pieces each that should fit to make 8 × 8-inch puzzles, mixed incorrectly. Pieces can be exchanged with others in order to complete a puzzle for each member, but members cannot talk. | Beg Mid End | Collaboration Social system | Cognitive Behavioral | Individual |
| Psyed Couns | 50. *The Eyes Have It:* Leader uses his or her eyes to influence member behavior. | Beg Mid End | Interconnection | Behavioral | Individual |
| Psyed Couns Psyther | 51. *Special Visitors:* Invite spouse, parents, and/or children of group members to a session. | Beg Mid End | Context Interconnection Collaboration Social system Meaning making | Cognitive Affective Structural | Individual Interpersonal Group |
| Psyed Couns Psyther | 52. *Secret Pooling:* Members anonymously write a "secret" about themselves that they have not shared in group and place the paper in middle of group. Members draw a secret (not their own) and empathize about what it might feel like. | Beg End | Interconnection | Structural | Interpersonal |
| Psyed Couns Psyther | 53. *Exaggerations:* Have a member exaggerate his or her behavior to see it clearly, to tire of it, or to gain insight into its sources. | Mid | Meaning making | Cognitive Affective Behavioral | Individual |
| Counseling | 54. *Physiogram:* Members physically place themselves in relation to the center of the room and in relation to each other. | Mid | Social system Meaning making | Cognitive | Group |

| Group Types | Best Practice Area: PERFORMING Techniques | Stage(s) | Ecological Concept(s) | Focus(i) | Level(s) |
|---|---|---|---|---|---|
| Psyed Couns Psyther Task | 55. *Diamond Dialogue:* Pass out sheets of paper with a large four-sided diamond in the center. Have group members write a goal in the center of the diamond. Write obstacles to that goal on the sides inside the diamond shape. Share with the group and try to find options which can be written outside the diamond shape opposite the obstacles. | Mid | Collaboration Meaning making | Cognitive | Individual |
| Psyed Couns Psyther Task | 56. *Vicarious Behavior:* A member can act out some behavior by using another member as a puppet (of sorts), directing that person to act, talk, and react in ways that relive some part of herself, her family, or her work, etc. Check responses from others. | Mid | Collaboration Meaning making | Cognitive Affective Behavioral Structural | Individual Interpersonal |
| Psyed Couns Psyther Task | 57. *Role Reversal:* Have members switch roles with other members or with the leader. | Mid | Interconnection Collaboration Social system Meaning making | Cognitive Affective Behavioral Structural | Individual Interpersonal Group |
| Psyed Couns Psyther Task | 58. *Inner Circle:* For multiple silent members, have them form an inner circle and talk about what it is like to be silent. For the active members, form an inner circle and talk about what it is like not hearing from others and not knowing what they are thinking. | Mid | Interconnection Social system Meaning making | Cognitive Affective Behavioral Structural | Interpersonal Group |
| Psyed Couns Psyther | 59. *Strength Bombardment:* Members present to each other what they see as the other's strengths. | Mid | Collaboration Meaning making | Structural | Interpersonal Individual |
| Psyed Couns Psyther Task | 60. *To Be or Not to Be:* Have the member act as if he or she is the person he or she wants to be. | Mid End | Meaning making | Cognitive Affective Behavioral | Individual |
| Psyed Couns Psyther Task | 61. *Be Me:* Group members choose from a stack of cards without looking at the label it signifies. The label is attached to the person's back, so that through interacting with others, the member has to guess what the card says. Labels can signify disabilities, such as "I am deaf"; stereotypes, such as "I am gay," feelings, such as "I am depressed," etc. | Mid End | Meaning making | Cognitive Affective Behavioral | Individual Interpersonal |

| Group Types | Best Practice Area: PERFORMING Techniques | Stage(s) | Ecological Concept(s) | Focus(i) | Level(s) |
|---|---|---|---|---|---|
| Psyed Couns Psyther Task | 62. *Hand out the Hugs:* Have members cut a long narrow piece of paper with a hand on each end. Once labeled with a name, the papers are passed around the group for each one to write an affirmation to the person the "hug" belongs to. | Mid End | Interconnection Social system Meaning making | Cognitive Affective Behavioral | Interpersonal |
| Psyed Couns Psyther | 63. *Arm Wrestling:* Invite members to compete in arm wrestling in order to vent emotions. | Mid End | Interconnection Collaboration Meaning making | Affective Behavioral | Individual Interpersonal |
| Psyed Couns Psyther Task | 64. *Advice Fix:* Have a "fixer" go around and give advice to each member and then say to each member "and from you I want . . . " to allow the member to do what's easy (give advice) and to do what's hard (ask for something from others). | Mid End | Interconnection Collaboration Social system Meaning making | Cognitive Affective Behavioral | Individual Interpersonal Group |
| Psyed Couns Psyther | 65. *Using a Medium:* Member 1 sits in the center facing Member 2, who represents the helper. Member 1 talks about a situation, feelings, or concerns and the group offers insights through Member 2 as the "medium." | Mid End | Collaboration Social system Meaning making | Cognitive Affective Behavioral Structural | Individual Interpersonal Group |
| Psyed Couns Psyther Task | 66. *Use of Silence:* Leader remains silent to encourage members' reflection and/or participation. | Mid End | Interconnection | Cognitive Affective Behavioral | Interpersonal Group |
| Psyed Couns Psyther Task | 67. *Role-Plays:* Leader asks a member; for example: "Leonard, you said that your father was very critical. Could you role-play your father and continue with your criticisms as though you are him — how he would phrase it?" | Mid End | Meaning making | Cognitive Affective Behavioral | Individual |
| Psyed Couns Task | 68. *Look Out Below:* Each member stands on a chair and speaks about who they see as "below" them, or the leader stands on the chair and the members speak about who is "above" them. | Mid End | Meaning making | Cognitive Affective Behavioral | Individual |
| Psyed Couns Psyther | 69. *Epitaphs:* Have members write their own epitaph. Invite sharing. | Mid End | Meaning making | Cognitive Affective | Individual |
| Psyed Couns Psyther Task | 70. *Johari Window:* Have members do a Johari Window. Share in the group. | Mid End | Interconnection | Cognitive Affective | Individual |

| Group Types | Best Practice Area: PERFORMING Techniques | Stage(s) | Ecological Concept(s) | Focus(i) | Level(s) |
|---|---|---|---|---|---|
| Psyed Couns Psyther | 71. *Pillow Fight:* Invite members to hit pillows in order to vent emotions. | Mid End | Social system Meaning making | Affective Behavioral | Individual |
| Psyed Couns Psyther Task | 72. *Therapeutic Fairy Tale:* Members write a fairy tale in 6–10 minutes. Begin with: "Once upon a time . . ." (with or without structured directions), in order to respond differently to a negative memory or situation. | Mid End | Collaboration | Cognitive | Individual Group |
| Psyed Couns Psyther Task | 73. *Hold Out:* Members stand holding hands while trying to keep another member (who is circling the group) from breaking in. | Mid End | Collaboration | Cognitive Affective Behavioral | Group |
| Psyed Couns Psyther Task | 74. *Experiential Focusing:* (1) The member describes an issue. (2) The group may clarify facts – not feelings. (3) Feelings are added to the narrative. (4) Focus for the member shifts from the issue to the member's feelings, while the member focuses on the direct inner reference of experiencing the emotions. (5) The member defines the issue in terms of feelings in order to work with it in a personal way. (6) The member gains a sense of active involvement with resolution or acceptance. The feelings themselves may change or shift. | Mid End | Meaning making | Cognitive Affective | Individual |
| Psyed Couns Psyther Task | 75. *Feelings Faces:* Form pairs. Using pictures of faces showing emotions, members choose a face (a feeling) and share a time when they experienced that feeling. Allow 4 minutes. Change feelings and change the person sharing. Go up to 5 feelings and regroup with all members. | Mid End | Interconnection Meaning making | Cognitive Affective Structural | Individual Interpersonal |
| Psyed Couns Psyther | 76. *Decision Making:* A member stands in front of group to make a decision. Using pros and cons approach, individual exhausts his list and asks group to then help. | Mid | Collaboration Meaning making | Cognitive Behavioral | Individual Group |
| Psyed Couns Psyther Task | 77. *Wish List:* Give each member a sheet of paper labeled "_____'s Wish List" and have the members exchange papers at 1-minute intervals. *(Continued)* | End | Interconnection Meaning making | Cognitive Affective Behavioral | Individual Interpersonal Group |

| Group Types | Best Practice Area: PERFORMING Techniques | Stage(s) | Ecological Concept(s) | Focus(i) | Level(s) |
|---|---|---|---|---|---|
| | *(Continued from p. 230)* Each member writes a wish to the person named on the paper. Pass the papers until each member receives his or her own. | | | | |
| Psyed Couns Psyther Task | 78. *Wizard of Oz:* Each member thinks of two things each in five areas: physical, mental, emotional, spiritual, and social. Each reads their list to the group while others take notes. Use whatever you have learned about each other to make a temporary gift to each member using whatever you have in your pockets, your wallet, your purse, etc. Pick a different gift for each. Go around and tell your gift's symbolism. | End | Interconnection Social system Meaning making | Cognitive Affective Behavioral | Individual Interpersonal Group |
| Psyed Couns Psyther Task | 79. *Follow-Up Session:* Hold a follow-up session weeks or months later and review what was gained in the initial experience. | End | Interconnection Social system Meaning making | Cognitive Affective | Group |
| Psyed Couns Psyther Task | 80. *Group Identification:* Group members identify context and purpose of their group. | Beg Mid End | Context | Cognitive | Individual Group |
| Psyed Couns Psyther Task | 81. *Revisit Group Rules and Expectations:* Rechecking what was decided can be helpful and necessary through exploring members' recall. | Beg Mid End | Context | Cognitive | Individual Group |
| Psyed Couns Psyther Task | 82. *How Did It Go?:* Simple and direct questions, such as this one, asked at appropriate times during a session can promote reflective participation. | Mid End | Meaning making | Cognitive | Individual |
| Psyed Couns Psyther Task | 83. *Systems-Centered Subgrouping:* Members are encouraged to identify subgroups within the group as a way of exploring interconnections and meaning. | Beg Mid | Interconnection Meaning making | Cognitive Affective | Interpersonal Group |
| Psyed Couns Psyther Task | 84. *String Activity:* Members use string to connect to each other all the possible relationships existing within the group. | Beg Mid | Context Interconnection Social system | Behavioral Cognitive Structural | Group |
| Psyed Couns Psyther Task | 85. *Thank You. I'm Wondering If We Could Hear from Others:* A simple question intended to open up discussion to involve others. | Beg Mid End | Collaboration | Cognitive | Group |

| Group Types | Best Practice Area: PERFORMING Techniques With Technology | Stage(s) | Ecological Concept(s) | Focus(i) | Level(s) |
|---|---|---|---|---|---|
| Psyed Couns Psyther Task | 1a. *Use of a Personal Responder System* with interactive software for classrooms or presentations, allowing for anonymous responses to group questions. | Beg Mid End | Context Collaboration Social system Meaning making | Cognitive Behavioral Structural | Individual Group |
| Psyed Couns Psyther Task | 2a. *Online Group:* Hold a group session using Web-based chat room, video imaging systems, etc. | Beg Mid End | Context Interconnection Collaboration Social system | Cognitive Affective Behavioral Structural | Individual Interpersonal Group |
| Psyed Couns Psyther Task | 3a. *Virtual Classrooms:* Hold a class using Web-based classroom management tools or video teleconferencing equipment, etc. | Beg Mid End | Context Collaboration Social system | Cognitive Structural | Individual Interpersonal Group |

| Group Types | Best Practice Area: PROCESSING (Within) Techniques | Stage(s) | Ecological Concept(s) | Focus(i) | Level(s) |
|---|---|---|---|---|---|
| Psyed Couns Psyther | 1. *Say It in One Word:* Have each member go around and say one word that describes how he or she feels after the meeting. | Beg | Meaning making | Cognitive Affective | Individual |
| Psyed Couns Psyther Task | 2. *Process Points:* Leader makes summary statements pointing out process, accomplishments, and future actions. | Beg Mid End | Context Social system Meaning making | Cognitive | Group |
| Psyed Couns Psyther Task | 3. *Confidentiality Review:* Review confidentiality and discuss its meaning with the group. | Beg Mid End | Context Interconnection Social system Meaning making | Cognitive | Interpersonal Group |
| Psyed Couns Psyther Task | 4. *My Group Experience:* Allow members to express their feelings about being in a group (or being forced into a group). | Beg Mid End | Context Social system Meaning making | Cognitive Affective | Individual Group |
| Psyed Couns Psyther | 5. *Say It Another Way:* Have each group member write to another person those things that he or she cannot say face-to-face. | Beg Mid End | Context Interconnection Meaning making | Cognitive Affective Behavioral | Individual Interpersonal |
| Psyed Couns Psyther | 6. *Awfulizing:* Imagine the worst thing that could happen to you in this group (to identify fears). Elicit sharing. | Beg Mid End | Context Meaning making | Cognitive Affective | Individual Group |

| Group Types | Best Practice Area: PROCESSING (Within) Techniques | Stage(s) | Ecological Concept(s) | Focus(i) | Level(s) |
|---|---|---|---|---|---|
| Psyed Couns | 7. *TA Diagrams:* Pass out Transactional Analysis diagrams and ask members to analyze their interpersonal interactions and label the appropriate Parent, Child, and Adult relational elements. | Beg Mid End | Interconnection Collaboration Social system Meaning making | Cognitive Behavioral | Individual |
| Psyed Couns Psyther Task | 8. *Diversion Tactics:* Divert attention from one member by addressing group behavior and reactions. | Beg Mid End | Interconnection Collaboration Meaning making | Cognitive Affective | Individual Interpersonal Group |
| Couns Psyther | 9. *The Real Me:* Ask the members to tell the group how they might be different outside the group versus in the group. | Beg Mid End | Interconnection Meaning making | Cognitive Affective | Individual |
| Psyed Couns Psyther | 10. *Group Sociogram:* Have members do a sociogram of the group's interactions and relationships. | Beg Mid End | Interconnection Social system Meaning making | Cognitive Affective Behavioral | Interpersonal Group |
| Psyed Couns Psyther | 11. *Interactional Journaling:* Have the group journal and then share among all members and leaders with reactions and summaries. | Beg Mid End | Interconnection Collaboration Social system Meaning making | Cognitive Affective Behavioral | Individual Interpersonal Group |
| Psyed Couns Psyther Task | 12. *Increased Awareness:* For the next session, ask members to consider: "What were you most aware of since the last session? Did you have any reactions since that time?" | Beg Mid End | Context Social system Meaning making | Cognitive | Individual Interpersonal Group |
| Couns Psyther | 13. *My Expectations:* Have a silent member face each member and say, "When I look at you I think you expect me to . . . " (to explore silent member's expectations of others). | Beg Mid End | Interconnection Social system Meaning making | Cognitive Affective Structural Behavioral | Individual Interpersonal Group |
| Psyed Couns Psyther Task | 14. *Group Assessments:* Add group assessment and/or self-evaluation for accountability and self-discovery at the end of each session. | Beg Mid End | Context Collaboration Meaning making | Cognitive Affective Behavioral | Individual Group |
| Psyed Couns Psyther Task | 15. *Deep Processing Model:* (1) *Transpose* the group meeting by recording objective observations. (2) *Reflect* on your subjective awareness of the meeting. (3) *Discover* meaning through integration of objective and subjective awareness. (4) *Apply* increased awareness through action plan derived from the evaluation. (5) *Evolve* as the plan grows with integration of best practices into action plan. | Beg Mid End | Context Meaning making | Cognitive | Group |

| Group Types | Best Practice Area: PROCESSING (Within) Techniques | Stage(s) | Ecological Concept(s) | Focus(i) | Level(s) |
|---|---|---|---|---|---|
| Psyed Couns Task | 16. *Power LineUp:* Have members position themselves in terms of some ranking order (e.g., birthday order, likes group work the most, etc.). | Mid | Meaning making | Cognitive Structural | Interpersonal |
| Couns Psyther | 17. *My Learning:* Leader asks group members to respond to "What have you learned?" | Mid End | Meaning making Sustainability | Cognitive | Individual |
| Psyed Couns Psyther Task | 18. *My Participation:* Leader: "Imagine yourself as you are now — silent — and it is the last session. What have you gotten from the group? How do you feel about your level of participation?" Elicit sharing. | Mid End | Context Meaning making Sustainability | Cognitive Affective | Individual |
| Couns Psyther | 19. *Be Direct:* Ask one group member to speak directly to another to tell how he affects him or her. | Mid End | Interconnection Social system Meaning making | Cognitive Affective Behavioral | Individual Interpersonal Group |
| Couns Psyther | 20. *Memory Connection:* Have a member who is disturbed by another member say, "When I feel your defensiveness I am reminded of . . . " | Mid End | Interconnection Social system Meaning making | Cognitive Affective Behavioral Structural | Individual Interpersonal Group |
| Couns Psyther | 21. *Self-Exposure:* Have members state how they feel about exposing themselves when someone has not reciprocated (silent member). | Mid End | Context Interconnection Social system Meaning making | Cognitive Affective Behavioral | Individual Interpersonal Group |
| Couns Psyther | 22. *Highlight the Behavior:* For a monopolizer, audiotape or videotape so member can evaluate himself or herself. | Mid End | Context Collaboration Meaning making | Cognitive Structural Behavioral | Individual Interpersonal |
| Psyed Couns Psyther Task | 23. *Questionnaire Round 2:* Redistribute a questionnaire on how well the members are coping with an area of concern. | Mid End | Context Collaboration Meaning making | Cognitive Affective Behavioral | Individual Interpersonal Group |
| Psyed Couns Psyther | 24. *Free Association:* Ask a member to name something she or he is afraid of, adding how that reminds her or him of something else. | Mid End | Meaning making | Cognitive Affective | Individual |
| Psyed Couns Psyther | 25. *Group Poll:* Check with members to see if they are getting from the group what they had expected. | Mid End | Interconnection Meaning making Sustainability | Cognitive Affective | Individual Interpersonal Group |
| Psyed Couns Psyther Task | 26. *Past vs. Present:* Have members reflect on the first meeting comparing to the present. Members can share verbally, journal, or be creative in representing their feelings. | Mid End | Context Interconnection Social system Meaning making | Cognitive | Individual Group |

| Group Types | Best Practice Area: PROCESSING (Within) Techniques | Stage(s) | Ecological Concept(s) | Focus(i) | Level(s) |
|---|---|---|---|---|---|
| Couns Psyther | 27. *Cathartic Meanings:* Ask the member who just experienced catharsis to summarize what just happened at each stage in order to make meaning of it and remember it. | Mid End | Context Interconnection Meaning making | Cognitive Affective | Individual |
| Psyed Couns Psyther | 28. *Reactions:* Leader asks members to imagine how different people will react to them "if you let them know. . ." Share with the group. | Mid End | Context Interconnection Collaboration | Cognitive Affective | Individual Interpersonal Group |
| Psyed Couns Psyther | 29. *Feedback as Poetry:* Give one member paper and a pen and tell him or her to write the first line of a poem that describes the group. Pass the pen and paper and each member adds a line to the poem. Read aloud to the group. | Mid End | Interconnection Collaboration Meaning making | Cognitive Affective Behavioral | Individual Interpersonal |
| Psyed Couns Psyther Task | 30. *Six-Month Reminders:* Write a note to yourself to open in 6 months about what you hope to have achieved. The leader returns them in 6 months unopened. | End | Context Social system Meaning making | Cognitive Affective Behavioral | Individual |
| Psyed Couns Psyther Task | 31. *Exit Interview:* Hold an exit interview with each group member to finalize the group experience. | End | Context Collaboration Meaning making | Cognitive Affective | Individual |
| Psyed Couns Task | 32. *Group Chant:* Group members make a circle. Leader: "Listen to the scoop on a really great group. Give a cheer for the group here." Members take turns stepping forward to share a success while others say one of these lines: "Now take a pause for a little applause." Or "Let's say it loud, we're feeling proud." Clapping adds fun! | End | Interconnection Collaboration Meaning making | Cognitive Affective Behavioral Structural | Group |
| Psyed Couns | 33. *Relative Goals:* Leader asks group members to respond to "How does this relate to your goals?" | End | Meaning making Sustainability | Cognitive | Individual |
| Psyed Couns Psyther Task | 34. *Rearview Mirror:* Leader: "Say you are in a car being driven (by someone else) away from the group immediately following the last session; all other members are visible through the rearview mirror. What would you say to members about what you have learned from them or from the group?" | End | Meaning making Sustainability | Cognitive | Individual |

| Group Types | Best Practice Area: PROCESSING (Within) Techniques | Stage(s) | Ecological Concept(s) | Focus(i) | Level(s) |
|---|---|---|---|---|---|
| Psyed Couns Psyther Task | 35. *Leader Points:* Leader asks, "What's happening now?" | End | Meaning making | Cognitive | Group |
| Psyed Couns Psyther Task | 36. *My Accomplishments:* Leader asks, "What have you accomplished?" | End | Meaning making Sustainability | Cognitive | Individual |
| Psyed Couns Psyther | 37. *Application Proclamation:* Leader asks, "How will you apply this?" | End | Meaning making Sustainability | Cognitive Behavioral | Individual |
| Psyed Couns Psyther Task | 38. *Grid for Experiences and Events in Group Work:* Ask members to process group experience by attending to what and how they talk in the group. | Mid End | Meaning making Sustainability | Cognitive Affective | Individual Interpersonal Group |
| Psyed Couns Psyther Task | 39. *Systems-Centered Subgrouping:* Members are encouraged to identify subgroups within the group as a way of exploring here-and-now interconnections and meaning. By recognizing subgroups, restraining forces are weakened. | Beg Mid | Interconnection Meaning making | Cognitive Affective | Interpersonal Group |

| Group Types | Best Practice Area: PROCESSING (Between) Techniques | Stage(s) | Ecological Concept(s) | Focus(i) | Level(s) |
|---|---|---|---|---|---|
| Psyed Couns Psyther Task | 1. *Session Review:* Leader reviews each session and determines if adjustments need to be made. | Beg Mid End | Social system Sustainability | Cognitive | Group |
| Psyed Couns Psyther Task | 2. *Supervision Journal:* Leader writes reflections in a journal, usually right after the group, planning, or supervision sessions. | Beg Mid End | Context Interconnection Social system Meaning making Sustainability | Cognitive Affective | Individual |
| Psyed Couns Psyther Task | 3. *Supervision Readings:* Leader is assigned readings that will aid the reflection and supervision process. | Beg Mid End | Context Meaning making | Cognitive Affective Behavioral | Individual |
| Psyed Couns Psyther Task | 4. *Supervision Reports:* Leader writes a weekly report reviewing group process, resources needed, attendance, etc. | Beg Mid End | Context Meaning making | Cognitive Affective | Group |

| Group Types | Best Practice Area: PROCESSING (Between) Techniques | Stage(s) | Ecological Concept(s) | Focus(i) | Level(s) |
|---|---|---|---|---|---|
| Psyed Couns Psyther Task | 5. *Coleader Checks:* Coleaders ask each other, "How am I doing?" and/or "How are we doing?" | Beg Mid End | Meaning making Sustainability | Cognitive Affective | Individual Interpersonal |
| Psyed Couns | 6. *Recording Review:* Leader/ coleaders review recordings made of session(s). | Beg Mid End | Meaning making | Cognitive | Individual Group |
| Psyed Couns | 7. *Goal Review:* Leader reviews goals he or she set in the planning stage. | Mid End | Meaning making | Cognitive | Interpersonal |
| Psyed Couns Psyther Task | 8. Pass out worksheets with sections labeled Assessment, Benefits, Consequences, Duty and Education, leaving room for group members to write. Useful for issues that arise which need attention to ethical decision making. | Mid End | Interconnection Collaboration Social system Meaning making | Cognitive Behavioral | Individual Group |
| Psyed Couns Psyther Task | 9. *Deep Processing Model:* (1) *Transpose* the group meeting by recording objective observations. (2) *Reflect* on your subjective aware-ness of the meeting. (3) *Discover* meaning through integration of objective and subjective awareness. (4) *Apply* increased awareness through action plan derived from the evaluation. (5) *Evolve* as the plan grows with integration of best practices into action plan. | Beg Mid End | Meaning making Sustainability | Cognitive | Group |
| Psyed Couns Psyther Task | 10. *Letter Review:* Members unseal their letters from the first session to see how they did. | End | Context Meaning making | Cognitive Affective Behavioral | Individual |
| Psyed Couns Psyther Task | 11. *Group Assessments:* Add group assessment and/or self-evaluation for accountability and self-discovery at the end of each session. | Beg Mid End | Context Collaboration Meaning making | Cognitive Affective Behavioral | Individual Group |

# Subject Index

# Author Index